THE SAVINGS AND
LOAN INDUSTRY

New Titles from QUORUM BOOKS

The International Law of Pollution: Protecting the Global Environment
in a World of Sovereign States
ALLEN L. SPRINGER

Statistical Concepts for Attorneys: A Reference Guide
WAYNE C. CURTIS

Handbook of Record Storage and Space Management
C. PETER WAEGEMANN

Industrial Bonds and the Rating Process
AHMED BELKAOUI

Of Foxes and Hen Houses: Licensing and the Health Professions
STANLEY J. GROSS

Telecommunications America: Markets Without Boundaries
MANLEY RUTHERFORD IRWIN

Pension Fund Investments in Real Estate:
A Guide for Plan Sponsors and Real Estate Professionals
NATALIE A. McKELVY

Growth Industries in the 1980s: Conference Proceedings
FEDERAL RESERVE BANK OF ATLANTA, SPONSOR

Business Strategy for the Political Arena
FRANK SHIPPER and MARIANNE M. JENNINGS

Socio-Economic Accounting
AHMED BELKAOUI

Corporate Spin-Offs: Strategy for the 1980s
RONALD J. KUDLA and THOMAS H. McINISH

Disaster Management: Warning Response and Community Relocation
RONALD W. PERRY and ALVIN H. MUSHKATEL

THE SAVINGS AND LOAN INDUSTRY

CURRENT PROBLEMS AND POSSIBLE SOLUTIONS

WALTER J. WOERHEIDE

Q

QUORUM BOOKS
Westport, Connecticut • London, England

Library of Congress Cataloging in Publication Data

Woerheide, Walter J.
    The savings and loan industry.

    Bibliography: p.
    Includes index.
    1. Building and loan associations—United States.
I. Title.
HG2151.W63 1984   332.3'2'0973   83-13686
ISBN 0-89930-038-3 (lib. bdg.)

Library of Congress Catalog Card Number: 83-13686
ISBN: 0-89930-038-3

First published in 1984 by Quorum Books

Greenwood Press
A division of Congressional Information Service, Inc.
88 Post Road West, Westport, Connecticut 06881

Printed in the United States of America

10 9 8 7 6 5 4 3 2 1

To my parents, Winston and Art,
who have done so much for me.

Contents

Tables

Acknowledgments

The idea for this book started when I was fortunate enough to be invited to participate in the Visiting Scholar program in the Office of Policy and Economic Research at the Federal Home Loan Bank Board. My own concerns about the quality of the regulatory efforts in the savings and loan industry have been easily put to rest after getting to work with many of the competent, dedicated staff at the Bank Board. I would like to thank especially Henry Cassidy, my supervisor at the Bank Board, for his frequent, helpful suggestions during my stay there.

As with most manuscripts, there are colleagues who have been willing to read and provide many useful comments on earlier versions of this book. I would like to thank Rich Cohn, Gene Carter, Margaret Monroe, and Owen Gregory for their willingness to share their time, even though the savings and loan industry is not exactly a topic near and dear to their hearts. I also appreciate the efforts of our Word Processing Center at the university. Anybody who can read through ten chapters of my handwriting truly deserves a special commendation.

Walt Woerheide

Introduction

Observers of the savings and loan industry today are nearly unanimous in their opinions that the industry is dying. Illustrative of their comments is the recent statement by one authority that "most of the nation's 4,000 thrifts will go under in merger or outright failure . . . leaving maybe 1,000, maybe 500."[1] It is easy to share this pessimism when one looks at recent trends in industry profits and net cash flows.

The purpose of this book is to provide answers to three questions:

1. How did the industry get into its current situation?
2. What is being done to save the industry?
3. What are the probable consequences of current actions?

While there might be general agreement on the answers to the first two questions, the answer to the third query can only be speculative. The first two questions are addressed in Chapter 1, which traces the history of the Federal Home Loan Bank System and reviews recent legislation affecting the industry. Speculation about the answer to the third question forms the basis for the other nine chapters in this book.

There is no obvious order for the last nine chapters, but there are some reasons for the order in which they have been placed. One of the problems that exists in the savings and loan literature is that some of the writers and researchers do not fully understand the factors that influence the profitability of savings and loans. These factors include such basic features as the organizational form of the association and the state in which the thrift operates, as well as such operating characteristics as the types of mortgages the thrift acquires, the amount of reselling of mortgages undertaken by the thrift, and the magnitude of nondeposit borrowing utilized by the thrift. For this reason, the determinants of profitability comprise the second chapter. This provides a better background for understanding the ramifications of some of the changes which are occurring in the industry.

The basic problem experienced by the thrift industry is that its interest rate risk exposure has been too large. This, of course, should come as no surprise to even the most casual industry observer. There is, however, a large step between this identification of the problem and a more specific statement as to the exact magnitude of this problem. In fact, it is rather difficult to discuss the various developments in the industry and their effects without a framework in which to visualize how these changes will exactly affect interest rate risk exposure. Chapter 3 solves this problem by offering the necessary analytical framework. The primary tool of analysis is a measure referred to as "duration," a concept that originated in the literature that deals with bonds but which is readily applicable to the assets and liabilities of savings and loans.

Chapter 3 will also show how another basic problem—the industry's financing of long-term assets (mortgages) with short-term liabilities (deposits)—can be defined more precisely. In terms of duration, one would say that the average duration of the assets is substantially longer than that of the liabilities. The interest rate risk exposure of a savings and loan then becomes a function of the difference between the average duration of its assets and that of its liabilities. As a result, the value of congressional and regulatory solutions can be analyzed by how they affect both the average asset and liability durations and the asset and liability yields.

Whereas the first three chapters provide the necessary background for an understanding of the history and problems of the thrift industry, the next six chapters look at the major developments. The first three of these examine several developments affecting the asset side of the thrift's balance sheet. The two most significant of these are the growth in what are referred to as alternative mortgage instruments and the expansion of authority to trade in financial futures contracts. Although the use of alternative mortgage instruments has certainly spread more rapidly than the use of financial futures, it is not clear to this writer which of these tools will have the more significant impact on the industry and its interest rate risk exposure problem. Therefore, the discussion on alternative mortgage instruments in Chapter 4 appearing prior to the discussion of financial futures and forward commitments in Chapter 5 is fairly arbitrary with respect to sequence.

The third major development in terms of asset powers for the industry is growth in consumer lending authority. It appears, however, that this tool will not be nearly as significant as the two mentioned above. Thus, the discussion of consumer lending is allocated to Chapter 6.

From the asset side of the balance sheet, we turn to the major developments affecting the liability side of the same sheet. Although developments have been many, especially during the writing of the final draft of this book, the two classifications which best summarize these developments are the elimination of interest rate ceilings and the introduction of negotiable order of withdrawal accounts. As in the case of consumer lending, perhaps neither of these developments is as significant as the changes involving alternative mortgage instruments and financial futures, although they are important. Thus, these topics are placed in

Chapters 7 and 8, so that they follow the discussion on the changes in asset powers.

Not all significant developments in the industry directly affect the balance sheet. The industry is undergoing substantial structural changes accomplished through voluntary and involuntary mergers as well as charter and organizational form conversions. Chapter 9 looks at how these mergers and conversions are affecting the industry and its prospects.

When all of these foregoing issues have been discussed, there will remain two questions regarding the future of thrifts. One is in what manner the typical thrift institution of the future will function once all of the developments discussed in the earlier chapters have been fully incorporated into its operations. The other is whether there will be a role for the small thrift in the future. Both of these questions are dealt with in Chapter 10.

The reader will notice that proposals involving government subsidies for the thrift industry are not discussed in any detail. Such proposals include an extension of the All-Savers Certificate and the government providing a warehouse service for the low-coupon mortgages held by the industry. The reason for this omission is that these subsidies involve only transitory financial aid rather than any permanent change in the operation of the thrift industry. It is this latter issue to which this book is directed and which is the basis for the topics selected.

NOTE

1. Thomas G. Donlan, "Fall from Grace," *Barron's,* December 7, 1981, p. 30.

Abbreviations

ACD	acquired
ACG	acquiring
AMI	Alternative Mortgage Instrument
AMIC	American Mortgage Insurance Company
AMLs	Adjustable Mortgage Loans
AMMINET	Automated Mortgage Market Information Network
ARMs	Adjustable-Rate Mortgages
ATs	Automatic Transfer Accounts
CBs	commercial banks
CBT	Chicago Board of Trade
CD	Certificate of Deposit
CD GNMA	Certificate Delivery GNMA
CDR	Collateralized Depository Receipt
CLS	Kent Colton, Donald Lessard, and Arthur Solomon
CRA	Community Reinvestment Act
DIA	Depository Institutions Amendments
DIDC	Depository Institutions Deregulation Committee
DIDMCA	Depository Institutions Deregulation and Monetary Control Act
DPM	Deferred-Payment Mortgage
ECOA	Equal Credit Opportunity Act
ERISA	Employee Retirement Income Security Act
FHLMC	Federal Home Loan Mortgage Corporation
FHA	Federal Housing Administration
FHA-VA	FHA-Veterans' Administration
FHLBA	Federal Home Loan Bank Act
FHLBB	Federal Home Loan Bank Board
FHLBs	Federal Home Loan Banks
FHLBS	Federal Home Loan Bank System
FIA	Financial Institutions Act
FIR	Federal Insurance Reserve
FNMA	Federal National Mortgage Association
FSLAC	Federal Savings and Loan Advisory Council

FSLIC	Federal Savings and Loan Insurance Corporation
GAAP	Generally Accepted Accounting Principles
GEHL	Growing Equity Home Loans
GNMA	Government National Mortgage Association
GPAML	Graduated-Payment Adjustable Mortgage Loan
GPM	Graduated-Payment Mortgage
HCDA	Housing and Community Development Act
HPAs	High-Performance Associations
HOLA	Home Owner's Loan Act
HOLC	Home Owner's Loan Corporation
HUD	Housing and Urban Development
IPC	Individuals, Partnership, and Corporation
IRAs	Individual Retirement Accounts
MMCs	Money Market Certificates
NM	nonmerging
NOW	Negotiable Order of Withdrawal
PAM	Pledged Account Mortgage
PLADs	Price Level Adjusted Deposits
PLAM	Price Level Adjusted Mortgage
PSID	Panel Study of Income Dynamics
PTs	Pass-Through Securities
RAM	Reverse-Annuity Mortgage
Repos	Reverse Repurchase Agreements
RESPA	Real Estate Settlement Procedures Act
RN	David Rochester and Walter Neely
RRM	Renegotiable-Rate Mortgages
SAM	Shared Appreciation Mortgage
SCSA	Standard Consolidated Statistical Area
SEM	Shared Equity Mortgage
SEP	Simplified Employer's Pension
SFPM	Standard, Fixed-Payment Mortgage
SLAs	Savings and Loan Associations
SKF	David Smith, Donald Kaplan, and William Ford
SMSA	Standard Metropolitan Statistical Area
VG	James Verbrugge and Stephen Goldstein
VRMs	Variable-Rate Mortgages
VST	James Verbrugge, Richard Schick, and Kenneth Thygerson
WRAP	Wraparound Mortgage

THE SAVINGS AND LOAN INDUSTRY

History of the Federal Home Loan Bank System

The history of the savings and loan industry since the Great Depression is primarily the story of the creation and development of the Federal Home Loan Bank System (FHLBS). The FHLBS is composed of the Federal Home Loan Bank Board (FHLBB), 12 regional Federal Home Loan Banks (FHLBs), and the member institutions. The member institutions include mostly, but not exclusively, savings and loan associations (SLAs).[1] All of the significant developments within the SLA industry have either produced changes in the regulatory stance of the FHLBB or have emanated from regulatory developments by the FHLBB. That is why the modern history of the SLA industry is also a history of the FHLBB.[2]

THE CREATION OF THE MODERN FHLBS, 1932-1935

The most rapid period of growth for SLAs in terms of the establishment of new associations was the decade from 1915 to 1925. At the end of 1915 there were 6,806 associations, and by the end of 1925 there were 12,403.[3]

Many of these institutions were set up by real estate people, insurance agents, lawyers, and contractors with the intention of using the associations as sources of income for their own businesses.[4] This control of SLAs by real estate concerns has been and remains a dominant feature of the thrift industry.

The concept of an FHLBS had been discussed by Congress in 1919, 1920, and 1927. No legislation materialized from these discussions because the proposals included granting authority to a government agency to issue tax-free bonds and because the banking industry viewed the creation of an FHLBS as detrimental to its own interests. Thus, it took the Great Depression to stimulate sufficient interest for Congress to formulate the final legislation. The Federal Home Loan Bank Act (FHLBA) was signed into law on July 22, 1932 by Herbert Hoover. The primary objectives were that the system would: (1) provide secondary liquidity to mortgage lending institutions which had temporary cash flow problems, (2) transfer loanable funds from saving surplus to saving deficit areas, and (3) attempt to stabilize the residential construction and financing industries. To accomplish these objectives the FHLBs would sell stock to its members and then loan this money back to its members. A loan from an FHLB was called an "advance."

The FHLBS was modeled to some extent upon the Federal Reserve System. The most obvious point of similarity is that there are 12 regional FHLBs just as there are 12 regional Federal Reserve Banks, although the district lines for the two systems differ because the FHLBA forbids the Federal Home Loan Bank Board from dividing a state into different districts.[5]

The name "Federal Home Loan Bank Board" refers both to the agency and to the Board members that control the agency. When it was originally created, there were five Board members appointed for six-year terms. The members of the Board were appointed by the President of the United States with the advice and consent of the Senate, and the Chairman of the Board was designated by the President. The first Board was appointed by President Hoover but was never confirmed by the Senate. President Roosevelt then made a new set of appointments upon taking office, and these appointees were approved.

After the FHLBS was established, Congress became concerned that the benefits granted to the SLA industry under the Federal Home Loan Bank Act were not being passed on to the country's homeowners. Specifically, the benefit of additional liquidity provided to SLAs through advances was not being passed on to homeowners in the form of easier mortgage terms and fewer foreclosures. In 1933, Congress passed the Home Owner's Loan Act (HOLA), which created the Home Owner's Loan Corporation (HOLC). The HOLC exchanged its own bonds for delinquent mortgages held by various mortgage lenders and then rewrote these mortgages for longer terms at lower interest rates. As a result of the exchange, the HOLC issued $770 million in bonds and acquired 13 percent of the mortgage portfolio held by SLAs.[6] During its life, the HOLC purchased and refinanced over 1.8 million delinquent mortgages, amounting to $6.2 billion.[7] The HOLC ceased purchasing and refinancing loans in 1936 because it had exhausted the $3 billion initial lending authority and the $1.5 billion additional lending authority granted it by Congress.[8] The HOLC auctioned off its remaining mortgage loans in large blocks in the early fifties and was liquidated in 1954.[9]

A second feature of the HOLA was that Congress gave the FHLBB authority to grant federal charters. Congress intended that the new chartering authority would facilitate the establishment of SLAs in communities which were not then served by an association. It was hoped that the expansion of the number of associations would enable more people to receive the intended benefits from the creation of the FHLBS. In the early days, FHLBB employees travelled around the country talking to local business people to encourage the creation of federally chartered SLAs.[10] Despite the intention and efforts of the FHLBB, the majority of federally chartered SLAs today are a result of conversions of state-chartered associations to a federal charter rather than *de novo* applications.

In 1934, Congress passed the National Housing Act in order to provide federally guaranteed home-mortgage insurance. The administration of the program was given to the newly created Federal Housing Agency because, although the Bank

Board proposed the legislation, the SLA industry opposed it. In fact, this was the first legislation promoted by the Bank Board which lacked industry support.[11] Opposition was based on the fact that the insurance would also apply to mortgages made by banks and insurance companies, and this was viewed by the SLAs as encouragement for these two industries to encroach on SLA turf.

The industry opposition was overcome and passage attained by the inclusion of Title IV, which created the Federal Savings and Loan Insurance Corporation (FSLIC) and authorized it to insure savings accounts for $5,000. The intention of insurance coverage was twofold. First, it provided safety for the small saver, and second, it provided an element of integrity to the entire system of thrift institutions. The annual premium for the insurance was initially set at .25 percent of insured savings.[12] Over the years, the amount of insurance coverage has been steadily increased to where it now stands at $100,000 per account holder, and the premium has been reduced to .12 percent of insured savings.[13]

The last major component of the FHLBB to be created in this period was the Federal Savings and Loan Advisory Council (FSLAC).[14] The FSLAC meets two to three times a year and submits a list of suggestions to the FHLBB for possible actions. The FSLAC has served little purpose other than to add a formal channel for the exchange of information between regulators and regulatees to the informal structure that already exists.

A QUIET PERIOD OF GROWTH, 1935-1965

From 1935 to 1965, there was little change in the regulatory structure of the industry, but substantial growth in assets and concentration within the industry occurred. The simplest statistic with which to demonstrate concentration is the decrease in the actual number of associations. At the end of 1935, there were 10,266 SLAs. By the end of 1965, only 6,185 associations were in existence. The decline has not been gradual, however. By the end of 1950, the number of SLAs was down to 5,992. This number then increased to a peak of 6,320 at the end of 1960 and has been on the decline ever since.[15]

In 1935, the SLA industry owned assets totaling $5,875 million, and the average association held assets of $572,277. By the end of 1965, industry assets totaled $129,580 million, and the average association held assets of over $20.9 million. Over this 30-year period, the total assets owned by the industry grew at an annual geometric mean rate of 10.9 percent, and those of the typical association grew at an average rate of 12.7 percent.

During the war years, the SLA industry found itself in the unusual situation that it was being inundated by deposits and had little opportunity to engage in mortgage lending due to the lack of private sector wartime construction. Although the industry was able to dispose of much of the real estate it had picked up as a result of foreclosures in the prior years, some desire was expressed toward placing restrictions on the amount of new deposits they would accept.[16]

There were several cosmetic changes in the FHLBB during this period. As a wartime economy measure, the Board was reduced to one member under the authority given to the U.S. President under the First War Powers Act of 1941.[17] On July 26, 1947 the Board was expanded under President Truman's Reorganization Plan No. 3 to its present arrangement of three members having four-year terms.[18] The only restriction on the Board membership is that all of the members cannot be from the same political party. Thus, as long as a Republican, for example, holds the presidency, there will likely be two Republicans and one non-Republican on the Board. Vacancies that develop on the Board are filled for the balance of the original term, although those appointed to fill a vacancy are eligible to be reappointed for a new term. Like most federal agencies, the Board has a recurring problem in that vacancies are not always promptly filled. For long periods of time, at least one and sometimes two Board positions are vacant.

Another cosmetic change during the 1935-1965 period was that the Board itself was moved several times within the bureaucratic framework. It had been originally created as an independent agency. Under President Roosevelt's Reorganization Plan No. 1 in 1939, it was placed within a large agency in the executive branch called the Federal Loan Agency, and in 1942 it was transferred to the National Housing Agency.[19] In 1947 it was moved to the Housing and Home Finance Agency, and under the Housing Act of 1955 it was returned to its original status as an independent agency.[20] This last move came as a result of efforts by industry trade associations.[21]

In the post-World War II period, the FSLIC itself started to undergo changes. The insurance coverage was increased to $10,000 in 1950 and to $15,000 under the Financial Institutions Supervisory Act of 1966. In terms of resources, the FSLIC was given authority in 1950 to borrow up to $750 million from the U.S. Treasury, along with the authority to make premium assessments on its members to cover expenses and losses and the authority to ask for deposits equal to one percent of its members' total savings. In 1961, the FSLIC was allowed to set up a "secondary reserve," which enabled it to more than double its reserves, and associations were required to prepay their premiums.[22]

The reason for these changes was the rapid growth in the number of insured associations during the fifties. In 1950 there were 2,860 FSLIC-insured associations with total assets of $13,691 million, and by 1960 there were 4,098 FSLIC-insured associations with total assets of $67,430 million. Because of this rapid growth, the ratio of FSLIC's reserves to its insured liability had dropped to a relatively low value of .62 percent compared to more typical levels of 1 to 2 percent. The FSLIC was then given the authority in 1965 to borrow from all insured associations, should the need arise.

One oddity that occurred during this period was that the FSLIC became a corporation without shareholders. In 1948, the $100 million in FSLIC stock was transferred to the Secretary of the Treasury from the HOLC. In 1950, a statute was passed allowing the FSLIC to buy back its stock, and the complete repurchase was accomplished by 1958.

In case the establishment and activity of the FHLBS to this point were not sufficient to demonstrate the government's preference for the housing sector, Congress passed the Housing Act of 1949, which declared explicitly that housing was worthy of special treatment.

During the fifties, the Bank Board's regulatory role was enhanced in several ways. For example, in 1950 the FHLBA was amended to give the FHLBB the power to set liquidity requirements. The original rules specified that liquid assets were to be defined as cash and U.S. obligations, and the FHLBB was restricted to setting the liquidity requirements at no less than 4 percent and no more than 8 percent of total savings accounts.[23] Also in 1950, the Bank Board allowed federal SLAs to rewrite their charters, giving them greater flexibility in structuring their savings accounts. The price of such changes was that the Bank Board obtained more authority over the associations.[24] In 1954, Congress granted the Board the power to enforce specific orders against federal associations that violated a law or regulation. When the FHLBB was first created, it could take action against a wayward federal institution either by seizing it or by using moral suasion. The former was usually too drastic, and the latter was frequently ineffective. The problem with this power of specific order was that an SLA could block the action by taking the issue into the federal courts and thereby force the FHLBB to take several years and substantial legal expense to achieve its goals.[25]

In 1959 the Bank Board received limited jurisdiction over holding companies, under the National Housing Act.[26] In this same year the Board started to implement formally its desire to coordinate the policies of the FHLBs with each other and with the Federal Government. This was accomplished by holding the first meeting of the bank presidents that year.

In 1951, SLAs were made subject to the federal corporate income tax. SLAs had previously been able to avoid taxation by successfully arguing that the mutual nature of the industry made it one that should not appropriately be taxed.[27] The imposition of income taxes on SLAs resulted from lobbying by the commercial banking industry, which felt competitively disadvantaged because of its own taxation. The initial tax provisions were not very stringent, achieved in the final bill from a compromise developed by Bank Board Chairman William K. Divers.[28] Initially, SLAs could deduct all additions to reserves as long as net worth did not exceed 12 percent of savings balances. Thus, taxes paid in 1955 amounted to only 1.8 percent of taxable income, and by 1960 they were down to .61 percent of taxable income. The Revenue Act of 1962 substantially increased the tax liability of SLAs, and many associations which had previously avoided taxes altogether now had to pay. By 1965, income taxes took 16.0 percent of taxable income, and by 1980, taxes were up to 34.3 percent of taxable income.[29]

A final piece of legislation during this period was the congressional authorization given to federally chartered associations to invest in service corporations. The Bank Board, however, placed such restrictive regulations on these operations that few were actually started at this time.

Two trends that began during the fifties and would prove significant in the next two decades were the development of a national market for SLA deposits and loans, and the use of a secondary mortgage market by SLAs.[30] The national market for deposits started because of recurring net debtor positions by California thrifts. The dearth of deposits and the excess of mortgage demand led the California institutions to offer higher deposit rates and eventually resulted in the attraction of money from other regions. A national mortgage market started when the FHLBB granted federal SLAs the authority to purchase Federal Housing Administration (FHA) mortgages nationwide.[31] The start of a secondary mortgage market might well be designated with the initiation of an annual conference on the subject in 1956 by a major trade association.[32]

The mid-1960s marked the change in the relationship of the FHLBS to government financing. Before 1965, the FHLBS was frequently a net supplier of funds to the government security market in that holdings of government securities by FHLBs and by members frequently exceeded the debt issues of the FHLBs. After this point in time, the System moved to an unequivocable debtor position.[33] Concurrent with this change in the financial relationship with the government, the Bank Board also changed the method it used to compute the rate on advances. Prior to 1965, the Bank Board employed an average cost rule under which the rate on advances equaled the average cost of each FHLB's share of the consolidated debt plus a small markup. Since this policy occasionally produced periods in which the rates on advances were below the rates paid on deposits, it also required nonprice rationing of advances by the FHLBs. Since 1965, the advances rate is based on the average cost of an FHLB's share of only the most recent consolidated obligations. Hence, it is now priced somewhat on a marginal rate concept.

In many respects, the fifties and early sixties were the best days for the savings and loan industry. In 1955, the return on net worth for the industry hit a peak of 16.9 percent. By 1967, that ratio had declined to a relative low of 4.9 percent.[34]

THE WORLD IN TRANSITION, 1966-1979

In 1966, the world that the SLAs had known started changing. The primary impetus for this change was economic in nature. Interest rates started rising, and short-term rates rose more rapidly than long-term rates. SLAs then found themselves in a position of paying rapidly rising passbook rates just to retain the money that they had. Three other events at this time also resulted in significant changes in the environment in which thrifts operated. First, by this time the commercial banks had begun issuing certificates of deposit and were competing aggressively for consumer deposits. Second, government agencies commenced issuing securities that were more attractive to SLA depositors than they had previously been. Third, depositors were becoming more interest-rate conscious.[35]

As the interest rates were rising in 1965, the FHLBB feared that rate competition among SLAs and from the commercial banks would create a large number of thrift failures. The Board first tried to stem the intra-industry competition by declaring that, "with few exceptions, no expansion advances could be made by District Banks to S&Ls paying more than 4.25 percent on its savings accounts."[36] This policy proved to have little effect. The next move by the Board to limit what it viewed as disruptive competition was to have Congress pass the Interest Rate Adjustment Act of 1966. This act gave the FHLBB the power to set interest rate ceilings for SLAs and the authority to confer with the Federal Reserve Board and the Federal Deposit Insurance Corporation in order to coordinate the ceilings for banks and SLAs so that the SLAs would be given higher ceilings, or what has become known as an interest rate differential. This coordination was accomplished by the creation of the Interagency Coordinating Committee.

It is interesting to note that the FHLBB had several times previously tried to have Congress pass this legislation. While those previous attempts had been opposed by the SLA industry, in 1966 the industry supported the legislation, primarily because it feared competition from the banks. However, the support was strictly viewed as transitional given that the industry had Congress incorporate into the bill a provision that the power to set ceilings would be terminated one year later. When the expiration date approached, an extension was obtained because the industry feared another bout of tight money in 1968. The extensions eventually became a permanent feature as the SLA industry found that life was actually quite pleasant when half of the important, recurring decisions that SLA management must make were regulated.[37]

When the interest rate ceilings were first imposed, the structure was quite simple. Passbook accounts were restricted to a ceiling rate of 4.75 percent, and the only certificate rate was 5.25 percent for a certificate with a $1,000 minimum balance and a maturity of at least 180 days. During the seventies the ceilings were raised several times, and the types of certificates that could be offered were expanded. In addition, the interest rate differential between the ceilings on SLA deposits and on commercial bank deposits was narrowed. Initially, the differential was set at 75 to 100 basis points; in 1970 the differential was reduced to 50 basis points; and in 1973 it was reduced to 25 basis points on most accounts and was eliminated on some types of accounts.[38] In 1975, Congress gave the regulators the authority to eliminate the differential on any categories of accounts established after December 10, 1975.[39]

Passage of the Interest Rate Adjustment Act in 1966 was followed by a fall in market interest rates. Since it was the rise in interest rates that had created the problems for the thrifts, the fall in rates and subsequent return to profitability by the SLA industry may have left some observers with the impression that the ceilings had saved the industry.[40] If there was such an impression, it should have been destroyed by the credit crunches which started in late 1969, mid-1973, and 1979. The academic community and many in the industry recognized that every time market rates moved above the ceilings, the interest rate ceilings created the problem of disintermediation (the withdrawal of money on deposit at financial institutions).

The other key piece of legislation from 1966 is the Financial Institutions Supervisory Act, which gave the FHLBB the authority to issue cease-and-desist orders that were effective immediately on any SLA.[41] Overcoming the deficiency in the similar 1954 law, this new act eliminated the ability of the recalcitrant SLA to tie up the FHLBB in the courts. Oddly enough, the SLA industry supported this legislation for two reasons, despite the broad power it gave to the industry regulator. First, the FHLBB had started in the early sixties to issue a large number of regulations with the intention of making it difficult for poorly managed SLAs to go out of business. Unfortunately, these restrictions also hindered the flexibility of the well-run associations. The industry therefore felt that with a cease-and-desist authority, the FHLBB would cease and desist from developing additional regulations and might even repeal some of the old ones. The second reason for industry support of the legislation was that the healthy SLAs were always concerned that the financial failure of the poorly managed associations might generate public concern about the entire industry and prompt a spate of withdrawals.[42]

The last of the sixties saw two more Congressional actions affecting the industry. One was the Holding Company Amendments of 1967, which gave the FHLBB the power to examine savings and loan holding companies. Under this authority, some of the recent interstate mergers have been authorized. The other was the Housing and Urban Development (HUD) Act passed in 1968. In terms of immediate consequences, this act amended the HOLA to give federal associations the authority to lend for housing fixtures and mobile trailer homes, as well as the authority to issue a wide variety of savings plans, notes, bonds, and debentures.[43] Of more significant long-term consequence is that this act created the Department of HUD. Indeed, it has been argued that "the creation of HUD represented the most important postwar change in both the type and the quality of government intervention in the housing and mortgage markets."[44] Finally, it was during this period that the Bank Board augmented SLA lending capability even further by granting thrifts the authority to make educational loans and investments in urban development projects, and the Board increased their apartment lending authorization.[45]

In August of 1968, the FHLBB lowered the liquidity requirement from 7.0 percent to 6.5 percent and expanded the definition of liquid assets. This change in the percentage rate was only the second change since the liquidity requirements were first established in December 1950. The definition of liquid assets was broadened from just cash and government securities to include such assets as Federal funds, reverse repurchase agreements (repos), and municipals. The real significance of these changes is that they marked the start of an active effort to control the liquidity levels and thus, presumably, the amount of mortgage lending that was occurring. From this point until the end of the seventies, there were 16 more changes in liquidity requirements, including the one in January 1972 when the overall liquidity requirement was left unchanged but a short-term liquidity requirement was imposed. There is some fairly strong evidence that the liquidity requirements have not actually had much of an effect on the actions of the thrift industry.[46]

In March 1969, Preston Martin became Chairman of the FHLBB. Concurrent with Martin's administration was a shift in FHLBB policy to make advances more attractive to the SLA industry in order to stimulate mortgage lending. The need to expand mortgage credit was a constant theme in speeches given by the members of the Bank Board during this period. For example, at the Annual Stockholders' Meeting of the Federal Home Loan Bank of New York on April 29, 1969, Chairman Martin stated that:

This country is faced with a mortgage credit gap and thus a housing supply shortage of serious proportions. Not enough housing units are being built. Not enough are being rehabilitated to satisfy current and anticipated demand. . . .

The extent of the mortgage gap can be influenced decidedly by the policies of the Federal Home Loan Bank System. Funds produced through the Bank System should be utilized to deepen, stabilize, and stimulate the mortgage market instead of allowing it to become nonresponsive to mounting demand.[47]

In 1969 the FHLBB sent questionnaires to members of the industry soliciting information about their interest in different types of advances programs. Not surprisingly, the survey results strongly supported the move to longer-term advances. At the time of the survey, the longest consolidated obligation outstanding had a maturity of slightly over two years.[48]

In Bank Board discussions of the advances policy, clear distinction was now made between expansion advances and withdrawal advances. Expansion advances were those used to meet new mortgage demand, and withdrawal advances were those used to replace liquidity lost through the withdrawal of savings. Since advances had previously been limited to maturities of one year, the Board was adamant that such short-term loans not be used for expansion purposes. The Board considered the advances program as underutilized and sometimes misunderstood by SLA managers. The perception of underutilization was due to the fact that no more than 60 percent of the members had used the advances program. It was considered misunderstood because many managers continued to view the FHLBB as a lender of last rather than first resort.[49] It should be pointed out that in this renewed emphasis placed on the advances program, the Board viewed Bank System credit as a supplement to, rather than a replacement of, over-the-counter savings.

The year 1969 marked the completion of a congressionally authorized, Board-financed study of the SLA industry. The study was first proposed by President Johnson in response to both the high rate of growth the industry had been achieving and the tight-money problems encountered in 1966.[50] The study, directed by Dr. Irwin Friend of the Wharton School of Finance and Commerce at the University of Pennsylvania, offered many recommendations which would become policy during the next decade.

The next major change in the SLA industry was initiated with the 1970 passage of the Emergency Home Finance Act, which singled out the Bank System as the principal vehicle of the Nixon administration's effort to revive a depressed housing industry. Title II of this act permitted the Federal National Mortgage Association (FNMA) to purchase conventional mortgages, and Title III created the Federal Home Loan Mortgage Corporation (FHLMC), which is usually referred to as "Freddie Mac." The primary purpose of the FHLMC was to facilitate the development of a secondary market for conventional mortgages. Another feature was that the act authorized the Bank Board to offer below-market interest rate loans totaling up to $250 million, provided the funds were used to make loans on low-and middle-income family homes.[51] A third feature of this act was its extension, from 20 to 30 years, of the amount of time that newly created SLAs had in which to meet the net worth requirements. During 1970, the Board made commitments to SLAs totaling over $150 million for up to 10 years at below-market rates for loans used to finance mortgages on HUD-subsidized projects.

By the end of 1970, a new advances policy was essentially in place. Even Chairman Martin was willing to admit "that the traditional distinction between liquidity advances and expansions advances blurs in meaning in the actual uses of these funds."[52] The real distinction between types of advances was viewed as one of long term versus short term. The FHLBs were by now offering firm loan commitments on a fee basis, and they were also offering SLAs fixed-rate as well as the previously offered variable-rate advances. The long-term advances allowed for early repayments. No prepayment penalty was imposed on the variable rate advances, but one was attached to advances with fixed rates.[53] To encourage greater use of advances, the Bank Board increased the limit on expansion advances that any one member could acquire, from 17.5 percent to 25.0 percent of savings deposits. It also removed its restrictions that advances could not be used to acquire loans or participations outside of an SLA's normal lending area.

In May 1970, the Board was becoming concerned that with the decline in interest rates after the credit crunch in 1969, depositors were returning their money to the thrifts, who were using it to repay the substantial amount of advances taken out in recent months. The Board preferred that the returning deposits be used for more mortgages and responded by offering below-market interest rate advances to any member who converted their maturing advances to one-year loans. With all the special programs that the Bank Board was offering on advances, along with their regular pricing policies, they maintained rates on the advances that were below the average cost of funds to the Bank System.[54] It should also be pointed out that during this period the Board was giving greater flexibility to the regional FHLBs in setting nonprice policies on advances.

Besides the major changes on advances, the Bank Board was increasing the types of certificates that SLAs could offer and reducing the restrictions on the money acquired through certificates. For example, on March 26, 1970, the Bank Board raised to 30 percent from 20 percent the percentage of total savings that could be in certificates which matured in two to four years. A 20 percent limit still applied to certificates maturing in one to two years and to certificates maturing in more than four years. In addition, in January 1970, SLAs were allowed to offer two-year certificates with higher yields.

The authorization of the two-year certificate set the pattern for deposit rate regulation during the seventies. As Jaffee and Rosen point out, such regulations during this decade were characterized by three patterns.[55] The first was a steady increase in the interest rate differentials between certificate and passbook accounts, whereby increases in the maturity of the certificates accompanied the increases in interest rate differentials. The second was the move in the late 1970s to variable-rate ceiling certificates, which had their precursor in 1973 with "wild card" accounts.[56] The final pattern was the extremely sluggish adjustment in the ceilings once they were set. For example, when ceilings were first established in September 1966, the passbook ceiling was 4.75 percent. This was not increased to 5.00 percent until January 1970. The 5.25 percent ceiling was introduced in July 1973, but the increase to 5.50 percent would not occur until July 1, 1979.

Still other changes during this period included the authorizing of third-party transfer payments and a relaxation of many of the regulations affecting service corporations.[57] Third-party transfer powers were granted because the SLAs argued that not granting them this power would exclude them from the development of future electronic funds transfer systems and would put them at an even greater disadvantage relative to commercial banks.[58]

This same period marked the start of political recognition of the need for major legislative reform of the financial institutions. The President's Commission on Financial Structure and Regulation, known as the Hunt Commission, presented its conclusions in December of 1971. Few of the Commission's recommendations were incorporated into law at the time, but the report "became a road map for regulatory change."[59] It also became the basis for many attempts at legislative reform such as the Financial Institutions Act (FIA) of 1973, which was passed in the Senate in December but was never considered in the House.[60] The FIA contained many of the reforms which were ultimately included in the Depository Institutions Deregulation and Monetary Control Act (DIDMCA) of 1980, such as the phasing out of interest rate ceilings and the interest rate differential, the granting of increased consumer lending authority, and the authority to offer other consumer financial services.[61]

The year 1970 also marked the introduction of pass-through securities (PTs).[62]

In 1970, $452 million in PTs were sold, and by 1979 this would grow to a volume of $24.6 billion.[63] Initially, all of the PTs had the sponsorship of federal agencies. PTs involving conventional mortgages were not issued until 1977.

By the end of the sixties, there were substantial changes in the major decisions that the typical SLA manager had been making in 1955. For example, many SLAs were now issuing FHA mortgages; aggressively promoting certificates; more likely to be involved in considering branches and mergers; planning to originate, sell, and service part of the mortgage portfolio; and making greater use of advances.

Regulatory actions during the seventies followed two conflicting modes. One was the continual relaxation of rules affecting asset and liability powers. The other was an increase in consumer-oriented directives. As an example of the relaxation trend, in 1971 the Bank Board expanded the primary lending territory for an SLA from an area within the state and within a 100-mile radius of the home office to an area within the state and within a 100-mile radius of any office or branch. It also passed regulations making it easier to buy or sell participation certificates, easing the method of computing the Federal Insurance Reserve (FIR) requirement by extending the computation of the deposit base to an average of the last three years, and giving SLAs the authority to make 95 percent conventional loans with certain restrictions.

In 1972, SLAs were granted the authority to make mortgages with diminishing monthly payments, and the FIR requirement was again relaxed by extending the computation of the average savings balance back over five years. One of the few more stringent regulations passed during this period was the addition of a short-term liquidity requirement to the total liquidity requirement.

In 1973 the Bank Board authorized 2.5-year and 4-year certificates along with the ability to offer subordinated debentures and capital notes with a minimum denomination of $50,000 and a minimum maturity of seven years, and increased from 5 to 10 percent of total savings the amount of savings that SLAs could have in large certificates paying over 6.75 percent.[64] In addition, the Board indicated that notes and subordinated debentures could be sold and would be allowed to count as net worth for regulatory purposes under certain conditions.[65]

Another change in the regulations affecting liabilities was the "wild card" experiment, which began on May 16, 1973 when authorities removed the interest rate ceiling from "jumbo" certificates of deposit (CDs) at both SLAs and commercial banks. It was expanded on July 5, 1973 when the ceilings were also removed from CDs with a maturity of at least four years and a denomination of at least $1,000. In addition, the FHLBB restricted the volume of "wild card" CDs that SLAs could acquire to 5 percent of each institution's total time and savings deposits. The experiment was terminated in November 1973 with the reimposition of ceilings on all but the jumbo CDs. One issue in debates about this experiment is the amount of savings that shifted from SLAs to commercial banks (CBs) because of the *de facto* removal of the differential. (The consequences of this experiment are discussed in Chapter 7.)

A final development during 1973 affecting the liabilities of SLAs was the adoption by the Board of regulations allowing SLAs in New Hampshire and Massachusetts to issue Negotiable Order of Withdrawal or NOW accounts.[66] These regulations lagged somewhat behind the actual introduction of NOW accounts, which were first offered at an SLA in Worcester, Massachusetts in 1972.

The asset side of the balance sheet also went through some changes in 1973. In March the Bank Board expanded the ability of SLAs to buy participation certificates. In June it increased the maximum allowable loan-to-value ratio on construction loans. September marked an increase in the list of allowable activities for service corporations and an expansion of the primary lending area to the entire state from the 100-mile radius rule. In October the Bank Board authorized the FHLBs to accept deposits paying daily interest, as well as short-term CDs, and started a program in which SLAs could invest in the federal funds market.

In September of 1973, the Bank Board announced another special advances program, the purpose of which was to stimulate commitments by SLAs to builders in the hope that this would promote construction. This program consisted of $2.5 billion in advances at 8.5 percent, which was substantially below market rates at that time, and was linked to a program by the FHLMC to purchase an additional $500 million in mortgages. The earliest allowable takedown on these advances was six months from the announced date of the program. The FHLBB did not intend to arrange for any financing until such time as the SLAs actually came in to borrow the money, thus committing itself to substantial interest rate risk exposure.

The changes in the industry in 1974 were primarily mandated by Congress, and many represented the start of the consumer-oriented directives. In 1974, Congress passed the Housing and Community Development Act (HCDA), the Employee Retirement Income Security Act (ERISA), the Depository Institutions Amendments (DIA), the Real Estate Settlement Procedures Act (RESPA), and the Equal Credit Opportunity Act (ECOA). The primary effects of these laws were as follows: the HCDA revised the loan limits for federal associations; the ERISA reduced restrictions on Keogh accounts and created Individual Retirement Accounts (IRAs); the DIA increased insurance coverage from $20,000 to $40,000, gave the FHLBB the same enforcement authority as the Securities and Exchange Commission over stock associations, and mandated a phase-out of the FSLIC's secondary reserve; the RESPA provided comprehensive guidelines for loan closing costs and settlement practices; and the ECOA prohibited discrimination on the basis of sex or marital status.

In May 1974, President Nixon announced a $10.3 billion program to help the housing industry. Of this total, $4 billion was to be provided through the

FHLBS and $3 billion through the FHLMC. The $4 billion portion of the program was to be given out in the form of five-year advances at below-market interest rates, and the money was to be distributed to the FHLBs at the rate of $500 million per month. The $3 billion that went to the FHLMC started a program of forward commitments to buy mortgages at below-market rates. The intention of the program was that the SLAs would charge the borrower the below-market rate and then pass the mortgage on to the FHLMC. Under this program, if the FHLMC was unable to borrow the necessary money in the private market, it was authorized to borrow from the U.S. Treasury.

AMMINET was started by the FHLMC in the spring of 1974. Standing for "automated mortgage market information network," AMMINET provides the quotations which facilitate a secondary market in mortgages. Other new developments during 1974 included the initial offerings by the FHLBB of discount notes with maturities of 30 to 270 days and the creation of a Consolidated Securities Fund operated by the Office of Finance. This fund is operated essentially as a mutual fund for the investment monies of the FHLBs. The FHLBs henceforth had the choice of investing their money themselves or letting the Office of Finance do it for them.

Within the industry itself, some state-chartered SLAs began experimenting with variable-rate mortgages (VRMs). This occurred despite Congress rejecting proposals for implementation of VRMs on a national basis. By the end of 1976, 81 institutions were offering VRMs, and the majority of these were in California.[67]

The year 1975 was a relatively quiet year from a regulatory perspective and one that witnessed additional consumer-oriented legislation. Congress passed the Regulation Q and Home Mortgage Disclosure Act, which prohibited the elimination or reduction of the existing interest rate differential between the SLAs and the banks without prior congressional approval, and required certain financial institutions to disclose publicly information about mortgage loans made. The Mortgage Disclosure Act developed as a response to accusations of "redlining"[68] and an increased desire on the part of Congress to force financial institutions to participate in accomplishing socioeconomic goals. In the preamble to the Mortgage Disclosure Act, Congress states that:

. . . some depository institutions have sometimes contributed to the decline of certain geographic areas by their failure pursuant to their chartering responsibilities to provide adequate home financing to qualified applicants on reasonable terms and conditions.[69]

Notwithstanding the statement by Congress that it believed "redlining" was occurring, recent empirical research suggests that was not the case.[70]

At this time, the Bank Board published its own thinking about the future of the SLA industry.[71] The basic theme was that both the public interest and self-interest would best be served by having SLAs become consumer finance specialists. Many of the ideas and proposals were consistent with those suggested in the Friend study and by the Hunt Commission.

In 1976, Congress passed an all-time high of seven laws affecting the SLA industry. These included the Real Estate Settlement Procedures Act Amendments, the New England NOW Accounts Act, the Equal Credit Opportunity Act Amendments, Employee Retirement Amendments, the Housing Authorization Act, the Energy Conservation Standards for New Buildings Act, and the Tax Reform Act.[72] The RESPA Amendments and the Employee Retirement Amendments eased various requirements mandated in the original acts while the ECOA Amendments expanded coverage of the original act. The New England NOW Accounts Act expanded NOW account authority to the previously uncovered states in New England. The Tax Reform Act was a mixed bag for the industry. It reduced certain allowable federal income tax deductions for the associations and increased the minimum tax rate, but it also liberalized IRA and Keogh account provisions. During the year, the FHLBs continued to expand the services to member associations as many offered open lines of credit to members and one bank even offered overdraft advances.[73]

In 1977, Congress passed another Housing and Community Development Act (HCDA), which among its many provisions required that regulatory agencies evaluate the records of the regulated institutions in meeting the credit needs of their communities "when considering applications for branches, charters, deposit insurance, holding company acquisitions, and office relocations."[74] The 1977 HCDA did ease several of the restrictions affecting the industry, such as the ceiling on single-family loan amounts for association lending, federal agency purchases, FHA insurance and security for FHLB advances, as well as the ceiling on conventional and FHA home improvement loans, and it broadened the FHA graduated-payment mortgage program.

The implementing regulation for the Community Reinvestment Act (CRA) portion of the HCDA required that the Board of Directors of each institution develop and review at least annually a community reinvestment plan. This plan was to be referred to as the CRA Statement, and public notice had to be given that the Statement was available for public inspection. At this same time that the CRA responsibilities were being imposed on the SLAs, the Bank Board reached an out-of-court settlement with a civil rights group which among other things called for each association to maintain a loan application register.[75]

One setback suffered by the industry in 1977 was that a U.S. Court of Appeals ruled that the FHLBs could no longer offer online accounting services to member associations.[76] This restriction was lifted in September 1980 when the FHLBB authorized the FHLBs to offer both data-processing and check-clearing services, but at competitive rates.[77]

The 1978 Revenue Act introduced the provision which allowed a one-time exclusion to certain homeowners of up to $100,000 worth of capital gains on the sale of a home, and introduced the SEP (Simplified Employer's Pension) IRA program. Also significant for the industry was the passage in 1978 of the Financial Institutions Regulatory and Interest Rate Control Act, which gave additional regulatory powers to the FSLIC, gave additional investment powers to SLAs, expanded the FHLMC's authority, authorized NOW accounts for New York and New Jersey, and extended the Regulation Q authority to December 15, 1980.

On June 1, 1978, the Board authorized what was to be the first of several money market certificates (MMCs). In this case they approved a certificate with a 26-week maturity, a $10,000 minimum deposit, and a yield 25 basis points above the auction yield on the most recent six-month Treasury bills. At the same time they approved an eight-year certificate with a $1,000 minimum balance and an 8 percent ceiling. The six-month MMC has been referred to as "perhaps the most significant innovation of the past decade,"[78] given that SLAs now had to offer market rates on one form of deposits. At the time of its introduction, many in the industry believed it would be a destructive element that would raise the average cost of their deposits without providing any real benefits. By September 30, 1981, these six-month MMCs were to account for nearly 40.4 percent of total deposits at SLAs.[79]

On June 8, 1978, the Board announced the establishment of a $10-billion Community Investment Fund.[80] This fund would provide up to $2 billion in advances annually for five years at a rate of 50 basis points below the market rate to local lenders supporting community revitalization plans. Participating institutions were not required to pass through their subsidy in the form of lower cost mortgages but were encouraged to utilize the differential for expenses connected with the programs.[81]

Still more liberalizing of the rules occurred with the passage of the 1979 HCDA Amendments. These amendments increased again the ceiling on single-family loan limits for association lending, federal agency purchases, and FHA insurance. It also exempted FHA loans from state usury laws.

Effective January 1, 1979, the Bank Board granted authority to federally chartered SLAs to offer VRMs, graduated-payment mortgages, and reverse-annuity mortgages.[82] Initially, the VRMs were restricted only to those federals operating in states where the state-chartered associations were also allowed to offer them. On July 1 of the same year, the Bank Board extended authority to all federals to offer VRMs. The idea to authorize VRMs was not new to the Bank Board. All of the FHLBB Chairmen during the seventies have recently indicated that among their major regrets as former chairmen was not having been able to implement VRM authority.[83] In fact, at one point during the early seventies the Board had actually finalized a variable-rate lending regulation. However, on the day it was to be sent to the *Federal Register,* the Board received "a petition signed by a number of prominent members of the House Banking Committee requesting" them not to publish the regulation.[84]

In June 1979, the Bank Board adopted its final rules and regulations with respect to chartering, examining, and regulating mutual savings banks. Some mutual savings banks had always been under Bank Board control because they were members of the FHLBS. Heretofore, all mutual savings banks had been state-chartered institutions and thus also subject to state regulatory control.

A NEW ERA STARTS, 1980-PRESENT

Throughout the seventies, there had been efforts to reform the financial institutions industry in general, and the thrift industry in particular, via the FIA. These reform efforts failed for two reasons. The first was a belief that financial reform would adversely affect the cost and availability of mortgage credit. The second was that while each sector within the financial institutions industry wanted reform that would benefit itself, each strongly opposed any reform that would help somebody else. One frequent stumbling block was the interest rate differential. The SLA trade associations would not accept any reform that eliminated the differential, and the banking associations would not accept any reforms that did not eliminate it.[85]

In April of 1979, Congress was given notice by the U.S. Court of Appeals for the District of Columbia that some financial legislation was almost mandatory. The Court had ruled that the various regulatory bodies had recently exceeded their authority in granting Automatic Transfer Accounts (ATs) to banks, drafts to credit unions, and remote service units to SLAs. The Court resolved that these services would have to be terminated by January 1, 1980 unless Congress validated them. This court-ordered deadline now gave some impetus to Congress to tack onto the validation legislation many of the reforms which had previously been considered. Legislation was subsequently introduced in both the House and Senate with the validation authority and several other reforms.

A problem quickly arose, however, in that because reform legislation had been bottled up for so long, there were too many ideas that people wanted to put into law. The three most controversial reforms were the authorization for nationwide NOW accounts, a phaseout of Regulation Q, and proposals dealing with membership in the Federal Reserve System. Of these three, the Regulation Q phaseout (that is, the elimination of all interest rate ceilings) was certainly the most controversial. It became clear that resolving the phaseout issue would require more time than was available under the court-ordered deadline. Senator Proxmire and Congressman Reuss arranged for a 90-day extension of the deadline, which was passed on December 28, 1979.

During the extension period, the House held its hearings on the phaseout proposal and became inclined to support a phaseout. Compromises were reached on all three key issues as to procedures and goals, and the final legislation, known as the Depository Institutions Deregulation and Monetary Control Act (DIDMCA), was signed into law on March 31, 1980, the deadline date provided by the 90-day extension.

The key feature of the DIDMCA was a six-year phaseout of deposit rate ceilings. Other features in the law which affected SLAs included the authority for federal SLAs to offer NOW accounts; to engage in credit card activities; to invest up to 20 percent of assets in consumer loans, commercial paper, and corporate debt securities; to offer trust services; to issue mutual capital certificates; and to make first or second mortgage loans without regard to size or geographic restrictions. The limitation on investment in service corporations was increased from 1 percent to 3 percent of total assets. The Bank Board was authorized to lower the federal insurance reserve requirement from 5 percent to 3 percent of the deposit base. Deposit insurance was increased to $100,000, and all state mortgage usury laws were preempted subject to the right of a state to reinstate them within three years. Another part of the package was that Congress left the issue of variable-rate mortgages to be decided by the various regulators.

Some indication of the expected effect of the DIDMCA on the SLA industry can be gleaned from a recent survey by Donald Fraser.[86] Receiving survey responses from managers at 205 SLAs, Fraser found that over one-half of the respondents expected that NOW accounts would provide at least 5 percent of their deposits by 1985, and 20 percent of the managers believed NOW accounts would provide at least 10 percent of their deposits by then. At least one-half expected that consumer loans would grow to at least 10 percent of assets by 1985, and 10 percent felt they would increase to as much as 25 percent of assets. All the managers believed that the DIDMCA would substantially improve their ability to compete, and the managers of the smaller associations were strongest on this point. The managers also agreed that ultimately the DIDMCA would lead to reductions in the amount of money that would otherwise have been available for single-family mortgages.

In view of the obvious problem of disintermediation created by the Regulation Q ceilings, an impartial observer might wonder why it took Congress so long and required so much effort to terminate them. There are at least two reasons. One is that many people honestly believed that the ceilings kept the cost of funds to SLAs lower than what they frequently would have been, and this meant that the SLAs could charge less for mortgages than they otherwise would have.[87] A second reason is that supporters of ceilings believed that the financial problems of SLAs would have been worse during the periods of disintermediation if there had been no ceilings.[88]

Several reasons are suggested as to why the DIDMCA passed when previous, less grandiose efforts such as the FIA failed. Ken McLean, Staff Director of the U.S. Senate Committee on Banking, Housing, and Urban Affairs during this period, suggests four reasons.[89] First, the high rates of inflation and the associated high market interest rates during this period meant that the savers in our society were being heavily penalized. Saving at depository institutions was in effect being discouraged, and this meant less money with which to finance capital expenditures. The second reason is that deregulation efforts in other sectors of the economy were deemed as having favorable results, and thus legislators were less fearful about the consequences of deregulating key aspects of the SLA industry. Third, by 1979 money market mutual funds were well established and had effectively eliminated the significance of interest rate ceilings for all but the smallest and most conservative savers. A fourth reason is that the American Bankers Association changed its position and now actively supported the spread of NOW accounts.

It has been stated often that the DIDMCA was "the most important piece of banking legislation since the 1930s."[90] However, there is some debate as to whether the act was one of deregulation or reregulation.[91] Whichever it is, clearly between the changes the law requires and those it approves, the typical SLA may move in the eighties to a position where it is a different institution even from what it was in the late sixties.

In order to accomplish the phaseout of ceilings by December 31, 1986, the DIDMCA created the Depository Institutions Deregulation Committee (DIDC), which is a new version of the old Interagency Coordinating Committee. The DIDC consists of the Chairmen of the Federal Reserve Board, the Federal Deposit Insurance Corporation, the FHLBB, the National Credit Union Administration Board, as well as the Secretary of Treasury as voting members, and the Comptroller of Currency as a nonvoting member. It is somewhat ironic that one of the first issues the DIDC considered was the elimination of merchandise premiums. The giving of premiums had provided a nonpecuniary method to bypass ceiling rates. The proposal to eliminate premiums thus would have made the ceilings more stringent rather than less. Lobbying pressure from the manufacturers of these premiums scuttled this proposal. Initial efforts by the Committee to raise the ceilings were met with protests by the SLA industry and the FHLBB Chairman that such a move was still too premature in view of the precarious health of the industry.

By the end of 1980, rising interest rates were taking their toll on the economic health of the SLA industry. Although the industry had a profit of roughly $800 million in 1980, 35 percent of the SLAs reported a loss in the second half of that year. In the first six months of 1981, the industry recorded its first semiannual loss since the FHLBB was created, and in the second half of 1981, the loss widened from $1.5 billion to $3.1 billion. The widespread nature of the problems is supported by the fact that in the second half of 1980, 85 percent of the SLAs reported losses.[92] Combined with these operating losses was a form of nonpublicized but massive disintermediation which has come to be referred to as a "silent run." In 1981 the insured associations had lost over $25 billion in net new savings.[93]

To help stop the outflow of deposits from the industry and to attract new deposits which could be used profitably, several new financial instruments were created. In 1980 a small saver's certificate was authorized. It is similar to the six-month MMC except that the allowable yield is keyed to the yield on 30-month Treasury notes. It differs from the MMC in that it has a 30-month maturity and no minimum denomination.[94] In March 1982, a 91-day certificate was authorized by the DIDC. Its maximum yield was to equal that on 13-week Treasury bills for thrifts and mutual savings banks. Commercial banks were restricted to paying a .25 percentage point lower rate. The 91-day certificate differed from the six-month MMC in that it would require a minimum of only $7,500 rather than $10,000.[95]

Then in June 1982 the DIDC approved still another new instrument. This time a $20,000 minimum daily balance account was authorized, and the maximum rate on this account was pegged to the three-month Treasury bill yield for SLAs and 25 basis points less for banks. The maturity on the account was allowed to range from 7 to 31 days, but this account could not be offered until September 1, 1982.[96]

At the same time that it approved the 91-day certificate, the DIDC also declared that beginning May 1, 1982, the ceiling would be effectively eliminated on all accounts that matured in at least 3.5 years. The Chairman of the FDIC was the only member of the DIDC to vote against this proposal. He argued that it was inconsistent to continue to give thrifts a competitive edge on new instruments when the Committee was charged with deregulating interest rates. This resulted in the additional decisions that the differential would last for only one year and that it would not apply when the Treasury bill rate was less than 9 percent.[97]

In the Economic Recovery Tax Act of 1981, two proposals were incorporated to help the SLA industry. One was the All-Savers Certificate. With a one-year maturity, this certificate paid a rate up to 70 percent of the yield on comparable one-year Treasury securities. The key benefit was that the interest income from this certificate was tax-exempt. The only restriction was that the tax-exempt income could not exceed $1,000 per person on a life-time basis. The other proposal in the Tax Act that was intended to bring deposits into the SLAs was the universal IRA. IRAs were previously restricted to workers who did not contribute to a pension fund in a particular year. The universal IRAs were made available to all workers.

In August 1982, interest rates finally started to decline and in a rather dramatic manner. By early November, they had fallen to a level where some industry observers were speculating that most SLAs would be out of danger of financial collapse by late 1983 provided the interest rates did not return to the earlier high ranges.[98] As an extra boost to the industry, Congress passed an additional aid package in October 1982. The most significant of the new changes allowed SLAs to make commercial loans totaling up to 10 percent of their assets after 1983 and to offer checking accounts to business customers. Other changes included an increased allowance in commercial real estate lending from 20 percent of assets to 40 percent, an increase in consumer loan authority from 20 to 30 percent of total assets, and the authority to offer NOW accounts to governmental units.[99]

CONCLUSIONS

The FHLBS was established in 1932 to help the housing industry by giving the SLA industry special privileges and services. Initial benefits included access to advances and the opportunity to sell problem loans to the HOLC. The belief that helping the SLA industry helped the housing industry continued to motivate Congress and the FHLBB to grant special privileges to SLAs in the postwar years. Some of these privileges included tax benefits which required an unusually heavy investment in long-term, fixed-rate mortgages, and "low-cost" passbook deposits which could not be acquired through direct price competition. It is unfortunate that this asset-liability structure tended to maximize the interest rate risk exposure of the SLAs. Thus it is no surprise that during the credit crunches of the fifties, sixties, and early seventies the SLA industry had some serious problems, and beginning in 1980 the industry started dying as a result of the higher interest rates.

Beginning in the mid-seventies, congressional actions began to turn against the SLA industry. SLAs were no longer being seen as the best route through which to promote the housing industry. Instead, they were seen as an inhibitor to congressional socioeconomic goals and found themselves imposed with the additional operating expenses associated with such acts as the CRA and RESPA. However, simultaneous with these restrictive laws were rules and regulations which began to "liberate" both the asset and liability powers of the SLA industry. Liberation of the liability side preceded that of the asset side. Some of the liberation came as a response to the developments in the economy. An example would be the money market and other special certificates which were authorized to offset the disintermediation resulting from the combination of high interest rates and the development of money market mutual funds. Other parts of the liberation came as a response to the dramatic problems of the industry. Examples of this form of liberation include the move toward adjustable mortgages, expanded consumer lending authority, commercial lending and deposit authority, and expanded powers in using financial futures contracts.

The industry today has the capability to be substantially different than it was ten or even seven years ago. The important question, however, is whether these new capabilities will really help the industry. That is the issue to which we turn in the remaining chapters.

NOTES

1. At the year-end of 1981, there were 4,034 members. Of these, 3,884 were SLAs, 148 were mutual savings banks, and two were life insurance companies. For further details see *'82 Savings and Loan Sourcebook,* United States League of Savings Associations, Chicago, Ill., p. 44.

2. Much of the material in the first half of this chapter is drawn from Thomas B. Marvell, *The Federal Home Loan Bank Board,* Praeger, New York, 1969.

3. *Savings and Loan Fact Book, 1973,* U.S. Savings and Loan League, Chicago, Ill., p. 57.

4. Marvell, *Bank Board,* p. 7.

5. Ruth Werner, "The Federal Home Loan Bank System," *Federal Home Loan Bank Board Journal,* April 1982, p. 16.

6. Werner, "Bank System," p. 17.

7. Ibid.

8. John M. Buckley, Jr., "The Federal Home Loan Bank Board," *FHLBB Journal,* April 1982, p. 5.

9. Werner, "Bank System," p. 17.

10. Marvell, *Bank Board,* pp. 26-27.

11. Buckley, "Bank Board," p. 5.

12. Werner, "Bank System," p. 32.

13. Ibid.

14. Marvell, *Bank Board,* p. 50.

15. *Fact Book, 1973,* p. 57. The pace of the decline in the number of associations has accelerated during the eighties, and there are only slightly less than 4,000 associations in operation today.

16. Buckley, "Bank Board," p. 7.

17. Ibid., p. 6.

18. Ibid.

19. Ibid.

20. Marvell, *Bank Board,* pp. 39-40.

21. Buckley, "Bank Board," p. 7.

22. *Savings and Loan '78 Fact Book,* United States League of Savings Associations, Chicago, Ill., p. 105.

23. Marvell, *Bank Board,* p. 30.

24. Buckley, "Bank Board," p. 7.

25. Marvell, *Bank Board,* p. 31.

26. Buckley, "Bank Board," p. 7.

27. This is, of course, the same argument used today by credit unions. However, as credit unions continue to increase their market share of deposits and increase their service offerings, the same fate of being made subject to taxation will likely befall them.

28. Statement by William K. Divers, *FHLBB Journal,* April 1982, p. 76.

29. *'82 Savings and Loan Sourcebook,* p. 40.

30. Buckley, "Bank Board," p. 7.

31. Ibid.

32. A.D. Theobald, *Forty-Five Years on the Up Escalator* (private printing), 1975, p. 200.

33. Dwight M. Jaffee, "The Federal Home Loan Bank System since 1965," in *Institutions, Policies and Economic Performance,* Carnegie-Rochester Conference Series on Public Policy, Vol. 4, 1976, p. 165.

34. *'78 Fact Book,* p. 88.

35. Dwight M. Jaffee, "What to Do about Savings and Loan Associations?" *Journal of Money, Credit and Banking,* November 1974, p. 540.

36. Buckley, "Bank Board," p. 10.

37. That is, the SLA manager has traditionally had only two basic price decisions to make. One is the price he pays for deposits, and the other is the price he charges for mortgages.

38. Andrew S. Carron, *The Plight of Thrift Institutions,* Brookings Institution, Washington, D.C., 1982.

39. Ken McLean, "Legislative Background of the Depository Institutions Deregulation and Monetary Control Act of 1980," *Savings and Loan Asset Management Under Deregulation: Proceedings of the Sixth Annual Conference,* Federal Home Loan Bank of San Francisco, 1980.

40. See, for example, the statement by John E. Horne, the Chairman of the FHLBB during 1966, in the *FHLBB Journal*, April 1982, pp. 79-80.

41. *'78 Fact Book*, p. 118.

42. Ibid., pp. 33-34.

43. *'78 Fact Book*, p. 118.

44. Jaffee, "What to Do?" p. 541. This comment was made in support of the same thesis developed in Kenneth J. Thygerson, "The Effect of Government Housing and Mortgage Credit Programs on Savings and Loan Associations," Occasional Paper No. 6, United States Savings and Loan League, Chicago, 1973.

45. Horne, p. 79.

46. See, for example, Maurice Weinrobe, "The Effectiveness of FHLBB Liquidity Policy, 1971-75," Federal Home Loan Bank Board Research Working Paper No. 66, March 1976.

47. "Martin Asks Bank Policy Changes to Help Close Mortgage Credit Gap: Says S & L Industry Must Maintain Home-Financing Lead," *FHLBB Journal*, May 1969, pp. 1-2.

48. A "consolidated obligation" is a bond sold by the Office of Finance of the FHLBB. The amount and frequency of sale of consolidated obligations are based on requests by the FHLBs. The proceeds from the sale are distributed to the FHLBs according to their requests.

49. "Martin Asks Bank Policy Changes," p. 4.

50. Marvell, *Bank Board*, p. 36.

51. R. Bruce Ricks and Harris C. Friedman, "The Housing Opportunity Allowance Program," *FHLBB Journal*, February 1971, p. 6.

52. Preston Martin, "New Credit Policies for the 1970's: A Discussion of FHLBB Objectives," *FHLBB Journal*, December 1970, p. 3.

53. Ibid., p. 4.

54. Ibid., p. 5.

55. Dwight Jaffee and Kenneth Rosen, "The Changing Liability Structure of Savings and Loan Associations," *Journal of the American Real Estate and Urban Economics Association*, Vol. 8, No. 1 (Spring 1980), p. 41.

56. "Wild card" accounts, which will be discussed more fully in Chapter 7, were certificates on which SLAs and banks were allowed to pay any rate of interest, provided there was a $1,000 minimum deposit.

57. Third-party transfer payments are payments made to a third party (such as a utility) by a second party (such as an SLA), upon request of a first party (such as the depositor).

58. See Jaffee, "Bank System since 1965," p. 192.

59. Robert O. Edmister, *Financial Institutions: Markets and Management*, McGraw-Hill, New York, 1980, p. 258.

60. Kent W. Colton, "Financial Reform: A Review of the Past and Prospects for the Future," Invited Research Working Paper No. 37, Office of Policy and Economic Research, Federal Home Loan Bank Board, September 1980, p. 15.

61. Buckley, "Bank Board," p. 11.

62. A pass-through security represents a claim on a portfolio of mortgages held by the issuer of the PTs. All payments on the mortgages, less a service fee, are passed-through to the holder of the security.

63. *'82 Sourcebook*, p. 51.

64. Prior to 1973, SLAs were able to issue certificates with 2.5-year and 4-year

maturities but could not pay a higher yield. The new rules allowed higher yields for these longer maturities.

65. Jaffee, "Bank System since 1965," p. 193.

66. A NOW account is, from the depositor's perspective, the same as an interest-bearing checking account at a bank. There are a few technical differences in how a bank and a thrift process these accounts.

67. Colton, "Financial Reform," p. 24.

68. "Redlining" is the practice of making the location of purchased property a major criterion in the decision of whether or not to grant a loan.

69. Title III, Pub. Law 94-200, Section 302(a).

70. A. Thomas King, "Discrimination in Mortgage Lending: A Study of Three Cities," Research Working Paper No. 91, Office of Policy and Economic Research, Federal Home Loan Bank Board, February 1980.

71. Federal Home Loan Bank Board, *A Financial Institution for the Future: Savings, Housing Finance, Consumer Services: An Examination of the Restructuring of the Savings and Loan Industry,* Washington, D.C., GPO, 1975.

72. *'78 Factbook,* pp. 119-20.

73. James L. Richter, "Office of the Federal Home Loan Banks," *FHLBB Journal,* April 1976, p. 25.

74. Michael L. Unger, "The Community Reinvestment Act and the Community Lending Activities of Savings and Loan Associations," a paper presented at the Mid-West Finance Association meeting, St. Louis, Missouri, April 5-7, 1979, p. 4.

75. Buckley, "Bank Board," p. 11.

76. James W. McBride, "The Office of the Federal Home Loan Banks," *FHLBB Journal,* April 1978, p. 26.

77. *Wall Street Journal,* September 19, 1980, p. 6.

78. Colton, "Financial Reform," p. 22.

79. *'82 Sourcebook,* p. 23.

80. Alvin Hirshen and Susan Evans, "Revitalizing America's Older Communities: More than 400 S&L's Using $1.13 Billion in CIF Funds," *FHLBB Journal,* February 1979, p. 2.

81. Unger, "Community Reinvestment Act," p. 13.

82. A reverse-annuity mortgage is one in which the borrower pledges real estate as collateral, but then the lender provides monthly payments to the borrower. When the mortgage matures, the borrower owes one lump-sum payment.

83. *FHLBB Journal,* April 1982, pp. 81-88.

84. Ibid., p. 82.

85. McLean, "Legislative Background," pp. 17-18.

86. Donald R. Fraser, "DIDMCA and the Savings and Loan Industry: Evidence from a Survey," *FHLBB Journal,* January 1982, pp. 2-8.

87. See, for example, Horne, p. 80.

88. McLean, "Legislative Background," p. 23.

89. Ibid., p. 27.

90. Robert Craig West, "The Depository Institutions Deregulation Act of 1980: A Historical Perspective," *Economic Review,* Federal Reserve Bank of Kansas City, February 1982, p. 3.

91. Edward Kane, "Reregulation, Savings and Loan Diversification and the Flow of Housing Finance," *Savings and Loan Asset Management under Deregulation: Pro-*

ceedings of the Sixth Annual Conference, Federal Home Loan Bank of San Francisco, 1980.

92. Timothy D. Schellhardt, "S&Ls Had Record $4.6 Billion Loss in '81; $6 Billion Deficit Seen Possible This Year," *Wall Street Journal,* April 6, 1982.

93. *'82 Sourcebook,* p. 21. Net new savings are new savings less withdrawals. A comparable statistic is the net savings receipts, which is new savings plus interest credited less withdrawals. In 1981 the net savings receipts were 2.7 percent of total savings deposits at the start of the year, which compares to a more normal range of 10 to 20 percent over the last two decades.

94. Based on this author's observations, most SLAs impose a $100 minimum denomination on these certificates.

95. "Banks, Thrifts Can Offer, Starting May 1, 91-Day Certificates Paying Market Rates," *Wall Street Journal,* March 23, 1982, p. 2.

96. "Savings Accord to Help Banks, S&Ls is Cleared," *Wall Street Journal,* June 30, 1982.

97. Ibid.

98. John Andrew, "Ailing S&Ls See Early Return to Health With New Powers, Lower Interest Rates," *Wall Street Journal,* November 19, 1982, p. 12.

99. "S&Ls Receive Expanded Lending Powers As Bank Board Carries Out Aid Package," *Wall Street Journal,* November 5, 1982, p. 4.

2

The Determinants of Profitability
for Savings and Loans

Although during recent years most SLAs have been losing money, some were still profitable and some were losing only small amounts of money. These differences in profitability have not been purely coincidental. Several reasons account for these differences and are important because they not only provide further insight as to how the industry got into its current problems, but they also provide insight as to the value of some of the changes which are occurring in the industry at the present time.

Before considering the determinants of profitability, it is important to understand what type of profitability should be measured. The type depends on the goals of the firm. Evidence suggests that the goals and objectives of SLAs are neither universally accepted nor without ambiguity. A simple description of a basic savings and loan operation, however, results in the definition of three basic decision areas affecting SLA profitability, all of which, in turn, are affected by the particular economies of scale associated with a savings and loan operation.

THE MANAGERIAL GOAL IN AN SLA

A common assumption in the financial theory literature is that the goal of the manager of a firm is to maximize the shareholder's wealth, and for stock corporations wealth would be measured in terms of the market value of the common stock.[1] The savings and loan industry, however, has traditionally been a mutual industry with a steadily growing representation of stock corporations. The concept of a maximization of owner-wealth as a goal for a mutual entity is at best ambiguous and at times rejected. Alfred Nicols has pointed out that:

Spokesmen from the mutual side of the business often attack their rivals, the stock companies, because of their interest in profit making. Mutuals are said to be superior because they have different goals: they are primarily interested in home financing; they are not watching the stock market; they are not interested in profits but rather the safety of the funds they invest for their savers. It is their proud boast that unlike the stock associations, profits plays [*sic*] no role in the mutual.[2]

Nicols' observation notwithstanding, most writers today identify some form of profitability maximization as the goal of both stock and mutual associations. For example, David Cole has suggested that return on assets is the best indicator of profitability for mutual associations and that return on equity is the best measure for stock associations.[3] In this case, the numerator of both ratios is net income, which he defines as income after taxes and after dividends paid on savings capital. The denominators are average total assets and average net worth, respectively. Eugene Brigham and R. Petit suggest that the appropriate measure of profitability for mutuals is net income plus interest on deposits to total assets.[4] Their argument is based on the fact that in a mutual, the depositors are the "owners."

Most other researchers in the area, however, opt for the assumption that the goal of all firms in the industry is to maximize return on net worth. Verbrugge, Schick, and Thygerson argue that this is more likely the uniform goal used at least in recent years because of the ceilings imposed on almost all of the types of deposits. In other words, mutual organizations have really not been free to pass through to the "owners" all of the profits that they might like because of the interest rate ceilings established in 1966.[5] Wilson, O'Connel, and Olson, in a similar vein, state that "the primary objective of managers should be to maximize income given that risk is controlled to acceptable levels."[6]

Another goal occasionally cited for mutuals is that of growth. For example, John Lapp suggested a dual goal of growth in combination with profit maximization.[7] He further suggests that growth as an objective is motivated by the fact that the salaries of management are usually keyed to the total assets of the association. It should be noted that Lapp also provides empirical support for growth as a co-objective. He shows through theoretical derivation that the yield on an SLA's existing mortgage portfolio will affect the growth rate of deposits if the growth rate is part of this dual objective. The empirical support for this point is that the average yield on mortgages held by SLAs lags one year and is a statistically significant variable in a regression which has the growth rate of per capita deposits as a dependent variable.

At about the same time that Lapp published his results, another study was produced by Lionel Kalish and Joseph McKenzie which provided a fair amount of evidence that profit maximization was the likely objective of SLAs.[8] Kalish and McKenzie show theoretically that under a goal of profit maximization, an SLA's past portfolio yield would not affect its current mortgage policy; and under a goal of deposit maximization, the higher the yield on the historic portfolio the lower the effective rate on the new loans. To test these hypotheses, the authors ran several regressions which had as the dependent variable the average effective rate on new, single-family mortgage loans charged by each of the associations in the sample during the first six months of 1976. Empirical support for their hypotheses depended on the signs and statistical significance of the independent variable representing the past portfolio yield.[9] The authors found that in regressions involving the total sample, and samples of stock, mutual, Chicago, and nonconcentrated markets, the past portfolio yield term was insignificant. Only in the regressions run with a sample of SLAs operating in concentrated markets did the coefficients of the past portfolio yield have the correct sign and statistical significance.

A third bit of evidence regarding growth as a goal was also provided by Nicols, who argued that the managers of mutuals would be motivated to redirect profits from the mutual SLA to what he refers to as the infrastructure.[10] The infrastructure is the group of businesses which provides services ancillary to the mortgage lending business and include such activities as mortgage banking and insurance. Nicols argues that this redirection of profits would reduce the potential contributions to reserves in mutuals relative to what stock associations would achieve, and those lower reserves would retard growth. Nicols supports this argument by noting that from 1950 to 1964 the stock associations in California increased their share of total assets and that of the federally chartered (mutual) associations from 41.9 percent to 66.3 percent. If deposit growth has been more of a goal of the mutuals than of stocks, then it would seem they have failed miserably. In general, the evidence regarding deposit growth as a goal for mutuals is contradictory.

It has also been suggested and empirically shown that lack of competitive pressures from the marketplace and absence of owner influence results in managerial decisions involving less risk exposure and greater operating costs.[11] These two conditions certainly describe much of the SLA industry. SLA managers are protected from market pressures in several ways. For example, one of the criteria used by the FHLBB in approving new charters is that existing associations not be damaged by the new entrant. As another example, since 1966 SLAs have had interest rate ceilings equal to or higher than those allowed commercial banks. The majority of SLA managers are also removed from owner influence in that a large portion of the majority of the industry is mutual as opposed to stock. In fact, Nicols argues that there is no legal support for depositor ownership of mutuals, nor is there any evidence that depositors direct mutuals or help in setting goals or procedures. This lack of any owner influence has led Nicols to refer to mutuals as "self-perpetuating aristocracies."[12]

In line with this idea that managers at the mutual SLAs may be prone to decisions involving less risk and more operating expenses, Nicols looked at various statistical measures of operating expense in an SLA as they relate to the production of new loans. As an example he cites the fact that in 1962 the California stock SLAs had twice as much new loan volume as the mutuals but only 60 percent again as much operating expenses; this, he suggests, would indicate that the mutuals had higher than necessary expenses.[13] James Verbrugge and Steven Goldstein have also tested this proposition.[14] Their two samples consisted of 126 California SLAs and an additional 50 associations located in the Los Angeles

Standard Metropolitan Statistical Area (SMSA). All of the tests were performed on both samples. To test for less risk exposure by mutuals, Verbrugge and Goldstein used linear regressions with the ratio of scheduled items to total loans as a proxy for loan quality. The independent variables included the association's size as measured by total assets, the age of the association, the average ratio of construction loans to total loans, the average annual rate of growth of total assets over the sample period, and a dummy variable for the organizational form of the association.[15] The coefficient for the organizational form was significant for both samples and showed that less risky portfolios were held by the mutual associations.

Verbrugge and Goldstein then looked at the effect of organizational form on operating expenses, using the same testing procedure. The results of these tests will be discussed in the section on operating expense management. Suffice it at this point to say that the tests showed that mutuals tended to have higher operating expenses. In a similar study by Verbrugge and Jahera, the authors found in a sample of only California SLAs that mutuals paid a significantly higher amount in wages and salaries. When the sample was expanded to include SLAs from Ohio and Texas as well, the authors also found that in highly concentrated markets, mutuals paid a significantly higher amount in wages and salaries. But, in those markets where there were more competitors, mutuals and stocks tended to pay the *same amount* of wages and salaries.[16] Nicols argues that compensation for managers at mutuals tends to vary inversely with their involvement in the infrastructure. For example, managers who own the insurance agency from which their borrowers must buy insurance tend to have lower compensation than managers without the insurance interest.[17]

A more recent study by Andrew Carron provides statistically significant evidence that the stock companies, and not the mutuals, have the higher operating expense ratios.[18] One of the major problems with Carron's tests, however, is that although he incorporates total assets into his regressions, he does not incorporate any variables which represent new loan activity.

The one thing that is clear from the foregoing discussion is that it is not clear that there exists an unambiguous, uniform goal for all savings and loans. In the case of stock associations, most researchers assume that the objective is to maximize return on equity. The empirical evidence supports the suggestion that stocks do a better job than mutuals of controlling expenses and that stocks are more prone to risk taking than mutuals. With this ambiguity in mind, we will now proceed to an examination of some of the factors which appear to create differences in profitability among all associations.

DETERMINANTS OF PROFITABILITY

The determinants of differences in profitability can be more easily discussed when classified within major decision areas faced by SLA managers. These decision areas can be easily defined by looking at a simple description of an SLA operation.

Table 2.1
1981 Balance Sheet

	Dollar Amount (in millions)	Percentage of Total
Mortgage Loans Outstanding	518,350	78.1
Cash and Investments Eligible for Liquidity	48,534	7.3
Other Assets	96,960	14.6
Total Assets	663,844	100.0
Deposits Earning Regular Rate or Below*	101,823	15.3
Deposits Earning in Excess of Regular Rate	422,551	63.7
Other Liabilities	111,078	16.7
Net Worth	28,392	4.3
Total Liabilities and Net Worth	663,844	100.0

SOURCE: *'82 Savings and Loan Source Book,* United States League of Savings Associations, Chicago, Ill., pp. 40-42. All figures are preliminary.

* "Deposits earning the regular rate" refers to accounts earning the passbook rate, which has a current ceiling of 5.50 percent. This awkward terminology is used here because it is the classification and terminology used by the FHLBB in its semiannual reports, and it is the terminology used by the U.S. League.

A traditional savings and loan is one of the simplest financial intermediaries to describe. A savings and loan accepts deposits and makes mortgage loans. Although these two activities are not exclusive lines of an SLA's business, they describe the vast majority of the activity performed by an SLA. This is easy to see if we examine a recent balance sheet and income statement for the industry, which are shown in Tables 2.1 and 2.2. Mortgages constitute nearly 80 percent of total assets, a figure which has not varied more than a few percentage points for many decades. Deposits constitute nearly 80 percent of total liabilities. Net worth, a figure which has been slowly declining in recent years, is 4.3 percent of assets. The income statement reflects the balance sheet in that slightly less than 90 percent of industry income was derived from mortgage interest and slightly more than 90 percent of total expenses was attributed to interest paid to depositors.

Based on this description, it would appear that there are three decision areas confronting the SLA manager. These can be categorized as asset management, liability management, and operating expense management.

Asset Management

The most comprehensive study in recent years on the determinants of profitability for SLAs was probably the previously mentioned work by Verbrugge, Shick,

Table 2.2
1981 Income Statement

	Dollar Amount (in millions)	Percentage of Total
Interest Income on Mortgage Loans	49,541	75.5
Interest Income on Investments	7,874	12.0
Other Income	8,203	12.5
Total Income	65,618	100.0
Interest Expenses	63,606	90.5
Other Expenses	8,209	11.6
Taxes	− 1,564	− 2.1
Total Expenses	70,251	100.0
Net Income	− 4,633	

SOURCE: *'82 Savings and Loan Source Book,* United States League of Savings Associations, Chicago, Ill., pp. 40-42. All figures are preliminary.

and Thygerson (VST). These researchers selected 478 SLAs from a stratified sample based on association asset size. They then selected financial ratios in each of the key decision areas which would be indicative of different strategies used by SLA managers. They next conducted an analysis of variance test and identified those ratios which were statistically significant in explaining the variance in the return on net worth ratios for the sample firms for the years 1971 and 1972. Under the asset management category, they tested the ratio of assets eligible for liquidity to total savings, interest on mortgage loans to total mortgage loans, fee income to total income, and nonoperating income to total income. The only ratios that were statistically significant in both years were the interest on mortgage loans ratio and the fee income ratio.

VST next analyzed why these two ratios varied for the different associations. In the case of fee income, they found a positive and significant relationship with the ratio of loans serviced to total loans in the portfolio, and they found the loans serviced ratio was more significant for the large associations. Somewhat less significant but nonetheless important in explaining the variance in fee income was the ratio of loans sold during the year to loans originated during the year.[19]

The authors also found that usury ceilings had a negative and significant influence on fee income. This means that the associations in states with effective usury ceilings were apparently not able to generate sufficient fees to offset the lower interest rates to which they were restricted. It also means that these associations were put in a position of having to purchase loans. Finally, the authors found that even after allowing for these other factors, the size of the association still had a positive and significant influence on fee income. One possibility is that the largest associations were able to "internalize" a greater proportion of the total fees involved in the origination process where such fees traditionally flowed to outside firms.

The authors then analyzed the determinants of mortgage yield and found several statistically significant influences. They found that higher ratios of conventional multi-family and construction loans to total loans and higher mortgage loan turnovers were positively associated with the mortgage yield. These first two ratios are easy to understand as multi-family and construction loans normally have higher rates than single-family loans. The turnover ratio is significant most likely because interest rates during the sample period (1971-1972) were substantially higher than they were during the previous decade.[20]

VST also found that the mortgage yield was inversely and significantly related to the number of savings and loans and mutual savings banks in the SMSA or county and to the presence of a below-market usury ceiling. It would appear that the competition that occurs when there is a larger number of neighboring institutions produced a lower mortgage rate. Finally, the authors found that the ratio of loans purchased to the total of loans purchased and originated was negatively related to mortgage yield. The suggested reason for this was that the SLAs which purchased a larger proportion of the mortgages that they acquired during the year were probably unable to invest their funds profitably in local mortgages.[21]

These results were similar to those provided in another study on profitability by David Smith, Donald Kaplan, and William Ford (SKF).[22] In their study, SKF divided SLAs into five categories based on asset size and then designated the top 10 percent within each category as high-performance associations (HPAs). They, too, found that their sample of 347 HPAs outperformed the average of all SLAs in terms of both mortgage yield and fee income. Their measure of performance was income per $100 of total assets in 1976, and most of the differences in net income were directly attributable to these revenue differences.[23]

SKF's results also concurred with those of VST in that they found that the high-performance associations had less income from securities and mortgage-backed bonds than the average for all associations. They emphasized the buyer-seller relationship for mortgages by pointing out that:

In 1976, the savings and loan industry sold $5.2 billion worth of loans and participations and purchased $6.7 billion worth. High performance associations, however, sold $1.0 billion of these loans and participations and purchased only $386 million of them.[24]

Some additional observations by SKF were not provided by VST. For example, while the high-performance associations had more assets invested in mortgages than the average association (84.3 percent compared to 82.2 percent), they also had larger portions of their mortgages in conventional as opposed to FHA-Veterans' Administration (FHA-VA) mortgages. Specifically, the high-performance associations had 93.0 percent of their mortgages in conventionals, compared to 89.6 percent for all associations. Finally, SKF note that the high-performance associations have less money invested in liquid assets, 8.4 percent compared to 9.0 percent for all associations. Also, they had a substantially lower ratio of scheduled items to net worth (14.2 percent compared to an industry average of 21.3 percent).

The negative effect of local competition on mortgage yields is reinforced in recent work by Lewis Spellman.[25] Spellman derived multiple regression estimates from a cross-section sample of 106 SMSAs for 1972. He found that, *ceteris paribus,* savings and loan profits in a market declined with the addition of either a unit bank or a unit savings and loan, and the amount of decrease was approximately the same for each. He also found that the addition of a bank branch also reduced aggregate profits, although the magnitude of reduction was about one-third the amount associated with the introduction of a unit bank. Unfortunately, Spellman chose his variables in such a manner that the channel through which the profit reduction occurred could not be identified.

Another comparison involving high-performance associations, this time with low-performance associations, was repeated recently with the result of still more insights about asset management at SLAs. James Verbrugge and Steven Goldstein (VG) computed and ranked the return on assets ratio for all FSLIC-insured SLAs for each year from 1978 to 1981.[26] They then defined a high-performance association as one which ranked in the top 25 percent of the associations in each of the four years, and a low-performance association as one which ranked in the bottom 25 percent of the associations in each of the four years. VG, as did VST and SKF, found that the high-performance associations had consistently higher ratios of loan fees to total loans, a larger percentage of conventional loans in their mortgage portfolio, a higher percentage of loans serviced for others, and a lower ratio of loans serviced by others than did low-performance associations. Contrary to SKF, VG found that a slightly lower portion of the assets of high-performance associations were invested in mortgages compared to the low-performance associations. This last observation may reflect the different time periods of these two studies. In the period covered by the VG study, the SLA industry had already begun to receive expanded asset powers. The evidence would seem to indicate that it was the more aggressive, profitable SLAs which were taking advantage of these expanded powers.

Another difference between the VG and SKF results is that VG found that the high-performance associations had a higher, rather than lower, percentage of their assets invested in liquid assets. In fact, VG report that while the average ratio of liquid assets to total assets for high-performance associations increased from 8.7 percent in 1978 to 12.15 percent in 1981, the ratio for low-performance associations declined from 7.3 percent to 6.7 percent over this same period.[27] In this case, the differences in the two studies may reflect the increased volatility of interest rates during the latter study along with changes in managerial strategy for dealing with these volatile rates.

Finally, VG found that high-performance associations were achieving relatively high rates of return from their investments in service corporations over the entire study period whereas low-performance associations had lower rates of return and actually lost money on their service corporations in 1980 and 1981.[28] The lack of a comparable result in VST and SKF probably reflects the lack of any investment in service corporations during these earlier time periods.

A more recent commentary on the thrift industry by Andrew Carron provides some similar observations about asset management. Carron's study, *The Plight of the Thrift Institutions,* differs from those by VST and SKF in that Carron attempted to identify those associations which would fail within the next few years. He defined the current financial position of the individual SLAs and projected their financial statements under three different economic scenarios. First he totaled under each scenario the number of associations viable only in a merger but which would be sufficiently attractive candidates that they would not require FSLIC assistance for the merger. He then totaled the number of associations that would require an FSLIC-assisted merger.

Carron argued that nearly all SLAs were earning a below-market rate of return on assets, but the troubled institutions were earning even less. The two principal factors are identified as low yield and low turnover. The low yields in some cases were due to imprudent decisions and in other cases to state usury laws.[29] Carron also suggests that the SLAs with the low turnovers in mortgages tend to be the ones located "in areas with stable or declining populations."[30]

Carron's last observation is certainly consistent with the other work cited. SKF found that slightly more than one-fourth of the high-performance associations were located in FHLB Districts 11 and 12, which include the far western states such as California and Washington. They also found few high-performance associations located in New England (District 1) and the Midwest (Districts 5, 6, 7, and 8).[31] VG found in their sample that the high-performance associations were dominant in the southeastern and western districts, and the low-performance associations were dominant in the northeastern districts.

In summary, the empirical evidence regarding asset management is fairly uniform in its implications. Profitable associations have high mortgage yields and a large amount of fee income. They obtain these through a rapid turnover of their mortgage portfolio and by servicing loans for others. In other words, they act like mortgage bankers.[32] They also locate in areas with fewer competitors, and they emphasize conventional, multi-family, and construction loans. Finally, during periods of stable interest rates they reduce their holdings in liquid assets and increase their holdings of mortgages, and reverse this pattern during periods of rising rates.

Liability Management

In the area of liability management, VST tested three variables: the ratio of total advances and other borrowings to total liabilities, certificates to total savings, and net worth to total savings. Only the latter two were statistically significant, and both were negatively related to return on net worth. VST analyzed only the factors influencing the certificates ratio and did not find particularly satisfying results. For example, they found the certificates ratio was inversely related to the number of savings and loans and mutual savings banks operating in the SMSA or county. Intuitively, one would expect greater competition to lead to more emphasis on certificates rather than less. They also found that the certificates ratio was inversely related to the median family income in the area. They suggested that this may be due to the fact "that many rapid growth markets for SLAs are areas populated by retirees (Florida, Arizona) whose income is relatively low but whose accumulation of financial assets is considerable."[33] These individuals would be more interested in the high yield, insured safety of certificates and would have the financial capability to buy large amounts of certificates. Finally, the researchers did find that the certificates ratio was positively and significantly related to the proportion of high-yielding loans in the portfolio. This suggests that the associations that are capable of acquiring high-yielding mortgages are willing to pay a higher price to acquire the funds necessary to finance these mortgages.

In the case of liability management, SKF and VG report results which are somewhat contradictory to those of VST. First, both SKF and VG found that the high-performance associations had a *higher* ratio of net worth to savings than did the comparable group. Second, both found that the average cost of money was virtually identical for high-performance associations and for the comparable group. SKF report that the mix between deposits and certificates was also nearly identical for the two groups. The only difference that SKF discovered in liability management between the high-performance associations and the average low-performance association was that the former used more jumbo CDs. VG, however, concur with VST in that the high-performance associations held fewer jumbo CDs.[34] VG also found that low-performance associations pay slightly more for nondeposit borrowings than do high-performance associations and have more of it primarily in the form of advances. Finally, they report that the high-performance associations at the start of their study period held a larger percentage of deposits in passbook form but that this proportion dropped more rapidly than it did for low-performance associations so that by 1981 the two groups had a nearly equal proportion of deposits in passbook form.

Carron's arguments and tests also generally support the results of the other research about liability management. For example, like SKF and VG, he found a positive and statistically significant relationship between profitability and the ratio of net worth to total assets. As with VST, he found that the critical cases have more certificate accounts. But unlike VG, he reported that the weak associations, rather than the strong ones, have more nondeposit liabilities.

In still another study, Kaplan and Smith studied SLAs' use of borrowed money. Using a classification scheme similar to that utilized in SKF, they found that the "high performance associations utilized greater debt financing than the average association in every category except reverse repurchase agreements, with the largest differences in mortgage-backed bonds and commercial bank borrowings."[35] They also found greater use of jumbo CDs by the high-performance associations. In a seemingly contradictory vein, they note that low-performance associations appeared to make heavy use of debt financing, but then they point out that the low-performance associations were heavy only in the use of reverse repurchase agreements (repos). If these repos were eliminated from the calculations, then the low-performance associations would be much closer in their liability structure to the average association than to the high-performance associations.

It should be mentioned that Kaplan and Smith provide no causal arguments about the heavy use of repos by low-performance associations. This is interesting because in a recent article in *Fortune,* Robert Dince and James Verbrugge argue that the heavy use of repos by SLAs could do more to save the industry today than any other single proposal that has been made.[36]

All of the above studies on profitability have used either some measure of profitability or operating expenses in order to categorize the SLAs. A completely different tact was taken by E. I. Altman and yielded additional insights.[37] Altman's interest was in identifying a set of prediction models based only on financial statement data that could distinguish problem-free SLAs from those with serious but temporary problems, and both of these from SLAs with serious and mortal problems. The technique used, discriminant analysis, involves looking for combinations of variables which together have identification capabilities beyond any value they might have individually. Among the variables Altman found best at discriminating among the categories were the ratios of borrowed money to total savings, FHLB advances to net worth, and the first difference between the borrowed money to savings ratio for this year and last year. The larger these variables, the greater the likelihood that an SLA was in financial trouble.

As in the case of asset management, the differences in the conclusions of these studies about liability management may be due to differences in the economy during the sample observation periods. VST did their testing during a relatively stable period when the more levered associations might certainly be expected to perform better. SKF, VG, and Carron used periods of more volatile interest rates. This means that the normal advantage of financial leverage may have turned to a temporary disadvantage. Certainly in the cases of VG and Carron, SLAs which had already suffered net losses or below-average net income would be more likely to have lower net worths. Since these same associations would be the ones most likely to continue showing poor profits, these researchers would likely find net worth negatively related to profitability.

Similar arguments could probably be made for most of the other characteristics of liability management. The real conclusion about liability management may therefore be that management should be flexible and that there is no one set or sets of strategies which are superior over long periods of time.

Operating Expense Management

Not unexpectedly, VST found the ratio of operating expenses to average assets to be negatively and significantly related to profitability.[38] Further investigation identified several significant determinants of operating expenses. It appears that higher proportions of conventional multi-family and installment loans[39] produce higher operating expenses, as do a higher proportion of loans sold to loans originated during the year and loans serviced for others to total loans in the portfolio. It was noted that the loans sold and loans serviced variables were not significant in regressions for those associations with more than $250 million in total assets. This suggests that larger associations can engage in secondary market operations with minimal effects on costs, yet smaller associations find the same tasks substantially more expensive in relative terms. Oddly enough, neither the ratio of construction loans to total loans nor the ratio of loans purchased to the total of loans purchased and originated had any significant effect on operating expenses.

VST also found that higher growth rates in total assets during the year produced higher operating expenses, yet larger associations had lower operating expense ratios. This would suggest that rapid growth is expensive, but economies of scale are available to the larger associations. Finally, the authors found that the number of branch offices was positively and significantly related to the operating expense ratio, except for associations with total assets greater than $250 million, in which case the number of offices was not significant. This suggests that economies of scale provide opportunities to the largest SLAs which are much more costly to smaller associations.

The results of SKF and VG provide only partial confirmation of those offered by VST. Both concur with VST that the high-performance associations had significantly lower operating ratios.[40] However, they differ from VST as to why. SKF find most of the differences in operating expense attributable to lower personnel costs and to slightly lower office occupancy, furniture, and equipment expenditures by high-performance associations. VST indicate they tested for differences in operating expenses such as personnel and occupancy costs and that they found no statistically significant relationships. VG concur with SKF that the high-performance associations spent lower percentages of operating expenses on office occupancy, but they also found that this group spent a higher percentage of operating expenses on personnel.

In addition, SKF noted that the high-performance associations had fewer installment loans, which supports VST's observations that installment loans were associated with higher operating expenses. However, SKF and VG found that the high-performance associations grew at a substantially faster pace than the average association. In line with VST's arguments, it may be that SKF and

VG were picking up an economies of scale phenomenon rather than a pure growth phenomenon.

Another examination of the operating expense ratio was the 1981 study by Verbrugge and Goldstein mentioned earlier in this chapter.[41] They used three different definitions of average operating expenses.[42] The independent variables in their regressions included an output variable which was measured alternatively with total assets and number of loans, loan composition variables, the average ratio of certificate savings to total deposits, the average ratio of loans purchased to total loans, the average ratio of loans sold to total loans, the average ratio of loans serviced for others to total loans, the number of offices operated by each association, and a dummy variable for organizational form. For all of the definitions used, and for both samples, the coefficient for the organizational form was statistically significant and showed that mutuals tended to have higher operating expenses. It is not clear from the tests whether the higher personnel costs took the form of higher salaries, more employees, or some combination of the two.

Both VG (1982) and SKF found the stock associations to be more profitable, which would reinforce VG's (1981) observation that mutuals had higher expenses. SKF attributed part of this higher profitability to the fact that most stock SLAs tended to be located in those states which had the most profitable SLAs. However, even within those states, they still noted the stocks to be consistently more profitable than the mutuals. They suggested that it was not clear whether the differences in profitability were due to different managerial goals or to differences in asset powers accorded the stocks, which were nearly all state chartered, and the mutuals, which were mostly federally chartered.[43] Nicols, using several sets of data for 1963, also found that the mutuals had higher levels of expenses.[44]

Carron argues that a significant source of problems for SLAs "are managerial decisions to pay high salaries to employees, officers, and directors; to build and maintain numerous large, lavish offices; and to provide a high level of service to customers."[45] He also performed some statistical tests with the operating expense ratio and the return on assets. He regressed both ratios against independent variables that included a dummy variable for a stock charter, a dummy variable for urban location, the assets less loans in process, and the square of assets less loans in process. The stock charter variable is highly significant in both regressions, but it indicates that stocks have higher rather than lower operating expenses and lower rather than higher returns on assets. These results are clearly contradictory to those suggested by SKF and VG (1981).[46] Carron does support SKF in that he finds the return on assets is positively and significantly related to the rate of growth in deposits. Oddly enough, the study by VST tested the relationship between the form of organization and return on net worth and found no statistically significant relationship between them. Finally, Carron and VG (1982) do concur that location in an urban area has a detrimental effect on operating expenses and profits. Both studies define an urban location as any which carries an SMSA designation.

George Benston also has studied the determinants of operating expenses and has identified several factors not mentioned by the other authors.[47] The two most significant variables identified by Benston are the negative effect of the percentage of loans made to loans serviced and the negative effect of the average dollar size of purchase mortgages made (as opposed to mortgages made as construction loans). Benston indicated that the more important component of the loans made to loans serviced ratio was the loans serviced.

Benston found that start-up costs seem to last about ten to fifteen years. Thereafter, the level of operating costs does not seem to be related to the age of the SLA. Also significant is the average cost of foreclosure in the state in which the SLA operates. Due to differences in state laws, there are substantial differences in average foreclosure costs, and these are related positively to the level of operating expenses.[48,49] Also, operating expenses were found to be positively related to the percentage activity in savings accounts,[50] negatively related to the size of savings accounts; positively related to the level of wages in the county in which the SLA operates; and positively related to the ratio of real estate owned to the total assets of an association.

More recently, Jay Atkinson used a similar methodology and provided several additional and somewhat conflicting observations about the determinants of operating expenses.[51] For example, in his first study he showed that operating expenses tend to be inversely related to the percentage of savings in CDs as measured by the ratio of interest paid on CDs to total interest paid.[52] He also found that operating expenses are positively related to the ratio of fixed assets to total assets,[53] the growth rate in the firm's total assets from the previous year, the amount of loans and participations sold relative to total asset holdings, and the amount of loans and participations the firm is servicing for other institutions relative to the firm's total assets. In his second study, Atkinson suggested that the effect of the composition of savings accounts is ambiguous and dependent on the sample used. The relationship of the ratio of loans serviced by others to total loans is also ambiguous, but the ratio of loans serviced for others to total loans is positively and significantly related to operating expenses. The ratio of "bad" loans to total loans has a positive relationship to costs as do the ratios of nonmortgage loans to total loans and the investment in service corporations to total assets.

Economies of Scale

As mentioned several times in the last three sections, size seems to play a role in producing the conditions that make it possible for some SLAs to be more profitable than others. The relationship between size and profitability is not, however, immediately obvious. VST tested size as a direct determinant of profitability and found no statistically significant relationship. Perhaps

Marcia Stigum expressed the relationship best when she stated:

> . . . there is some critical asset mass at which the character of management changes. Below that critical asset mass, management is small and officers concentrate on making loans and day-to-day operations. Above that critical mass management becomes large enough so that some individuals in it can devote time to analyzing their firm's position and to develop optimal strategies for it.[54]

The most recent empirical evidence, however, would seem to contradict Stigum's observation about size. After VG (1982) made the designation of high-performance associations and low-performance associations, they examined the percentage composition based on total asset categories. They found that within the three categories covering total asset sizes from $0 to $100 million, the number of high-performance associations easily dominated the number of low-performance associations. Within the three total asset categories from $100 to $1,000 million, the low-performance associations dominated.[55]

Several studies have examined directly the issue of economies of scale for SLAs. These include the already cited studies by George Benston and by Eugene Brigham and R. Richardson Petit, both of which are in Irwin Friend's *Study of the Savings and Loan Industry,*[56] as well as the two recent studies performed by Jay Atkinson.[57] Before we review their results, it would be appropriate to describe the data bases used in each study as well as the key working definitions.

The Brigham and Petit study used cross-sectional data for the years 1962-1966, as did Benston's. Atkinson's two studies used cross-sectional data for the years 1974 and 1975, respectively. Brigham and Petit limited their sample to a subsample of SLAs from four SMSAs. Benston used the population of reporting SLAs subject to certain screening conditions, as did Atkinson.

The studies are almost unanimous in their conclusions but disagree in scholarly yet vehement ways as to appropriate working definitions. For example, one major source of disagreement is the proxy for measuring the output of an SLA. Benston uses three different measures as his proxy. These include (1) the number of loans made, (2) the number of loans serviced, and (3) the number of savings accounts. He argues that the majority of the costs of making a loan tend to be fixed rather than variable with respect to the size of the loan, and therefore the number of loans made will provide a better measure of economies of scale for an SLA's operation than the amount of the loans made.[58] Brigham and Petit view the output of an SLA as the amount of intermediation it provides and use total assets as their proxy. They argue that the size of a mortgage approximates its social product. In other words, a $100,000 mortgage provides approximately ten times the social value as a $10,000 mortgage. Their argument suggests, however, that they should have used gross mortgages made during the year or total mortgages outstanding at year-end as their measure of output.

Atkinson uses two measures of output in his first study: total assets and "active assets." This latter is defined as the total assets of an SLA, less the dollar value of their loans serviced by others, plus loans serviced for others. Atkinson argues that this second definition is more consistent with the body of literature that views lending institutions as originators and servicers of loans rather than as lenders of money.[59] In his second study, he uses total assets.

Despite their differences in proxies for the output of an SLA, the four studies reached almost identical conclusions. For example, Benston concluded that "a principal finding of this analysis is that there are consistent, highly 'significant' economies of scale, for all definitions of output and years, which showed no trend during this period."[60] Brigham and Petit concluded that "it appears that heightened inter- and intra-industry competition after 1963 has tended to bring out latent economies of scale as cost consciousness has, to a degree, replaced the earlier emphasis on growth."[61] Atkinson added in his first study that "in spite of the remarkable growth of individual S&Ls in the interim between the earlier studies and the present, there is no sign that any has reached the point that marks the lowest ebb of the average cost curve."[62] In his second study, he notes that:

Our results indicated that economies of scale are not as easily demonstrated as others have concluded. Such economies turn out to be crucially dependent on the way in which they are specified. An examination of the likely biases of each functional form suggests that only relatively small firms (under $50 million in assets) would have lower average costs with growth.[63]

A fair summary of these four studies is that economies of scale exist, although their structure is somewhat in doubt, and that it would appear that the industry will continue to be able to take advantage of them.[64]

It would seem that this conclusion is contradictory with the empirical results of VG (1982). However, this contradiction is probably more superficial than real. The results by VG (1982) reflect variations in management strategies with regard to asset and liability mix and operating structure, while the studies on the economies of scale made allowances for these differences.

SUMMARY AND OTHER OBSERVATIONS ABOUT PROFITABILITY

The basic lesson of the foregoing discussion is that in order to maximize profitability, a savings and loan should locate well, act like a mortgage banker, organize as a stock corporation, and be large. These characteristics are not necessarily independent of each other. With respect to locating well, the SLA should clearly locate in states without restrictive usury ceilings and in areas with prospects for high mortgage turnover and little competition. The repeal of all state usury laws under the DIDMCA would seem to eliminate the asset yield problems, except that the law also gives states up to three years to reinstate the usury ceilings. Areas of high turnover and little competition should be those states with rapid population growth.

The suggestion to act like a mortgage banker follows from the fact that the associations able to turn over their mortgage portfolio more quickly and to sell and service mortgages were the more profitable ones. It also seems clear why everybody in the industry cannot act like mortgage bankers. A mortgage banker has to face a steady demand for new mortgage loans. An association whose growth in savings equals or exceeds its growth in mortgage loan demand simply has little choice but to hold its own mortgages. Thus the ability to act like a mortgage banker would seem to hinge on whether the association has located in an area with sufficient mortgage demand to allow it to do so. A second aspect of acting like a mortgage banker is that the association must be reasonably large so that it can afford the staff necessary to obtain and service its mortgages efficiently.

In order to be a stock corporation, the SLA would have to locate in a state which allows stock charters.[65] As of December 31, 1981, nearly 60 percent of all stock associations were located in only five states.[66] Several of these states, such as California, with its rapid growth in mortgage demand, have many of the other features which favor profitable operations by SLAs.

A major problem with the literature to date on the profitability of SLAs is that none of the studies has really taken into consideration the primary risk faced by a thrift, that is, the risk associated with interest rate changes. One reason for this deficiency is that it is difficult to estimate empirically differences in the risk exposure toward changes in interest rates.

NOTES

1. J. Fred Weston and Eugene F. Brigham, *Essentials of Managerial Finance,* 6th ed., Dryden Press, Chicago, Ill.: 1982, p. 8.

2. Alfred Nicols, *Management and Control in the Mutual Savings and Loan Association,* Lexington Books, D. C. Heath and Company, Lexington, Mass.: 1972, pp. 114-15.

3. David W. Cole, "Measuring Savings and Loan Profitability," *Federal Home Loan Bank Board Journal,* October 1971, pp. 1-7.

4. Eugene F. Brigham and R. Richardson Petit, "Effects of Structure on Performance in the Savings and Loan Industry," in Irwin Friend (ed.), *Study of the Savings and Loan Industry,* Vol. 3, Washington, D.C., GPO, 1969, pp. 971-1210.

5. James A. Verbrugge, Richard A. Schick, and Kenneth J. Thygerson, "An Analysis of Savings and Loan Profit Performance," *Journal of Finance,* December 1976, pp. 1427-42.

6. John Wilson, William O'Connel, Jr., and Ronald Olson, *A Model for Savings and Loans,* Robert F. Dame, Inc., Richmond, Va.: 1982, p. 5.

7. John S. Lapp, "The Determination of Savings and Loan Association Deposit Rates in the Absence of Rate Ceilings: A Cross-Section Approach," *Journal of Finance,* March 1978, pp. 215-30.

8. Lionel Kalish and Joseph A. McKenzie, "The Influence of Portfolio Drag on a Savings and Loan Association's Current Mortgage Lending Policy," Research Working Paper No. 69, Office of Economic Research, Federal Home Loan Bank Board, January 1978.

9. Several alternative definitions were used to estimate the past portfolio yield. The results were the same regardless of which definition was used.

10. Nicols, *Management and Control,* p. 29.

11. See, for example, Kenneth J. Boudreaux, "Managerialism and Risk Return Performance," *Southern Economic Journal,* January 1973, pp. 366-72; Cynthia A. Glassman and Stephen A. Rhoades, "Owner vs. Manager Control Effects on Bank Performance," *The Review of Economics and Statistics,* May 1980, pp. 263-70; Joseph R. Monsen, John S. Y. Chiu, and David E. Colley, "The Effect of Separation of Ownership and Control on the Performance of the Large Firm," *Quarterly Journal of Economics,* August 1968, pp. 435-51; and Nicols, *Management and Control.*

12. Nicols, *Management and Control,* p. 1.

13. Ibid., p. 36.

14. James A. Verbrugge and Steven J. Goldstein, "Risk, Return, and Managerial Objectives: Some Evidence from the Savings and Loan Industry," *Journal of Financial Research,* Vol. 4, No. 11 (Spring 1981), pp. 45-58.

15. The inclusion of the growth rate in total assets is consistent with Nicols' observation that the volume of new loans is the most significant determinant of expenses, and the inclusion of the construction loans would seem appropriate since these are the most expensive loans to make.

16. See James A. Verbrugge and John S. Jahera, Jr., "Expense-Preference Behavior in the Savings and Loan Industry," *Journal of Money, Credit and Banking,* November 1981, pp. 465-76.

17. Nicols, *Management and Control,* p. 115.

18. Andrew S. Carron, *The Plight of the Thrift Institutions,* Brookings Institution, Washington, D.C., 1982.

19. This latter ratio was more significant for associations with total assets less than $100 million.

20. See, for example, any issue of the *Federal Reserve Bulletin* from the early 1970s.

21. This argument is well supported by data presented by Nicols which showed that (1) in 1963, only the SLAs in the Greensboro and San Francisco districts were net sellers of mortgages and that the SLAs in all the other districts were net purchasers, and (2) for conventional first mortgage loans given in June 1964 on previously accepted single-family homes in various cities around the country, interest rates were the highest in the cities in these two districts. See Nicols, *Management and Control,* pp. 244, 295.

22. David L. Smith, Donald M. Kaplan, and William F. Ford, "Profitability: Why Some Associations Perform Far above Average," *FHLBB Journal,* November 1977, pp. 7-13.

23. They found that the high-performance associations had $6.91 in income per $100 of assets from mortgage loans, compared to $6.49 in income for all associations, and that the the former had $0.63 in loan, loan servicing, and miscellaneous fees per $100 of assets, compared to $0.42 for all associations.

24. Smith et al., "Profitability," p. 13.

25. Lewis J. Spellman, "Commercial Banks and the Profits of Savings and Loan Markets," *Journal of Bank Research,* Spring 1981.

26. James Verbrugge and Steven Goldstein, "Profitability and Operating Efficiency Differences among Savings and Loan Associations," a paper presented at the annual meeting of the Financial Management Association, San Francisco, California, October 13-16, 1982.

27. Ibid., p. 12.

28. Ibid., p. 16.

29. Carron, *Plight,* p. 33.

30. Ibid.

31. Smith, et al., "Profitability," p. 8.

32. The mortgage banker role explains the high fee income, it does not explain the high portfolio yield.

33. Verbrugge et al., "An Analysis," p. 1440.

34. Verbrugge and Goldstein, "Profitability and Operating Efficiency," p. 32.

35. Donald M. Kaplan and David L. Smith, "The Role of Short-Term Debt in Savings and Loan Liability Management," in *New Sources of Capital for the Savings and Loan Industry: Proceedings of the Fifth Annual Conference,* Federal Home Loan Bank of San Francisco, 1979, p. 167.

36. Robert R. Dince and James A. Verbrugge, "The Right Way to Save the S&Ls," *Fortune,* August 10, 1981.

37. Edward I. Altman, "Predicting Performance in the Savings and Loan Association Industry," *Journal of Monetary Economics,* October 1977, pp. 443-66. An expanded version of this same research is available in Altman's paper, "The Development of a Performance-Predictor System for Savings and Loan Associations," Invited Research Working Paper No. 10, Office of Economic Research, Federal Home Loan Bank Board, December 1975.

38. Altman found a variation of this ratio, net operating income to gross operating income, to be the single best predictor of financial problems.

39. Installment loans were defined as including mobile home loans, home improvement loans, and consumer loans.

40. SKF evaluated operating expense management in terms of the operating ratio, which they defined as operating expenses as a percentage of income. VST and VG used operating expenses as a percentage of average assets. For cross-sectional comparisons, this difference is probably immaterial. However, in time series studies, this difference is crucial, as the former ratio has been steadily falling over the last 30 years, while the latter has been on the rise since 1967. See Walt J. Woerheide, "Economies of Scale in the SLA Industry: The Historical Record," *Nevada Review of Business and Economics,* Summer 1980, pp. 2-8.

41. Verbrugge and Goldstein, "Risk, Return and Managerial Objectives." To avoid any confusion between references to the two works by these co-authors, this work will be subsequently referred to as VG (1981) and the other work ("Profitability and Operating Efficiency") will be referred to as VG (1982).

42. These included: (1) total operating expenses including advertising and interest costs, (2) all expenditures associated with personnel and staff, and (3) all expenditures associated with both personnel and office operations.

43. Only in 1973 did the Bank Board start granting federal charters to stock organizations. See Daniel J. Vrabac, "Savings and Loan Associations: An Analysis of the Recent Decline in Profitability," *Economic Review,* Federal Reserve Bank of Kansas City, July-August 1982, p. 4.

44. Nicols, *Management and Control,* pp. 265, 275-76.

45. Carron, *Plight,* p. 33.

46. In response to an inquiry from this author about the contradictory nature of his results, Carron acknowledged such was the case and suggested that the stock variable was reflecting some other effect.

47. George Benston, "Cost of Operations and Economies of Scale in Savings and

Loan Associations," in Irwin Friend (ed.), *Study of the Savings and Loan Industry,* Vol. 2, Washington, D.C.: GPO, 1969, pp. 667-761. Benston's study will be described more fully in the next section on economies of scale.

48. Nicols (*Management and Control,* p. 67) also argues the relevance of differences in foreclosure costs among states, and points out that these differences influence not only operating expenses but also the proportion of assets listed as real estate owned and contracts for sale.

49. For example, until September 1981, the state of Illinois had the longest redemption period on mortgages in the country, 12 months. This meant that between the time a borrower first misses a payment until the house is put on the market, as much as 18 months could elapse. During this period, the costs of monitoring the default, along with various legal fees, mount up. This stiff foreclosure law also had the effect of reducing the gross income of SLAs in the state because it meant that Illinois mortgages were among the least attractive in secondary markets and thus reduced the ability of the associations in the state to resell their mortgages. See Kathleen Myler, "Foreclosure Change Seen Aiding Illinois Mortgage Resales," *Chicago Tribune,* October 11, 1981.

50. The percentage activity in savings accounts is defined as annual deposits plus withdrawals divided by average savings balances times 100.

51. Jay Atkinson, "The Structure of Cost in the Savings and Loan Industry during 1974," Research Working Paper No. 67, Office of Economic Research, Federal Home Loan Bank Board, March 1977; and Jay Atkinson, "Firm Size in the Savings and Loan Industry," Invited Research Working Paper No. 29, Office of Economic Research, Federal Home Loan Bank Board, December 1979. The two studies by Atkinson will also be discussed more fully in the next section.

52. Recall that in the section on liablility management, both VST and VG (1982) found that the proportion of certificates to total deposits was inversely related to profitability. This would suggest that the increased interest expense on certificates exceeds the savings in operating expenses.

53. Nicols (*Management and Control,* p. 288) argues that buildings and furnishings are little more than surrogate variables for organizational form because of the propensity by mutual managers to take their income in the form of lavish working conditions.

54. Marcia L. Stigum, "Some Further Implications of Profit Maximization by a Savings and Loan Association," *Journal of Finance,* December 1976, p. 1425.

55. Verbrugge and Goldstein, "Profitability and Operating Efficiency," p. 3.

56. See George Benston, "Cost of Operations," and E. F. Brigham and R. R. Petit, "Effects of Structure."

57. Jay Atkinson, "The Structure of Cost," and Jay Atkinson, "Firm Size."

58. Nicols (*Management and Control,* p. 172) emphasizes the same argument and adds that mutuals attempt to keep their operating expenses "appearing" reasonable by limiting their growth through limits on the number of new loans made each year.

59. See Atkinson, "Structure of Cost," p. 29, footnote 13.

60. Benston, "Cost of Operations," p. 718.

61. Brigham and Petit, "Effects of Structure," p. 1027.

62. Atkinson, "Structure of Cost," p. 32.

63. Atkinson, "Firm Size," pp. *i-ii.*

64. It should be noted that Benston finds no differences in economies of scale between large and small associations. Atkinson concluded in his first study that economies of

scale are greater for large associations. In his second study, he suggests they exist only for the small SLAs.

65. The Garn-St. Germain Depository Institutions Act of 1982 allows Federal stock SLAs to operate in all states.

66. Specifically, California, Texas, Ohio, Florida, and Illinois. See *'82 Sourcebook,* p. 38.

3

Measuring the Interest Rate Risk
Exposure of Savings and Loans

Casual observers of the savings and loan industry identify the basic cause of current industry problems as the fact that interest rates have risen substantially in the last few years. This statement is true but somewhat of an over simplification. There are benefits which accrue to savings and loans when interest rates rise. Unfortunately, the disadvantages from the rise far outweigh the advantages.

For these reasons, an examination of the consequences of interest rate changes for savings and loans is in order. One of the best tools for this examination is a statistic referred to as duration. The next few pages will mathematically define duration and provide a discussion of the intuitive interpretation of the formulas. The emphasis of the discussion is on the intuitive concept, so any reader unfamiliar with the mathematics of the various formulas should nonetheless be able to grasp their significance. Once the meaning, significance, and limitations of duration have been clarified, we proceed to the concept of "immunization," which refers to the process of reducing or eliminating the effects of interest rate changes on the net worth of SLAs.

DURATION: AN INTRODUCTION

Duration is most easily described with examples drawn from its historical derivation as a tool for describing the interest rate risk of bonds. A bond is a fixed-return investment which usually has two features: a promise to repay principal at maturity and a promise to provide regular interest payments. There are several types of yields associated with bonds, but the one of most relevance is the yield-to-maturity. The yield-to-maturity has a very precise mathematical definition: the value of i which makes true the following equation for the price of a bond:

$$P_0 = \frac{C_1}{(1+i)^1} + \frac{C_2}{(1+i)^2} + \cdots + \frac{C_N}{(1+i)^N} + \frac{PAR}{(1+i)^N} \tag{1}$$

where P_0 = price of the bond today,

C_t = interest (coupon) paid at the end of the time period t,

PAR = maturity value of the bond,

N = number of time periods to maturity, and

i = yield-to-maturity quoted as a rate per period (e.g., semiannual or annual).

Equation (1) states that the yield-to-maturity on a bond is the interest rate i that equates the present value of the interest payments and the maturity value of the bond with the price of the bond today.

Whenever an investor buys a fixed rate of return investment such as a bond, he presumably has a planned holding period or time horizon and an expected holding period yield. Interest rate risk refers to the problem that the actual holding period yield may differ from the expected holding period yield because of changes in interest rates. To understand how this might occur, let us look at the definition of actual holding period return. We start with a description of the terminal value of the bond investment, which is

$$V_T = C_1(1+y)^{T-1} + C_2(1+y)^{T-2} + \cdots + C_T + P_T \qquad (2)$$

where V_T = value of the investment at the end of the holding period,

T = number of time periods in the holding period,

y = rate at which the coupon payments are reinvested, and

P_T = price of the bond at the end of the period T.[1]

Equation (2) states that the terminal value of the investment is equal to the value of coupons after they have been reinvested at the rate y, and the price of the bond at the end of the holding period.[2] We can now define the actual holding period yield as the value r which makes the following equation true:

$$P_0(1 + r)^T = V_T \qquad (3)$$

Equation (3) states that the actual holding period yield is the rate at which P_0 dollars will grow to V_T dollars in exactly T time periods.[3] From equations (2) and (3), it should be clear that the only reasons the actual holding period yield would differ from the expected holding period yield are if the reinvestment rate or the price of the bond at the end of the holding period is different than what had been anticipated.[4]

If the holding period corresponds to the maturity of the bond (that is, $T = N$ and $P_T = PAR$) and if the reinvestment rate equals the yield-to-maturity (that is, $y = i$), then the actual holding period yield will equal the yield-to-maturity. As an example, a five-year bond which has coupon payments of $100 per year and a yield-to-maturity of 12 percent will also provide a five-year holding period return of 12 percent if the $100 coupon payments are reinvested at a rate of exactly 12 percent. If the reinvestment rate is greater than the yield-to-maturity, then the actual holding period return will be greater than the yield-to-maturity. For example, if the $100 interest payments were reinvested at a yield of 15 percent, then the holding period return would equal 12.53 percent. But, if the reinvestment rate were less than the yield-to-maturity, then the actual holding period return would also be less than the yield-to-maturity. The point here is that the actual holding period return is sensitive to the reinvestment rate. This sensitivity is described by the term "reinvestment rate risk."

A bond investor does not have to buy a bond with a maturity equal to his intended holding period. He may buy a bond with a longer maturity and sell it at the end of the holding period (that is, $T < N$). If he sells the bond prior to maturity, then the interest rate risk includes both reinvestment rate risk and price risk. Price risk is the possibility that the price of the bond at the time it is sold will be different from what was anticipated. The amount of price risk in a bond is a function of two variables, the term-to-maturity of a bond and the level of interest payments. As a general rule the longer the term-to-maturity, *ceteris paribus,* the greater the price risk.[5] For example, let us assume an investor is looking at two bonds which have equal coupon payments of $100 per year, but one bond matures in five years and the other matures in ten years. If we also assume a $1,000 par value and a $1,000 market value, then both bonds would have a yield-to-maturity of 10 percent. If yields-to-maturity on comparable bonds were to suddenly rise to 12 percent, then the price of the five-year bond would drop to $927.88 and the price of the ten-year bond would drop to $887.02.[6] However, if the yields-to-maturity on comparable bonds were to drop suddenly to 8 percent, then the prices on the five-year and ten-year bonds would rise to $1,079.87 and $1,134.21, respectively. The point illustrated here is that the bond with the longer maturity has the greater percentage price variability and thus the greater price risk.

Now let us consider what happens when bonds have equal terms-to-maturity, equal yields-to-maturity, and different coupon payments. Suppose we have two five-year bonds with yields-to-maturity of 10 percent, and one bond pays annual interest of $100 while the other pays annual interest of only $50. The price of the first bond would be $1,000.00 and the price of the second would be $810.44. If yields-to-maturity suddenly rose to 12 percent, the prices of the two bonds would drop to $927.88 and $747.64, respectively. If, however, yields-to-maturity suddenly dropped to 8 percent, then the prices would rise to $1,079.87 and $880.24. The price changes for the $100 coupon bond are -7.21 percent and $+7.99$ percent, and for the $50 coupon bond are -7.74 percent and $+8.61$ percent. Note how the bond with the lower coupon rate has the greater percentage price fluctuations.

As long as an investor is considering two bonds with the same maturity and different coupon rates, or two bonds with the same coupon rate and different maturities, it is easy to identify which bond has the greater price risk. However, when an investor is comparing two bonds with different maturities and different coupon rates, then it is not so easy to identify which one has the greater price risk. For example, suppose an investor is considering a six-year bond which has coupon payments of $150 per year and a yield-to-maturity of 10 percent versus a five-year bond which has coupon payments of $20 per year and a yield-to-maturity of 12 percent. The investor would have to be extremely experienced to know intuitively which bond has the greater price risk.

Fortunately, the problem is resolved by computing for each bond a statistic that is referred to as *duration*. The larger the duration of a bond, the larger the change in price for any given change in interest rates. Like yield-to-maturity, duration can be expressed concisely in mathematical notation. Duration is defined as

$$d = \frac{\dfrac{C_1 \times 1}{(1+i)^1} + \dfrac{C_2 \times 2}{(1+i)^2} + \cdots + \dfrac{C_N \times N}{(1+i)^N} + \dfrac{PAR \times N}{(1+i)^N}}{P_0} \tag{4}$$

where d stands for duration, which is measured in years, and all the other symbols are the same as before. The numerator of the equation is similar to the right-hand side of equation (1). The major difference is that each term in the numerator is multiplied by the time period in which the payment is received. The denominator is the price of the bond today. The duration statistic is, in effect, a weighted average of the maturities of all the cash flows associated with the bond.

To illustrate the use of equation (4), let us compute the duration for the two bonds described above. The first step is to figure the price at which each bond would trade. This can be done by using equation (1). In the case of the six-year bond with a $150 coupon rate and a yield-to-maturity of 10 percent,

$$P_0 = \frac{150}{(1+.10)^1} + \frac{150}{(1+.10)^2} + \frac{150}{(1+.10)^3} + \frac{150}{(1+.10)^4} + \frac{150}{(1+.10)^5}$$
$$+ \frac{150}{(1+.10)^6} + \frac{1000}{(1+.10)^6} \tag{5}$$

$$= \$1,217.80.$$

Similarly, the price of the five-year bond with a $20 coupon rate and a 12 percent yield-to-maturity would be computed as

$$P_0 = \frac{20}{(1+.12)^1} + \frac{20}{(1+.12)^2} + \frac{20}{(1+.12)^3} + \frac{20}{(1+.12)^4} + \frac{20}{(1+.12)^5} + \frac{1000}{(1+.12)^5} \tag{6}$$

$$= \$639.50.$$

These two prices now become the denominators for the duration equation. Duration for the six-year bond is computed as

$$d = \frac{\dfrac{150 \times 1}{(1+.10)^1} + \dfrac{150 \times 2}{(1+.10)^2} + \dfrac{150 \times 3}{(1+.10)^3} + \dfrac{150 \times 4}{(1+.10)^4} + \dfrac{150 \times 5}{(1+.10)^5} + \dfrac{150 \times 6}{(1+.10)^6} + \dfrac{1000 \times 6}{(1+.10)^6}}{\$1,217.80} \tag{7}$$

$$= 4.51,$$

and duration for the five-year bond is computed as

$$d = \frac{\dfrac{20 \times 1}{(1 + .12)^1} + \dfrac{20 \times 2}{(1 + .12)^2} + \dfrac{20 \times 3}{(1 + .12)^3} + \dfrac{20 \times 4}{(1 + .12)^4} + \dfrac{20 \times 5}{(1 + .12)^5} + \dfrac{1000 \times 5}{(1 + .12)^5}}{\$639.50} \tag{8}$$

$$= 4.75.$$

It is clear that the five-year bond has the longer duration. This means that any immediate changes in market interest rates will produce larger percentage changes in the price of the five-year bond than in the price of the six-year bond. The duration statistic has incorporated into one number the effects on price risk of differences in maturity and differences in coupon rates.

One of the most important features about duration is that no value is unique to a single bond. In other words, there is an infinite number of combinations of yield-to-maturity, term-to-maturity, and coupon rate that will produce the same duration number.[7] Hence a bond with some particular yield-to-maturity, term-to-maturity, and coupon rate can be described as having price risk equal to that of another bond whose yield-to-maturity, term-to-maturity, and coupon rate are all different from those of the first bond.

For every combination of bonds which have the same duration, there is always one easily identifiable bond. It is the one referred to as a zero-coupon bond. A zero-coupon bond is one which provides no interest payments but has a redemption value, and it is sometimes referred to as a pure discount bond.

The duration of a zero-coupon bond is equal to its term-to-maturity. The validity of this last statement is easily demonstrated algebraically. From equation (1) we see that the price of a zero-coupon bond reduces to the following:

$$P_0 = \frac{0}{(1 + i)^1} + \frac{0}{(1 + i)^2} + \cdots + \frac{0}{(1 + i)^N} + \frac{PAR}{(1 + i)^N} = \frac{PAR}{(1 + i)^N} \tag{9}$$

because all of the interest payments are zero. Similarly, the duration for a zero-coupon bond reduces to the following:

$$d = \frac{\dfrac{0 \times 1}{(1 + i)^1} + \dfrac{0 \times 2}{(1 + i)^2} + \cdots + \dfrac{0 \times N}{(1 + i)^N} + \dfrac{PAR \times N}{(1 + i)^N}}{P_0} = \frac{\dfrac{PAR \times N}{(1 + i)^N}}{P_0} \tag{10}$$

If we then substitute the price of the zero-coupon bond from equation (9) into equation (10), we find that

$$d = \frac{\dfrac{PAR \times N}{(1 + i)^N}}{\dfrac{PAR}{(1 + i)^N}} = N. \tag{11}$$

This result gives us the basis for an intuitive understanding of the concept and significance of duration. Any bond whose duration is, say, 5.0 years will have the same price risk as a five-year, zero-coupon bond. Another bond with a duration of, say, 6.0 years will have the same price risk as a six-year, zero-coupon bond. Intuitively it is much easier to grasp that a six-year, zero-coupon bond has greater price risk than a five-year, zero-coupon bond. Since there are no coupon payments to affect the price risk, that risk becomes directly related to maturity.

The relationship between the price of a bond and the bond's duration is approximated as

$$\frac{\Delta P_0}{P_0} \approx -d \times \frac{\Delta i}{1+i} \times 100\% \tag{12}$$

where Δ represents the change operator and all the other symbols are the same as before.[8] To illustrate, we had previously computed the price and duration of a six-year bond which had coupon payments of $150 and a yield-to-maturity of 10 percent to be $1,217.80 and 4.51 years, respectively. If the yield-to-maturity were to change suddenly to 9 percent, then the approximate percentage change in the price of the bond should be

$$\frac{\Delta P_0}{P_0} \approx -4.51 \times \frac{(-.01)}{1+.10} \times 100\% = 4.1\% \tag{13}$$

The actual price of the bond at a 9 percent yield-to-maturity is $1,269.18, which represents a 4.22 percent change in the price.

The reason that equation (12) is stated as an approximation and the reason that the above example did not work out perfectly is that its accuracy depends on the magnitude of change in the yield-to-maturity. For small changes in yields on short-term bonds, the relationship in equation (12) is quite accurate. Large changes in yields produce percentage price changes somewhat different from those indicated by equation (12). The disparity increases as the term-to-maturity increases and is somewhat larger for decreases in yields than for increases in yields. Examples of the disparities in the percentage change indicated by equation (12) and the actual percentage change are shown in Table 3.1. The magnitude of the differences in the predicted and actual price changes in Table 3.1 are such that the user of the duration statistic should be aware of them, but the significance of the differences depends on the purpose for which the duration statistic is being used.

One of the most important characteristics about duration is that it increases at a decreasing rate. For example, as shown in Table 3.2, the 8 percent coupon bond with an 8 percent yield-to-maturity has a duration of 4.218 years when the term-to-maturity is 5 years, a duration of 7.067 years when the term-to-maturity is 10 years, and a duration of 10.292 years when the term-to-maturity is 20 years. Thus, when the maturity doubles from 5 to 10 years, the duration increases by only 67.1 percent, and when the maturity doubles again to 20 years, the duration statistic increases by only 45.6 percent. For the longer-term bonds (and mortgages, as we will see later), the differences in duration due to a few years' difference in the maturity are relatively insignificant. In

Table 3.1

Price Changes Implied by Duration versus Actual Changes from Given Changes in Yield on 8% Coupon Bonds with Selected Maturities

Term-to-Maturity (Yrs.)	Yield Change in Basis Points									
	−100		−50		−1		+50[a]		+100[a]	
	Duration	Actual	Duration	Actual	Duration	Actual	Duration	Actual	Duration	Actual
5	4.09	4.16	4.07	4.11	4.06	4.05	4.04	4.01	4.02	3.96
10	6.93	7.11	6.87	6.95	6.80	6.78	6.73	6.65	6.66	6.50
30	12.21	12.47	11.75	11.87	11.31	11.32	10.89	10.80	10.48	10.32

SOURCE: Stanley Diller, "Near-Term Optimization or Duration as Measure of Bond Price Volatility," *The Money Manager,* February 5, 1979. Copyright Institutional Investor, Inc., 1979, Reprinted by permission of Institutional Investor, Inc.

[a] The minus signs on the predicted and actual percentage price changes are withheld for clarity.

other words, with regard to interest rate risk, there is for practical purposes no significant difference between a 25- and a 30-year bond.[9]

It was mentioned earlier that usually the longer the term-to-maturity the longer the duration of the bond. The exceptions to this rule are the long-term bonds whose coupon yields are less than their yields-to-maturity. In these cases, a bond with a shorter term-to-maturity may nonetheless have a larger duration than another bond whose yield-to-maturity and coupon yield are the same but whose term-to-maturity is longer. This phenomenon can be observed in Table 3.2. For example, the 20-year bond with a 16 percent yield-to-maturity and a 4 percent coupon rate has a duration of 8.085 years. A 100-year bond with the same yield-to-maturity and coupon rate has a duration of only 6.75 years. So although this reversal phenomenon occurs, the magnitude of the reversal is not tremendous, and it occurs only on what may be described as unusually long-term bonds.

DURATION: ADDITIONAL ASPECTS[10]

The formula for duration which was given in equation (4) could be referred to as the classical definition and is the formula that will be used throughout this text.[11] However, other definitions have been proposed for the measure of duration, and the reader should have some understanding of them and why they have been offered.

The most common alternative suggested is one in which the discount rate used is not the yield-to-maturity but rather is the set of spot rates for zero-

Table 3.2
Duration in Years of Bonds with Semiannual Coupons

Years to Maturity	Promised Yield-to-Maturity											
	4 Percent*			8 Percent*			12 Percent			16 Percent		
	Coupon Rate			Coupon Rate			Coupon Rate			Coupon Rate		
	4%	6%	8%	4%	6%	8%	4%	6%	8%	4%	6%	8%
One	.990	.986	.981	.990	.985	.981	.990	.985	.980	.990	.985	.980
Five	4.581	4.423	4.290	4.533	4.361	4.218	4.481	4.295	4.141	4.424	4.223	4.059
Ten	8.339	7.859	7.497	7.986	7.454	7.067	7.585	7.011	6.608	7.142	6.539	6.132
Twenty	13.951	12.876	12.181	11.966	10.922	10.292	9.932	9.040	8.532	8.085	7.406	7.036
Fifty	21.980	20.629	19.903	12.987	12.743	12.406	8.929	8.868	8.864	6.806	6.780	6.776
One Hundred	25.014	24.535	24.293	13.029	13.006	12.995	8.835	8.834	8.834	6.750	6.750	6.750
Infinity	25.500	25.500	25.500	13.000	13.000	13.000	8.833	8.833	8.833	6.750	6.750	6.750

* These columns are the same as those found in L. Fisher and R. Weil, "Coping with the Risk of Interest Rate Fluctuation: Returns to Bondholders from Naive and Optimal Strategies," *Journal of Business*, October 1971, p. 418.

coupon bonds. In other words, the discount rate for money received at the end of the first time period is the yield-to-maturity for a one-period, zero-coupon bond. The discount rate for money received at the end of the second time period is the yield-to-maturity for a two-period, zero-coupon bond. These discount rates would be those taken from a yield curve derived from a series of zero-coupon bonds. In equation form this definition would be stated as

$$d = \frac{\dfrac{C_1 \times 1}{(1+i_1)} + \dfrac{C_2 \times 2}{(1+i_2)^2} + \cdots + \dfrac{C_N \times N}{(1+i_N)^N} + \dfrac{PAR \times N}{(1+i_N)^N}}{P_0} \qquad (14)$$

where i_t is the yield-to-maturity on a zero-coupon bond that matures in t time periods. Depending on the shape of the yield curve, all the discount rates could be different. However, if the yield curve were perfectly flat, then all of the discount rates would be identical, and the alternative definition would be equal to the classical definition.

The alternative definition has one very nice mathematical property which the classical definition lacks. That property is the ability to use market value weighted averages when dealing with a portfolio of bonds with different durations. That is, with the alternative definition, if an investor uses half of his money to buy bonds which all have a two-year duration and the other half to buy bonds with a four-year duration, then his portfolio will have a duration of three years, and changes in the market value of the portfolio due to changes in the yield curve are approximated by equation (12). However, if the durations are measured using the classical definition, then the market value weighted portfolio duration would still be three years, but it would not necessarily be an unbiased predictor of changes in the market value of the portfolio. Rather, such changes would be approximated as[12]

$$\frac{\Delta P_p}{P_p} \approx -D_p \Delta i_p + \sum_{j=1}^{m} \frac{P_j}{P_p} \Delta i_j (D_p - D_j) \qquad (15)$$

where P_p = the market value of the portfolio,

D_p = the market value weighted average duration of the portfolio,

i_p = yield-to-maturity for the portfolio,

P_j = the market value of the holdings of security j,

m = total number of securities in the portfolio, and

D_j = the duration of security j.

Still other definitions for duration have been suggested. Their formulations, however, are even more mathematically complex than the two definitions already discussed and will not be presented herein.[13] Definitions have proliferated because the accuracy of equation (12) depends upon the manner in which interest rates change. The classical definition is optimal when the yield curve begins as flat and then makes a single, parallel shift at the start of the holding period. The alternative definition is somewhat more flexible in that the yield curve need not be flat, but the other conditions still apply. Namely, it is expected that there will be a single, parallel (that is, additive) shift in the yield curve at the start of the holding period. The more complex definitions are based on more complex types of shifts in the yield curve (such as multiplicative). The key, however, is that all of these shifts are assumed to be one-time events at the start of the holding period. No definition of duration has been suggested that treats multiple random shifts in the yield curve during the holding period.

From the foregoing discussion it should be apparent that within a theoretical context the optimal definition of duration to be used depends upon the current shape and the expected form of shift in the yield curve. In actual applications, it may not make too much difference which definition is used because the calculated values are frequently quite close. For example, Table 3.3 is a partial reproduction of duration values using three different definitions derived by Bierwag and Kaufman under two different yield curve structures for two different coupon yields. The three definitions include the classical definition (D_1), the alternative definition (D_2), and a third definition they propose for a multiplicative shift in the yield curve (D_3). As they point out

Except at high coupons and long maturities, the values of the three definitions do not vary greatly. Thus, D_1 may be used as a first approximation for D_2 and D_3. The expression for D_1 has the additional advantage of being a function of the yield to maturity of the bond.[14]

One aspect of duration which is frequently misunderstood is that it is not necessarily a good *ex ante* relative measure of risk. Although it is clear that a bond with a larger duration will always have a larger price change for a given change in interest rates, it is not always the case that the two bonds will undergo a change in yields of the same magnitude. Recent work by Yawitz and by Yawitz and Marshall has shown that the volatility of yields has historically varied inversely with the term-to-maturity.[15] That is, long-term interest rates tend to have much smaller changes than short-term rates. Thus, even though a long-term bond may have a substantially larger duration than a short-term bond, its price volatility will not be nearly as large as the difference in duration would suggest because the long-term rate will likely change by less than the short-term rate.

IMMUNIZATION

At the start of the chapter, it was pointed out that the interest rate risk of a bond investor who sells his bond prior to maturity includes both price risk and reinvestment rate risk. These risks may be offsetting. If interest rates rise after an investor buys a bond, then the price of the bond declines and the

Table 3.3
Values of Alternative Definitions of Duration

Term-to-Maturity	Zero-Coupon Holding Period Yield (%)	Duration in Years					
		5% Coupon			10% Coupon		
		D_1	D_2	D_3	D_1	D_2	D_3
A. Upward Sloping Yield Curve							
1	6.10	.99	.99	.99	.98	.98	.98
5	6.50	4.47	4.46	4.48	4.13	4.12	4.16
10	7.00	7.83	7.78	7.92	6.93	6.86	7.03
15	7.50	10.23	10.00	10.36	8.92	8.68	9.04
20	8.00	11.82	11.24	11.87	10.36	9.80	10.37
25	8.50	12.81	11.74	12.61	11.41	10.42	11.18
B. Downward Sloping Yield Curve							
1	8.50	.99	.99	.99	.98	.98	.98
5	8.10	4.44	4.44	4.43	4.09	4.10	4.06
10	7.60	7.71	7.76	7.61	6.77	6.84	6.67
15	7.10	10.02	10.24	9.81	8.64	8.89	8.48
20	6.60	11.65	12.22	11.37	10.01	10.59	9.84
25	6.10	12.79	13.91	12.51	11.04	12.13	10.94

SOURCE: Bierwag and Kaufman, "A Note," p. 368. Copyright 1977 by the University of Chicago. Reprinted by permission of the University of Chicago Press.

Note: D_1 = classical definition (equation (2))
D_2 = alternative definition (equation (14))
D_3 = definition developed by Bierwag-Kaufman for a multiplicative shift in the yield curve

investor suffers a loss in the market value of his bond. However, because interest rates are higher, the bond holder will find that his returns from reinvesting the coupon payments will be higher than they otherwise would have been. In other words, part of what the bondholder has lost because of the drop in the market value of the bond will be made up by larger than anticipated returns from reinvesting the coupon payments. A similar situation develops when interest rates fall. The bondholder will observe that the market value of the bond rises, but the income from reinvesting the coupon payments will be lower than it would have been. Since the change in the price of the bond and the change in income from reinvesting the coupons are in opposite directions, it would seem that a bondholder might be able to use this phenomenon to minimize his total interest rate risk exposure for his assumed holding period.

A naive strategy to minimize the interest rate risk is to buy a bond whose maturity matches an investor's holding period. In other words, an investor who wishes to liquidate his portfolio in, say, five years would buy a five-year bond. This strategy eliminates price risk from the investment because, assuming no default occurs, the investor will receive the par value of the bond on the maturity date. There is no uncertainty as to what par value is. The problem with this strategy, however, is that the reinvestment rate risk has not been eliminated.

There is an alternative and usually superior strategy by which to minimize interest rate risk. The investor buys a bond whose duration equals his planning horizon. This means that in the previous example in which a five-year planning horizon was assumed, a bond with a five-year duration would be purchased. When the duration exactly matches the planning horizon, under certain conditions, the investor will have a risk-free investment! Any gain or loss in the market value of the bond at the end of the planning horizon might be *exactly* offset by the loss or gain in income due to the change in the reinvestment rates.

Perhaps an example would be useful to demonstrate this point. Let us consider, as before, an investor who has a five-year planning horizon. The naive strategy would suggest the purchase of a five-year bond. Suppose such a bond could be purchased which pays $90 interest per year and has a yield-to-maturity of 5 percent. Next, suppose that immediately after purchasing the bond, market interest rates decline to 2 percent and stay there for the next five years. The investor would have paid $1,173.15 for the bond, and he would receive $1,000 par value at maturity, $450 in coupon payments (five years' interest at $90 per year), and $18.36 from reinvesting the coupon payments at 2 percent until maturity. The actual holding period return then equals approximately 4.59 percent.

As an alternative strategy, the investor could purchase a bond with a five-year duration. In this case, one such bond would be a six-year bond which pays $90 interest per year and has a yield-to-maturity of 5 percent.[16] Let us again assume that immediately after purchase, interest rates drop to 2 percent and stay there for the next five years. At this time the investor sells his bond, which has one year left to maturity. The investor would have paid $1,203.00 for the bond and would receive $1,069.62 as proceeds from selling the bond, $450 in coupon payments, and $18.36 from reinvesting the coupons. The holding period return is then almost 5 percent.[17] It is not 5 percent exactly because the duration was not exactly 5.0 years.

In the above example, it should be noted that if interest rates had risen to 8 percent immediately after the purchase of each bond, then the holding period returns would have been approximately 5.43 percent and 5.00 percent for the naive and alternative strategies, respectively. In other words, regardless of what happens to interest rates immediately after the bond purchase, the purchaser of the bond with the five-year duration has little interest rate risk. However, the purchaser of the five-year maturity bond still faces that risk.

The strategy of setting the duration of the bond equal to the planning horizon provides what is known as *immunization*.[18] An immunized investment is one in which the actual holding period return is never less than the expected holding period returns.[19] This lower limit on the actual return is the basis for the earlier suggestion that an investor who sets the duration equal to the planning horizon would, under certain conditions, have a risk-free investment. It is risk-free in the sense that there is no possibility of earning less than the expected rate of return.

The ideal conditions under which the duration strategy may provide immunization depends upon the definition of duration employed. If the classical definition is used, then the optimal conditions are: (1) the yield curve changes only once during the holding period, (2) this one change occurs immediately after the bond is purchased, (3) the yield curve makes only a parallel shift, and (4) the yield curve is flat. Now, even the most casual observer of market interest rates has noted that one-time, parallel changes in flat yield curves at the start of planning periods is not an accurate description of our financial markets.[20] Indeed, a better description is that a nonlinear yield curve makes frequent, nonparallel changes, and in recent years the variance of these changes seems to have become larger.

It thus becomes an empirical question of whether the frequency and timing of interest rate changes are such that the duration strategy can provide an approximation of immunization. In what is now a classic article, Fisher and Weil provided some empirical evidence that this is indeed the case.[21] For the period from 1926 to 1965, they examined the rates of return that could have been achieved for different holding periods had an investor used, first, a naive strategy of buying bonds whose term-to-maturity equaled the various holding periods and, second, an optimal strategy of selecting bonds whose duration matched the various holding periods. They showed that in the vast majority of the time periods the duration strategy came closer to providing the expected yield than did the naive strategy. It should be noted, however, that the duration strategy did not always provide immunization. There were some time periods in which the immunization strategy provided less than the expected rate of return. So although the duration measure is not perfect with respect to eliminating interest rate risk, it is substantially superior to the use of maturity, and no other measure has been empirically documented as being superior.[22]

DURATION AND THE ASSETS AND LIABILITIES OF SLAs

The concepts of duration and immunization should now add substantial clarity and precision to the discussion about savings and loans. In the simplest

Table 3.4
Duration Estimates Based on the 1981 Balance Sheet

Category	Percentage of Total	Estimated Average Duration (years)
Mortgage Loans Outstanding	78.1	5.0
Cash and Investments Eligible for Liquidity	7.3	0.5
Other Assets	14.6	8.0
Total/Weighted Average	100.0	5.11
Deposits Earning Regular Rate or Below	15.3	0.5
Deposits Earning in Excess of Regular Rate	63.7	2.0
Other Liabilities	16.7	1.0
Total/Weighted Average	95.7*	1.58

* This total does not equal 100.0% because of the omission of net worth.

possible terms, the basic problem of SLAs is that the average duration of their assets is substantially larger than the average duration of their liabilities.

Furthermore, we can now estimate the magnitude of this duration mismatch as shown in Table 3.4. The percentage breakdowns for the asset and liability categories are the same as those provided in Table 2.1.

As we saw in Table 2.1, the dominant asset of SLAs is the mortgage. The typical mortgage has a term-to-maturity of slightly more than 28 years at the time it is issued.[23] A mortgage is, of course, much like a bond. For our purposes, however, there are three major differences between these two types of assets. The first is that the average mortgage is usually prepaid after one-third to one-half of its life, and most bonds are outstanding until their original maturity. The second is that the coupon payments on a bond include only interest and not principal, whereas mortgage payments include both interest and principal. The third is that coupon payments are paid only semiannually, whereas mortgage payments are paid monthly.

All of these differences are beneficial to savings and loans because they reduce the duration on a mortgage. For example, a 30-year bond with a 10 percent coupon yield paid semiannually and a 10 percent yield-to-maturity has a duration of 9.94 years.[24] A 30-year mortgage with a 10 percent yield and semiannual payments has a duration of 8.80 years. The difference is due to the inclusion of amortization of principal in the semiannual payments. If this same 30-year mortgage required monthly amortization payments, then its duration would be 8.49 years.[25] Finally, if the 30-year mortgage is repaid after 12 years, then its duration declines to 6.77 years. Clearly, the prepayment and monthly amortization features of the traditional mortgage combine to reduce substantially the price risk to savings and loans on their mortgage holdings from that of bonds of equal maturity.

One aspect of the recent historically high interest rates is that they have served to reduce further the duration on new mortgages. For example, a 30-year, 6 percent mortgage on which no prepayments are expected has a duration of 10.78 years. If this same mortgage is expected to be repaid after 12 years, its duration is 7.90 years. However, at a rate of 16 percent, the duration numbers become 6.08 and 5.34 years, respectively. This is clearly quite a reduction in interest rate risk exposure.

Although the duration for a new mortgage which has an expected repayment after 12 years is slightly less than seven years, the average duration of all mortgages will be less. This is because as mortgages move closer to maturity or closer to the expected date of repayment, their duration becomes smaller. The average duration of the mortgage portfolio is the weighted average of the durations of each mortgage, where the durations are weighted by the market values of the individual mortgages. Precise estimates of the average duration for the mortgage portfolio requires knowledge of the exact composition of the industry's holdings. For our purposes, an estimate of five years is sufficient.[26]

Because of their smaller percentage holdings, the duration estimates for the other asset categories can be even rougher. The category of cash and investments eligible for liquidity includes cash whose duration is clearly zero and various short-term securities whose durations probably do not exceed four years. The average duration is probably close to one-half year.[27]

The category of other assets includes such items as buildings, fixtures, and foreclosed property. Without substantial research, any estimates for this category are probably the most uncertain of the asset categories. However, an arbitrary selection of eight years may not be inappropriate.[28]

Using these estimates, the weighted average asset duration works out to be 5.11 years. We are now ready to estimate the average duration for the liabilities.

As we saw in Table 2.1, the major liability of savings and loans is the deposit. Before providing estimates on the duration of the deposits, a brief comment should be made about "deposit longevity." This term refers to the length of time that the money in an account remains on deposit. Deposit longevity affects the duration of a deposit in the same way that prepayment affects the duration of a bond. If there are homogeneous expectations about the expected market date of prepayment on a mortgage, then the market value of that mortgage will change in response to interest rate changes based on the expected prepayment date rather than the maturity date. In other words, the existence of an expected prepayment date on a mortgage reduces the duration of this mortgage.

In an analogous manner, homogeneous expectations about the deposit longevity of an account will affect the change in the market value of this deposit in response to changes in interest rates. This point is particularly crucial in any discussion about the duration of passbook deposits. Technically speaking, passbook deposits are constantly maturing securities and, as such, would have a duration equal to zero.[29] However, passbook deposits have an effective maturity that is substantially longer than zero. The value of these passbook deposits and, more importantly, the changes in the value of these deposits as interest rates change will depend on the expected deposit longevity. For example, if the expected deposit longevity of a passbook account is three years, then the duration of the deposit will be the same as if it had a three-year maturity.

One of the problems with computing durations for the actual assets and liabilities of SLAs is that changes in interest rates will alter the expected prepayment dates of mortgages and the expected deposit longevity of the liabilities. For example, when interest rates rise, a homeowner is less prone to move because it would mean replacing his or her current mortgage with a more expensive one. Hence prepayment dates become more distant and the durations of the mortgages become larger. Similarly, a rise in interest rates will reduce the deposit longevity of a passbook account. The greater the differential between the passbook rate (currently 5.5 percent) and market rates, the more likely depositors will be motivated to move their money out of passbook accounts and into higher yielding securities. This reduced deposit longevity thus means a shorter duration. For current empirical purposes, it is safe to assume that over short time periods and for "small" changes in interest rates, this effect of interest rate changes on prepayments and deposit longevity is negligible. However, it does provide a convenient explanation for the evolution of the interest rate risk of SLAs.

Until the early seventies, the deposits at SLAs were virtually all in the form of passbook accounts, and today's passbook accounts provide only about 20 percent of all deposits. Yet, prior to the seventies, the SLA industry had few of the problems it has today with interest rate risk exposure. Passbook accounts in the earlier periods had a long deposit longevity because market rates tended to be comparable to passbook rates and few alternatives were available to passbook account holders. So even though the passbook accounts technically had a maturity of zero years, the duration was large because of the lengthy deposit longevity. Therefore, SLAs were relatively immunized in those days and had little interest rate risk exposure. Currently, however, because of the high level of interest rates relative to passbook rates, the deposit longevity of passbook accounts is quite short. This shortness results in a greater mismatch between the asset and liability durations.

With the concept of deposit longevity in mind, we are now ready to return to our exercise of estimating the average liability duration for SLAs. Based on the rapid outflow of passbook accounts from SLAs in recent years, it would seem that the deposit longevity and duration of these accounts would be no more than six months.

Most of the certificates of deposit have the attractive feature that interest is allowed to compound. When allowed, the certificate becomes the equivalent of a zero-coupon bond. This is because the depositor does not receive any money until maturity, at which time he receives principal and all accrued interest. Although some of the certificates issued by SLAs have maturities of up to eight years, many now issued have maturities which range from 30 days to six months. For our purposes, it is probably sufficient to estimate a two-year duration for the deposits earning in excess of the regular rate.[30]

Finally, the category of other liabilities includes variable-rate and long-term, fixed-rate advances as well as subordinated debentures. As in the case of the category of other assets, substantially more data on the breakdown of this category would be necessary to make a precise estimate. Employed here instead will be a rather arbitrary assumption of a duration of one year.[31]

As in the case of assets, the average duration of liabilities is the weighted average of the duration of individual liabilities. With the estimate described above, the weighted average liability duration works out to be 1.52 years. Thus, *the basic problem of SLAs can be described by the fact that their average asset duration is about five years and their average liability duration is about one and one-half years.*[32]

IMMUNIZATION OF SLA BALANCE SHEETS

In the previous discussion of immunization, the strategy described involved immunizing the investor from interest rate risk for the intended holding period or planning horizon. In the case of SLAs, there is no obvious planning horizon, but there is nonetheless an opportunity to apply the concept of immunization. The SLA manager administers two portfolios: an asset portfolio and a liability portfolio. The market value of each portfolio is affected by the level of interest rates. The SLA manager could achieve *portfolio immunization* if interest rate fluctuations caused the change in the market value of the asset portfolio to be exactly matched by the change in the market value of the liability portfolio.

If the market values of the assets and liabilities of an SLA are initially equal, then portfolio immunization simply requires that the asset portfolio duration be set equal to the liability portfolio duration. Because part of their assets are financed by such items as net worth, reserves, and surplus, the market value of the assets more typically exceeds the market value of the liabilities.[33] Under these circumstances, portfolio immunization requires that the liability portfolio duration exceed the asset portfolio duration by the same relative amount that the market value of the assets exceeds the market value of the liabilities. Specifically, portfolio immunization requires that

$$\frac{d_A}{d_L} = \frac{L}{A} \tag{16}$$

where d_A, d_L = the average asset and liability portfolio durations,

$\qquad A$ = the market value of the assets, and

$\qquad L$ = the market value of the liabilities.

Another way of viewing equation (16) is that if a portfolio is immunized when

$$d_A A = d_L L, \tag{17}$$

then the failure of equality in this relationship implies that the SLA is not immunized.[34] Furthermore, the magnitude by which the inequality fails to hold would indicate the magnitude of interest rate risk exposure of a particular institution.[35]

The reader should not infer from this discussion that an SLA manager would always seek to be immunized. Rather, the optimal degree of immunization depends upon such features as the manager's expectation of future interest rate changes,[36] the uncertainty of future interest rate changes, the size of the association, and the manager's attitude toward risk aversion.[37] For example, if a manager were fairly certain that interest rates would rise by a large amount, he would substantially lengthen the duration of his liability portfolio relative to the duration of his asset portfolio. Conversely, if he were fairly certain that interest rates would drop by a large amount, he would substantially lengthen the duration of his asset portfolio relative to that of his liability portfolio. In fact, the only condition under which a rational, risk-averse manager would seek to immunize his balance sheet perfectly is when "he expects that interest rates are not going to change."[38] In such a case, a nonimmunized portfolio creates risk without any expectation of gain from interest rate movements.

Any duration imbalance should also be affected by the degree of uncertainty about future interest rate changes. The greater the uncertainty, the less the imbalance the manager is willing to undertake.

A second aspect of the portfolio immunization issue is that it deals only with interest rate risk exposure and not with expected rates of return. For example, suppose a manager has a zero-coupon, seven-year liability with a yield-to-maturity of 9 percent. If he uses the money to purchase a ten-year bond with a 6 percent coupon yield and a 12 percent yield-to-maturity, then he will have a nearly immunized balance sheet as the bond has a duration of 7.011 years and the liability has a duration of 7.0 years. This combination is nonetheless highly profitable as the manager is achieving an expected average yield spread of 3 percent (12 percent minus 9 percent) for the next seven years that is virtually free from interest rate risk.

Depending on the asset combinations that are available, a manager may find that for "reasonable" increases in interest rate risk exposure, he can substantially increase his expected yield. Ideally, therefore, a portfolio manager would first set his asset and liability portfolios to achieve the highest possible yield spread. Then the manager would adjust the portfolios for differences in durations based on his own forecast of interest rates. The adjustment process would continue only so long as the reduction in expected profits is sufficiently offset by the reduction in interest rate risk exposure.

In the case of SLAs, managers have had little control over their assets and liabilities. Tax laws and regulations have forced the associations to hold the vast majority of their assets in long-term, fixed-rate mortgages. Similarly, regulations have restricted the associations to offering short-term liabilities. So the SLA manager has been forced, under the threat of stringent penalties, to hold a portfolio with a high interest rate risk exposure. In fact, based on their duration mismatch, SLAs have been one of the institutions with the largest interest rate risk exposure in our economy today. It is little wonder that they have been one of the industries which has been hurt the most by the rapid rise in interest rates in recent years.

NOTES

1. Implicit in equation (2) is the assumption that the holding period T is less than or equal to the maturity of the bond.

2. For simplicity, I have assumed that all coupon payments are reinvested at the same rate of y.

3. A more proper, but not necessarily more insightful, formulation of the holding period yield would be:

$$r = \sqrt[T]{\frac{V_T}{P_0}} - 1.$$

4. Also for simplicity of exposition, I have omitted the possibility of default.

5. This is not always true, and the exceptions will be discussed later in the chapter.

6. The numbers in this example, as in all the examples to follow, unless otherwise noted, are derived with the assumptions that coupon payments are paid and compounded annually, that the bonds are noncallable and nonconvertible, and that the bonds have a par value of $1,000.

7. See, for example, Richard W. McEnally, "Duration as a Practical Tool for Bond Management," *Journal of Portfolio Management,* Summer 1977, pp. 53-57.

8. Ibid., p. 55.

9. A second characteristic of note in Table 3.2 is that even if bonds have a maturity of infinity, they still have a finite duration. Furthermore, the coupon rate is immaterial in computing this value. The formula to compute the duration of a perpetual bond is

$$d_\infty = (r + p)/rp$$

where d_∞ = the duration of a bond with a maturity of infinity,

r = the annual yield-to-maturity expressed as a decimal fraction, and

p = the number of interest payments per year.

For example, a bond which has a maturity of infinity, a 6 percent yield-to-maturity, and pays interest semiannually would have a duration of 2.06/.12 = 17.166 years. This formulation is covered in L. Fisher and R. Weil, "Coping with the Risk of Interest Rate Fluctuations: Returns to Bondholders from Naive and Optimal Strategies," *Journal of Business*, October 1971, p. 418.

10. This section discusses some of the technical limitations of the duration statistic and may be skipped by the less technically inclined readers without loss of continuity.

11. The classical definition was developed by Frederick R. Macaulay in *Some Theoretical Problems Suggested by the Movements of Interest Rates, Bond Yields, and Stock Prices in the United States since 1856*, Columbia University Press, New York, 1938.

12. See George Kaufman, "Duration, Planning Period, and Tests of the Capital Asset Pricing Model," *The Journal of Financial Research*, Spring 1980, p. 5.

13. For examples of some of the more complex formulations, the reader is referred to G.O. Bierwag and George G. Kaufman, "Coping with the Risk of Interest Rate Fluctuations: A Note," *Journal of Business*, July 1977, pp. 364-70; and John C. Cox, Jonathon E. Ingersoll, Jr., and Stephen A. Ross, "Duration and the Measurement of Basis Risk," *Journal of Business*, January 1979, pp. 51-61.

14. Bierwag and Kaufman, "A Note," p. 367.

15. See Jess Yawitz, "The Relative Importance of Duration and Yield Volatility on Bond Price Volatility," *Journal of Money, Credit and Banking*, February 1977, pp. 97-102; and Jess Yawitz and William Marshall, "The Shortcomings of Duration as a Risk Measure for Bonds," *The Journal of Financial Research*, Summer 1981, pp. 91-101.

16. The duration is actually 4.997 years, but the 5 percent figure is close enough for our purposes.

17. More precisely, it is 5.0221 percent.

18. Sometimes this strategy has been referred to as innoculation. However, the correct term is immunization.

19. This definition of immunization was suggested by L. Fisher and R. Weil in "Coping with the Risk of Interest Rate Fluctuations," p. 415.

20. For the reader who skipped the previous section, some alternative definitions of duration were discussed which were designed for nonparallel shifts in the yield curve.

21. Fisher and Weil, "Coping with the Risk of Interest Rate Fluctuations."

22. Additional empirical tests on this point have been provided by G.O. Beirwag, G.G. Kaufman and A.L. Toevs, "Management Strategies for Savings and Loan Associations to Reduce Interest Rate Risk," in *New Sources of Capital for the Savings and Loan Industry: Proceedings of the Fifth Annual Conference*, Federal Home Loan Bank of San Francisco, 1980.

23. According to the series published in the *Federal Reserve Bulletin*, the average maturity on new mortgages has fluctuated between 28 and 29 years since at least 1978.

24. If this bond had a maturity of infinity, its duration would be only 10.5 years.

25. Although the change from semi-annual to monthly payments reduces the duration by .3 years, a shift to semi-monthly payments would further reduce the duration by only .03 years. It would seem unlikely that this incremental risk reduction would be worth the expense.

26. In a similar attempt to estimate the average asset and liability durations, Harvey Rosenblum also estimates the *average* mortgage duration at 5.0 years. See Harvey Rosenblum, "Liability Strategies for Minimizing Interest Rate Risk," in *Managing Interest Rate Risk in the Thrift Industry: Proceedings of the Seventh Annual Conference*, Federal Home Loan Bank of San Francisco, 1982.

27. This also agrees with the estimate provided by Rosenblum.

28. Rosenblum uses ten years as the duration for the fixed, long-term assets, which is only one component of the other assets category.

29. Rosenblum, in "Liability Strategies," assigns a duration of .05 years to passbook accounts. See also Walt Woerheide, "The Evolution of SLA Susceptibility to Interest Rate Risk during the Seventies," *Journal of the Midwest Finance Association,* 1980, p. 127.

30. Rosenblum divides this category into several subcategories with durations that range from 0.1 year to 2.5 years.

31. Rosenblum uses only the category of advances and assigns these a duration of .5 years.

32. Similar estimates were derived in Harvey Rosenblum, "Interest Rate Volatility, Regulation Q, and the Problems of Thrift Institutions," in *Proceedings of a Conference on Bank Structure and Competition, May 1 and 2, 1980,* Federal Reserve Bank of Chicago, pp. 16-42.

33. During the last few years, the market value of the assets of many SLAs has probably been less than the market value of the liabilities. This problem does not invalidate any of the issues concerning the immunization framework.

34. See, for example, Alan C. Hess, "Duration Analysis for Savings and Loan Associations," *Federal Home Loan Bank Board Journal,* October 1982, p. 14.

35. Bierwag, Kaufman, and Toevs, "Management Strategies," suggest that differences in the asset and liability durations are useful measures of interest rate risk exposure, and thus regulatory agencies would find them useful in evaluating capital adequacy (p. 196).

36. More formally, it is not the manager's expectation of interest rate changes per se which is germane but the relationship between the manager's expectation of interest rate changes and the expected interest rate changes which are implicit in the yield curve.

37. For a discussion of the strategies of portfolio adjustments and interest rate risk exposure, see M.A. Grove, "On 'Duration' and the Optimal Maturity Structure of the Balance Sheet," *The Bell Journal of Economics and Management Science,* Autumn 1974, pp. 696-709.

38. Grove, "Optimal Maturity Structure," p. 703.

4

Alternative Mortgage Instruments

During the 1970s, the SLA industry underwent a "revolution" in its liability structure as passbook accounts diminished from the dominant liability to minority status, and liabilities changed from strictly fixed rate to a situation where the majority of deposits were variable rate. During the first half of the 1980s a similar revolution is occurring within the industry's assets. This revolution is the rapidly decreasing use of what is called the standard, fixed-payment mortgage (SFPM) and the equally rapidly increasing use of alternative mortgage instruments (AMIs).

An AMI is any mortgage that is not an SFPM. A major problem in talking about AMIs is the variety of different types of AMIs that exist and the many different names used to describe them. Not only is there a plethora of names, but different names are frequently used to describe identical mortgages. Regardless of their names, various AMIs will affect the risk exposure and the expected returns of SLAs. A key ingredient to the growth of these instruments is the willingness of consumers to accept them.

THE SFPM AND TYPES OF AMIs

What we today call the standard, fixed-payment mortgage has been in existence for a long time. Indeed, it was the most common type of mortgage in use in the late 1920s, but it accounted for slightly less than one-half of the total mortgages written.[1] The conversion of the mortgage loan industry to the near universal use of the SFPM has been attributed to both its use as the FHA-insured mortgage in 1934 and to its use by the Home Owner Loan Corporation.[2]

The SFPM is characterized by equal monthly installments which include both principal and interest. SFPMs typically have a maximum maturity of 30 years but can be written for terms of as few as five or ten years. As with any debt instrument, the lender can always ease any of the covenants of the mortgage but cannot unilaterally make them more restrictive. The collateral for any mortgage is by definition real estate, and many mortgages have a due-on-sale clause. The mortgage becomes assumable when the due-on-sale clause is omitted. Mortgages also allow prepayments of principal, although prepayment penalty fees may sometimes be required.

The Adjustable or Variable-Rate Mortgages

One reason for the variety of names given to different AMIs which to most laymen would appear to be identical is that these mortgage instruments were put into use over a period of time during which the regulatory constraints on mortgage terms were being relaxed. A brief review of this evolution would be helpful in understanding current mortgage instruments. The first such AMI approved by the FHLBB is referred to as the Variable-Rate Mortgage or VRM. [Since the names "variable," "renegotiable," and "adjustable" are frequently used to describe all of these types of mortgages, the discussion will be simplified if the capitalized abbreviations are used only to refer to each specific type of mortgage and the noncapitalized names to refer to a category of mortgages.] The VRM was approved in 1978 and compared to subsequent AMIs was quite restricted. The basic terms of the VRM are shown in Table 4.1. Under the VRM, the lender is allowed to alter the effective interest rate subject to several restrictions. These include the monthly mortgage payment not increasing by more than 7.5 percent per year, the mortgage interest rate not increasing by more than 50 basis points per year and not changing by more than 250 basis points cumulatively, and not being changed more than once a year.[3]

In a VRM, the index for adjusting the mortgage rates is an industry cost of funds index. Decreases in the index must be matched by mandatory decreases in the interest rate on the mortgage, but increases in the index are treated as optional by the lender. With a VRM, the borrower must be given a 90-day notice of any changes in the interest rate, and no prepayment penalties can be imposed if made within 120 days of any notification. Changes in the interest rate on a VRM can be accomplished by either altering the monthly mortgage payment or by changing the maturity of the mortgage. However, the maturity cannot be increased by more than one-third its original term.[4]

On April 3, 1980, the FHLBB passed regulations authorizing Renegotiable-Rate Mortgages or RRMs. The RRMs are substantially less restricted than their VRM predecessor. For example, although the interest rate on the RRM can change by no more than 50 basis points per year, the total cumulative change in the interest rate is restricted to only 5 percent. Also, there is no option for extending the maturity of an RRM,[5] no minimum adjustment on interest rate changes, and no restrictions on prepayment penalties.[6] As in the case of the VRM, the lender must give a 90-day notice before any interest rate change, but the prohibition against prepayment penalties applies only to the first notification. The key difference between a VRM and an RRM is in the frequency of adjustment. The change period for the interest rate on RRMs is three to five years. The allowable indices for the RRM are the Bank Board's series of the monthly national average mortgage

Table 4.1

Major Characteristics of Recent Federal Regulations Governing Adjustable-Rate Home Mortgage Lending

Major Characteristics	VRM Regulations* (July 1, 1979)	RRM Regulations* (April 3, 1980)	Adjustable Mortgage Loan**	Adjustable Rate Mortgage**
Requirement to offer fixed-rate mortgage instrument to borrower	Yes	None	None	None
Limit to amount of ARMs that may be held	50%	None	None	None
Indexes governing mortgage rate adjustments	U.S. SLA cost of funds or other approved index	U.S. mortgage rate	Any interest rate index that is readily verifiable by the borrower and not under the control of the lender, including national or regional cost-of-funds indexes for SLAs.	One of three national rate indexes—a long-term mortgage rate, a Treasury bill rate, or a three-year Treasury bond rate.
Limit on frequency of rate adjustments	Once a year or longer	3 to 5 years	None	Not more often than every six months.
Limit on size of periodic rate adjustments	.5%/year	.5%/year	None	1 percentage point for each six-month period between rate adjustments, and no single rate adjustment may exceed 5 percentage points.

Limit on size of total rate adjustment over mortgage life	2.5% Overall	5% overall	None	None
Allowable methods of adjustment to rate changes	Change maturity or monthly payment by no more than 7.5%	Change monthly payment only	Any combination of changes in monthly payment, loan term, or principal balance.	Changes in monthly payment or rate of amortization.
Limit on amount of negative amortization	None	None	No limit, but monthly payments must be adjusted periodically to amortize fully the loan over the remaining term.	Limits are set, and monthly payments must be adjusted periodically to amortize fully the loan over the remaining term.
Advance notice of rate adjustments	90 days	90 days	30 to 45 days before scheduled adjustment.	30 to 45 days prior to scheduled adjustments.
Prepayment restrictions or charges	None within 120 days of notification	None after first notification	None	Prepayment without penalty permitted after notification of first scheduled rate adjustment.
Disclosure requirements	Compare VRM and an SFPM, including worst case	Show worst case only for first adjustment	Full disclosure of AML characteristics no later than time of loan application.	Full disclosure of ARM characteristics no later than time of loan application.

* *SOURCE:* Henry J. Cassidy, "Comparison of the VRM and RRM Regulations and Rollover Recommendations," in "Comparison and Analysis of the Consumer Safeguards of Variable Rate and Renegotiable Rate Mortgage Instruments," Research Working Paper No. 95, Office of Policy and Economic Research, Federal Home Loan Bank Board, 1980.

** *SOURCE:* David F. Seiders, "Changing Patterns of Housing Finance," *Federal Reserve Bulletin*, Board of Governors of the Federal Reserve System, June 1981, p. 468.

Table 4.2
Description of the Eight ARMs Purchased by the FNMA

Plan #	Index	Rate Adjustment Period	Limit on Interest Rate Change	Payment Adjustment Period	Limit on Increase in Monthly Payment
1	6-mo. T-bill	6 mo.	none	6 mo.	7.5%
2	6-mo. T-bill	6 mo.	none	36 mo.	none
3	1-yr. T-note	12 mo.	none	12 mo.	7.5%
4	3-yr. T-note	30 mo.	none	30 mo.	18.75%
5	3-yr. T-note	30 mo.	5%	30 mo.	none
6	5-yr. T-note	60 mo.	none	60 mo.	none
7	FHLBB mortgage index	12 mo.	none	12 mo.	none
8	FHLBB mortgage index	12 mo.	2%	12 mo.	none

contract interest rates on the purchase of previously occupied houses. As with VRMs, it is mandatory that decreases in the index be passed on, but increases in the index are optional.[7]

On March 23, 1981, the Comptroller of the Currency issued regulations for Adjustable-Rate Mortgages (ARMs) for national banks, and on April 23 the FHLBB issued regulations for Adjustable Mortgage Loans (AMLs). Essentially, the regulations for the AMLs subsume the regulations for the VRMs and the RRMs because of their encompassing nature. The major characteristics associated with ARMs and AMLs are also shown in Table 4.1, which clearly indicates that the AML is a much less restricted instrument than even the ARM. The key features of the AML are that virtually any index may be used to adjust the mortgage rate and that there are no limits on the frequency, size, or cumulative size of interest rate changes. Also, any combination of changes in monthly payment and loan term is permitted; this includes the possibility of "negative amortization."[8] Advance notice of rate adjustments must be given only 30 to 45 days prior to any change, and there are no prepayment restrictions.

In August 1981, the Federal National Mortgage Association (FNMA or "Fannie Mae") began buying eight standard types of ARMs. Because the existence of a secondary market should be an attractive feature for any mortgage, it is likely that some of these eight types of ARMs will become the most common used. The basic features of these eight plans are highlighted in Table 4.2.[9] Six of the eight use Treasury securities which range in maturity from six months to five years as the index number, and the other two use the FHLBB's index of mortgage rates on loans closed on existing residences. A common feature to all of them is that negative amortization is acceptable. The rate adjustment period varies from six months to five years, and six of the eight have no limit on the interest rate change. The payment adjustment period also ranges from six months to five years, but only five have no limit on the increase in the amount of monthly payment.

Two other types of mortgages which closely resemble an adjustable mortgage are the "interest-only" balloon mortgage and the "partially amortizing" balloon mortgage. A balloon mortgage is one in which the principal comes due in one large, final payment after a series of smaller, equal installment payments. An interest-only balloon mortgage has payments that consist only of interest, and a partially amortized balloon mortgage has regular payments that would be the same as if the mortgage were being amortized over a much longer period. The partially amortized balloon mortgages may have fixed or variable interest rates, and maturities range from 1 to 15 years.[10] These balloon mortgages are like adjustable mortgages in that at maturity they can be rewritten at the current market rate.

During 1980, SLAs in Wisconsin offered one-, two-, and three-year partially amortized balloon mortgages based on 30-year maturities, and found that virtually all their mortgage applications were for these loans.[11] One reason for this popularity is that these loans were offered with only a 5 percent down payment and at a 12 percent rate with two points, when comparable 30-year loans were costing 14 percent. At the time of renewal, the SLAs were only charging $50 to $100 to roll over the mortgage.

A rather serious constraint on the use of balloons by the federal SLAs had been Bank Board restrictions. Balloons required a 40 percent downpayment and had a maximum allowable maturity of five years. In October 1981 the FHLBB modified these terms to require only a 5 percent downpayment and to permit a 40-year maturity. It also allowed the federal associations to insert an adjustable interest rate into a balloon mortgage.[12]

Although all of the AMIs discussed so far differ in terms of the mechanics, they are quite similar in terms of the general approach and the purpose they are intended to serve. The general approach is that the interest rate on the mortgage is allowed to fluctuate, and the purpose is to transfer at least some of the interest rate risk from the lender to the borrower. These instruments differ by the pattern of permitted interest rate changes and in the amount of interest rate risk exposure that is transferred to the borrower.

Several other types of mortgage instruments have been developed or proposed in recent years. Some of these are intended to deal with a different issue, namely, the "tilt" problem. The "tilt" phenomenon occurs because during inflationary periods the interest rate on mortgages incorporates an expected inflation premium while the incomes of borrowers at the time of the mortgage loan cannot be so adjusted. Under an SFPM the mortgage payment will be quite large because of the inflation premium, while the borrower's income will be low initially compared to what it will be later. Thus, mortgage payments that would be almost impossible for the borrower to pay in the early years could be considered absurdly low in later years. An obvious solution is to have a mortgage whose payments rise over the life of the mortgage.

The Graduated-Payment Mortgages

A mortgage currently in use today which deals with the tilt problem is the graduated-payment mortgage or GPM. In a GPM the initial payments are less than what they would have been under an SFPM. They then increase each year for a certain number of years and finally level off. For example, under one popular GPM plan, the payments increase by 7.5 percent each year for the first five years and then stabilize.[13] A not uncommon consequence of the low initial payments is negative amortization. Thus the principal actually grows in the early years of a GPM.

A modified version of the GPM is the pledged account mortgage or PAM. In a PAM the borrower agrees to set up a pledged account, and when the monthly mortgage payments are insufficient to cover the interest portion, the difference is taken out of the pledged account rather than added to the principal.[14]

Another twist to the GPM is to combine it with the features of the AML. This creates what is referred to as the graduated-payment adjustable mortgage loan or the GPAML. The tricky feature of the GPAML is that there are two interest rates involved in the mortgage, a debit rate and a payment rate. The debit rate is that at which interest accrues, and the payment rate is that used to determine the size of the mortgage payment. The GPAML was authorized by the Bank Board on July 14, 1981 for use by federal SLAs and federal mutual savings banks. The primary restrictions on the GPAML are that the payment amount has to be adjusted within ten years to an amount sufficient to amortize the principle over the remaining term of the loan, and it must be so readjusted every five years if there is a change in the debit rate. As in the case of AMLs, there are no restrictions on the amount by which the monthly payment, the interest rate, or the loan term may be adjusted, except that the term of the loan may never exceed 40 years from the date of the closing.[15]

The most recently developed version of the GPM is the growing equity mortgage. These will be referred to as GEHLs for "growing equity home loans" rather than GEMs because the latter term is registered as a service mark by Merrill Lynch with the permission of GEM Savings Association of Dayton, Ohio.[16] GEHLs in general, including Merrill Lynch's, start off with a monthly payment based on a 25- or 30-year maturity. At the end of each year the monthly payment is automatically increased by an amount that typically ranges from 2.5 percent to 7.5 percent.[17] All of the increase in payment is applied to repayment of principal, with the result that these mortgages have maturities ranging from 10 to 15 years. The advantage to the borrower from this mortgage is that it is issued at a lower rate than comparable SFPMs, and it results in substantial savings in interest payments over the life of the mortgage.[18] It also has an apparent psychological benefit of offering many homeowners a reasonable chance of owning a mortgage-free home. A drawback is that after about the sixth year the decline in the interest portion of the mortgage payments results in the loss of most of the tax benefits of having a mortgage.[19]

The Profit Sharing Mortgages

One of the more exotic mortgages that has come into existence in recent years is the shared appreciation mortgage or SAM. Essentially, the lender provides a below-market rate on the mortgage in exchange for part of the price appreciation on the house. The price appreciation is shared either at the time the house is sold or at some predetermined date, whichever comes first. In the latter case the appreciation has to be based on an appraised value. One version of the SAM which has been marketed by Advance Mortgage Corp. provides mortgage money at one-third off from the current mortgage rate, in exchange for one-third of the price appreciation when the house is sold.[20] The popularity of SAMs among lenders will probably follow the inflation rate of real estate prices. SAMs will surely lose their appeal during periods of stagnant or deteriorating real estate prices.

In 1980 the FHLBB promulgated its proposed regulations for SAMs, but at the time of this writing, final approval for SAMs has still not been given to federal SLAs. The proposed regulations limit the proportion of price appreciation payable as contingent interest to 40 percent, the maximum term to ten years, and require the lender to guarantee refinancing at market rates upon maturity of the SAM with something other than an SAM.[21] The proposals also define the net appreciated value as either the net selling price or appraised value less the cost of the property, the cost of any capital improvements, and the cost of the appraisals needed to determine market value.[22] A major drawback of SAMs for SLAs is that, if the FHLBB approves them, the FHLMC has no proposals to create a secondary market in them.[23] Thus, they would have to be held until maturity.

Another version of the SAM is the shared equity mortgage or SEM. In the SEM, an investor provides part or all of the equity downpayment for a home buyer. The investor may also provide some of the monthly mortgage payment and pay some of the real estate taxes and insurance premiums. The investor thus becomes a co-owner of the home and will receive an agreed-upon percentage of the price appreciation when the home is sold. In addition, the investor obtains annual tax deductions for his share of the interest expense and taxes as well as depreciation and insurance write-offs.[24] As with SAMs, few SEMs are being made, and they have not been approved by the FHLBB.[25]

The creation of an SEM has benefits for both the buyer and the investor. The buyer needs substantially less downpayment, and the investor can participate in a more attractive conventional mortgage than would otherwise be available. This is because the FHLMC and the FNMA will buy mortgages only on owner-occupied residences. Lenders thus tend to charge higher rates on investor mortgages because these will likely have to be held in their own portfolios.[26]

A major drawback to an SEM is the possibility of default on the payments by either the owner or investor. The owner would presumably have to obtain another investor or lose his property,[27] and the investor would presumably have to tie up additional money and time during foreclosure proceedings.

Because SEMs are so new, many of the legal issues surrounding them are still unresolved. For example, some SEMs may qualify as securities and thus be subject to state "blue sky" laws and the various federal securities laws.[28] Also, there are still many questions about the circumstances under which the investor will be entitled to take depreciation charges.[29]

A version of the SAM which is more likely to be approved is a deferred-payment mortgage or DPM. In a DPM, the borrower makes mortgage payments on only a portion of the mortgage. The balance of the mortgage is treated as a zero-coupon note with a specific maturity. For example, a 30-year, $100,000 mortgage might be acquired with an agreement to defer payment on 20 percent of the mortgage balance for ten years.[30] At a contract rate of 12 percent, the monthly payment to amortize the $80,000 portion over 30 years is $823. After ten years, the deferred $20,000 portion would be due along with accrued interest of $46,000. This deferred payment could then be converted to a 20-year mortgage. The combined monthly payments would then total $1,550. The primary difference between the SAM and the DPM is that with the SAM the magnitude of the balloon payment is based on the house's price appreciation and is speculative. With the DPM, the magnitude of the balloon payment is based on the deferred portion of the mortgage and is known with certainty.

The PLAM

One type of mortgage which has been proposed often but is not yet commercially used is referred to as the price level adjusted mortgage or PLAM.[31] Behind a PLAM is the idea that the high mortgage rates today are based on the sum of a real interest rate and the expected inflation rate. This combination creates the tilt problem described earlier and results in the possibility that either the lender or borrower will receive a windfall gain if the actual inflation rate turns out to be different from the expected rate. These problems can be substantially reduced if the borrower is charged only for the actual inflation rate. The mechanics of the mortgage might work along the following lines.[32] Suppose a lender believes that in the absence of inflation, the real interest rate would be 5 percent. On a 30-year, $60,000 mortgage, the monthly payment would be $322.09, and after one year the balance due on the principal would be $59,115. If the inflation rate during the year were 8 percent, then the balance due would be increased by 8 percent. The monthly payment due during the second year is then computed from the adjusted principal based on a 5 percent, 29-year amortization. The increase in the monthly mortgage payment will equal the inflation rate. Now, if the borrower's income has also gone up at the rate of inflation, then the tilt problem will have been transferred from the borrower to the lender. This transferrence has occurred because the lender presumably would still offer deposit rates based on expected or *ex ante* inflation rates and would be earning money on its assets based on the real rate and *ex post* inflation rates.[33]

The removal of the tilt problem from the lender can be seen graphically as shown in Figure 4.1. The numbers in Figure 4.1 represent a 30-year, $50,000 mortgage.[34] The PLAM is at an initial rate of 4 percent and assumes an annual realized inflation rate of 10 percent. The SFPM is at a 14 percent rate. The vertical axis in Figure 4.1 represents the real or inflation-adjusted value of future monthly payments in today's dollars. The real value of the SFPM payments declines (hence the tilt phenomenon), but the real value of the PLAM payments is constant (hence the removal of the tilt). Figure 4.1 also shows the nominal values of the outstanding balances of both mortgages and the nominal values of the monthly payments. Under the PLAM, what had started out as a $50,000 mortgage has grown by the end of 25 years to a principal balance due of $158,615. The monthly payments have similarly grown from $239 in the first year to $2,351 during the twenty-fifth year. A borrower who does not realize that his income is also assumed to grow at a 10 percent rate in this example would easily be shocked at the magnitude of the numbers associated with the PLAM as it approaches maturity.

The previous example demonstrates a "pure" PLAM in which the initial mortgage rate is the "pure" real rate of return. Modified PLAMs could also be structured. As an example, if the real rate of return were believed to be 4 percent and the long-term inflation rate were expected to be 10 percent, then a modified PLAM might charge an initial mortgage rate of 9 percent which represents the real rate of return plus one-half the expected inflation rate. Subsequent adjustments might then be based on one-half the realized inflation rate.

One drawback to the prospective homebuyer from the PLAM is that it reduces much of the benefit of home ownership because of its potential to be an inflation hedge. The tilt phenomenon makes it difficult for people to buy a home and frequently causes them to buy a home smaller than what they initially might desire. However, it also enables their real disposable income to grow at a faster rate than it otherwise would. This faster growth comes in part from the inflation hedge of home ownership.

A technical problem with the PLAM is that at the time the lender adjusts the principal for the *ex post* inflation rate, the amount of the adjustment becomes taxable income. This is a problem because it can create a substantial increase in the tax liability without a concomitant increase in cash inflows.[35] In the 30-year, $60,000 mortgage example cited above, if there were a constant 8 percent inflation rate, then there would be several years in which the principal adjustment is well in excess of $4,000.

The RAM

There is one type of instrument which technically qualifies as an AMI but is substantially different from all of the above-described instruments. This is

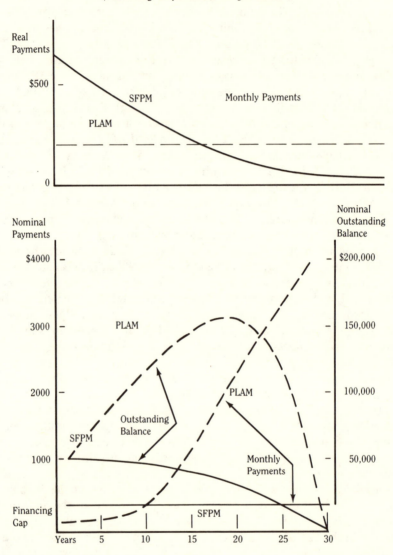

Figure 4.1
Comparisons of Monthly Payments and Outstanding Balances
(Assuming 10 percent steady inflation)

SOURCE: Henry J. Cassidy, "Price-Level Adjusted Mortgages versus Other Mortgage Instruments," *FHLBB Journal,* January 1981, p. 5.

the reverse-annuity mortgage or RAM. In all the other AMIs, the lenders provide money to facilitate the purchase of a house. In an RAM, the lender makes a loan to the current homeowner with the already-owned house as collateral. An RAM enables a homeowner to obtain benefits from the equity in his house without having to sell it. Like SAMs and SEMs, it appears that few SLAs offer RAMs, so a description of how the standard RAM works cannot be offered. Frequently suggested is that the borrower takes a lump-sum loan and purchases an annuity from an insurance company. The loan becomes due at a specified date, when the homeowner dies, or when the house is sold, whichever comes first.[36] An alternative structure is that the lender provides monthly payments to the borrower, and then at maturity all of the monthly payments and accrued interest would be due.[37] Still another possibility is to structure a sale and leaseback arrangement. The ideal arrangement from the homeowner's viewpoint would be a lifetime lease.[38]

SLAs may offer RAMs under current Bank Board regulations, but there can be no interest rate adjustments or prepayment penalties.[39] The Bank Board formerly required but now no longer insists on guaranteed refinancing upon maturity of the RAMs, and the Bank Board must review all proposed plans.[40] The Board is currently considering proposals to permit interest rate adjustments, eliminate the refinancing requirement, and delete the mandatory review.[41]

Other Types of New Mortgages

Three other mortgage instruments which have received attention recently are the "no-interest" loans, second mortgages, and "blends." "No-interest" or "zero-percent financing" loans typically are mortgages with relatively large downpayments, short maturities, and payments that are ostensibly principal only. Conceptually, these loans reflect that the seller is incorporating the financing charges into the price of the real estate. The difference between the normal market value of real estate and an inflated price which incorporates the financing costs is referred to as seller's points. However, some "no-interest" loans do include what are referred to as monthly carrying charges or service fees. Although it is not legally mandatory to disclose seller's points as financing charges, it is necessary to disclose carrying charges or service fees as such.[42] One disadvantage to the buyer under a no-interest loan is that since the financing charges become incorporated as part of the purchase price, they are not immediately deductible.[43] There is some compensation from the tax code in that if the seller provides the mortgage, a no-interest loan becomes an installment sale. If the stated interest rate on an installment sale is less than 9 percent, then the Internal Revenue Service will impute a 10 percent interest rate on the payments.[44] Thus, some of the monthly payment on a no-interest loan is still tax-deductible as interest.

Second mortgages are not really as innovative as the other forms discussed herein, but they are among the faster growing in terms of annual volume. In fact, some SLAs in recent years have at times ceased to provide new first mortgages and have offered instead only second mortgages and refinancing of first mortgages already on the books.[45]

A "blended" mortgage is usually a combination of an assumable mortgage and additional financing. This is also referred to as a wraparound mortgage or WRAP.[46] A blended mortage may be provided by the seller, in which case the original lender is affected only in that an old mortgage is not paid off that otherwise would have been. But a blended mortgage may also be provided by the original lender. The benefits in this case are that the original lender can receive normal financing charges and may take the opportunity to increase the interest rate on the old loan. The new blended rate may still be less than current rates. The new borrower receives the benefit of a below-market interest rate, and the seller is able to sell his property free and clear.[47]

The Due-on-Sale Problem

The practice of seller-provided, blended mortgages was probably dealt a death-blow by a U.S. Supreme Court decision in June 1982. Seller-provided blendeds could be arranged whenever the lender had failed to include a due-on-sale clause, or when the lender could not enforce such a clause which had been included in the mortgage contract. The legal conflict began when, in recent years, 18 states had developed state laws or state court rulings which supposedly voided the due-on-sale clause. In 1976, however, the FHLBB approved regulations giving all federal SLAs the right to enforce such clauses.[48] In California, the conflict between state law and federal regulation was temporarily resolved in a 1978 California Supreme Court ruling, known as the Wellenkamp decision, in favor of state law.[49] The U.S. Supreme Court ruling of 1982 reversed the Wellenkamp decision and could be applied retroactively. The final court ruling applied ostensibly only to federal associations, but "some states have parity laws that automatically give state thrifts any new powers granted federal S&Ls."[50] Those states which do not have such parity laws will probably grant such parity in this case, because they risk having many of the state associations convert to federal charter.

The irony of the due-on-sale controversy is that it has pitted two traditional allies, the real estate industry and the thrift industry, against each other. The real estate industry argued that the assumption of existing mortgages was providing the ability to close the majority of home sales in some areas.[51] The SLA industry argued that continued allowance of assumables could cost them as much as $1 billion annually in lost earnings.[52] However, there is some indication that this estimate may be high. For example, Mark Meador, based on an empirical analysis of the behavior of repayment rates at California SLAs, estimates that during the first half of 1981, the affected state-chartered SLAs suffered an opportunity loss of repayment inflows on an annual rate of $1.27 billion, which would have produced additional profits at an annualized rate of $58 million.[53] In a similar piece of research, Larry Ozanne estimated the loss in net income to the state-chartered SLAs in 1981 to be between $58 and $170 million.[54]

THE EFFECT OF AMIs ON THE RISK EXPOSURE OF SLAs

Because of the various ways in which they are structured, AMIs will affect the risk exposure and the expected returns of SLAs. The primary risk exposure affected will be that of interest rate. However, other forms of risk exposure such as default risk will also be affected.

The Adjustable-Rate Mortgage

A mortgage with an adjustable interest rate has a substantially shorter duration than an SFPM. For a mortgage of a given maturity, the decline in duration is a function of the ability of the contract rate to adjust to new market rates. At the extreme, an adjustable mortgage whose contract rate change matches every change in market rates would always have a duration of zero. This is because the mortgage would always be worth the principal due and there would be no change in the value of the mortgage due to changes in market interest rates.

A more realistic situation is that the interest rate would change at intervals ranging from six months (ARMs) to five years (RRMs) with no restrictions on the magnitude of change. In these cases, the duration of the mortgage would range from slightly less than six months to somewhat more than four years. In other words, the process of adjusting the contract rate to market rates is analogous to the mortgage being paid off and the lender immediately relending the money. Since the original VRMs had relatively tight restrictions on the total change allowed, they did not substantially lower the durations of the mortgages.

In view of the radical difference in the duration of an SFPM and the more recently authorized adjustable mortgages, it would seem that these latter instruments virtually eliminate the interest rate risk exposure of SLAs. In fact, that is the case. The massive losses that SLAs are sustaining today accrue from the old, low-rate SFPMs in their mortgage portfolios. They are suffering no losses and bear little interest rate risk exposure from the more recent RRMs and AMLs in their portfolios.

It should be pointed out that the use of adjustable mortgages does not *eliminate* the interest rate risk exposure; it *transfers* that risk to the borrower. This transfer is a touchy political issue and represents one of the reasons that the regulatory authorities have taken so long to authorize adjustable mortgages. In fact, political displeasure with the adjustables continues to be voiced, as evidenced by recent testimony before the Subcommittee on Financial Institutions Supervision, Regulation and Insurance.[55]

Yet, there is some evidence that all borrowers are not necessarily worse off with adjustable mortgages. Two key factors appear to affect the relative riskiness. One is the source of change in market interest rates, and the other is the composition of the borrower's portfolio. If the market interest rate changes due to a change in the real interest rate, then an adjustable mortgage is unquestionably riskier for the borrower. If, however, market interest rates change due to changes in the rate of inflation, then many borrowers will find the adjustable mortgage less risky than the SFPM. These would be the borrowers whose portfolios contain large portions of "variable coupon assets, common stocks, real assets, and fixed coupon liabilities."[56]

The initial coupon rate on an adjustable mortgage should be less than that on an SFPM that has an equal maturity. The reason is that an SFPM is equivalent to issuing an adjustable mortgage and simultaneously writing a put option on the level of bond prices.[57] [A put option is an agreement whereby the buyer of the option has the privilege of selling a specified asset to the seller of the option at an agreed upon price prior to an agreed upon expiration date.] Since the put option has a positive value, the adjustable mortgage would have to be worth less than the SFPM. This reduction in value is achieved with a lower initial coupon rate. There are potential exceptions to the relative pricing of SFPMs and adjustable mortgages. For example, if everyone were convinced that interest rates were about to experience a substantial decline such that holders of SFPMs could profitably refinance even after paying the refinancing costs, then an adjustable mortgage might be priced slightly above an SFPM.[58]

The selection of an index for adjustable mortgages can be quite a problem. The two basic choices are a cost of funds index and a mortgage rate index. If the lender specifies a cost of funds index, then he creates arbitrage opportunities for the borrower. For example, if the cost of funds index rises and the rate on new mortgages does not, then the borrower may find it profitable to refinance the mortgage. If the cost of funds index drops and the rate on new mortgages does not, then the borrower will likely continue to hold the mortgage and the lender suffers an opportunity loss. If the lender selects a mortgage index, then he still suffers from a form of interest rate risk exposure. For example, if the index drops while cost of funds does not, then the lender will have a squeeze on earnings. If the index rises and his cost of funds does not, then the lender will have an unexpected increase in profits.

Although these problems associated with the selection of an index may make it sound like the variable-rate mortgages are not really transferring interest rate risk, that is not the case. Interest rate risk, as we have described it so far, has been restricted to changes in the level of interest rates. The problems associated with the selection of an index are actually part of the risk associated with a "twist" in interest rates. A twist is defined as moves in opposite directions of long-term (mortgage) rates and short-term (deposit) rates, which leave average rates unchanged. Neither the SFPM nor any of the AMIs deal with the risk of interest rate twists.

One potential political problem with the use of a cost of funds index has been suggested by the Director of Economic Research at the FHLB of Boston, who fears that such practice may invite profit margin regulation.[59] If the index chosen is highly or perfectly correlated with the lender's own cost of funds, then such an index generates a guaranteed and highly visible profit margin, which could then be easily regulated. Despite this political issue, the same writer notes that cost of funds indices tend to immunize management from errors in their decisions about deposits and deposit rate offerings. This risk of setting inappropriate deposits rates then gets transferred to the mortgage holders. The suggested implication is that regions such as the West Coast which have shortages of loanable funds could afford to incorporate cost of funds indices, and regions such as New England which have surpluses of loanable funds would have to use mortgage rate indices.[60]

These arguments overlook several economic issues. The first is that as long as the prepayment privilege exists, no one SLA can transfer all of its risk of increases in its cost of funds to borrowers if there have not been corresponding increases in rates on new mortgages. The second is that SLAs have never been allowed to use their own cost of funds as an index. Thus, even if the managers at an SLA pay unnecessarily high rates for its funds, the cost of funds index would not necessarily change. Finally, it is not clear why the interest rates on mortgages would not fully reflect regional differences in the availability of funds, and thus why contract terms could be used to adjust for these differences.

The effect of adjustable mortgages on the incomes of SLAs would depend on the terms of the mortgage. Some simulation evidence suggests that the income effects would be beneficial but not dramatic. In one such simulation, Joseph McKenzie constructed a hypothetical mortgage portfolio for the SLA industry at the end of 1978.[61] The parameters for the portfolio were based on "actual aggregate lending volumes, rates, and terms from 1954 through 1978, along with an assumed constant payment factor of 9 percent per year."[62] The reasonableness of the simulation parameters can be judged by the fact that the simulation portfolio had a year-end 1978 average yield of 8.60 percent and an outstanding stock of $453.2 billion, compared to an actual yield of 8.54 percent and an actual stock of $432.9 billion. McKenzie found that the highest attainable portfolio yield at the end of 1978 would have been 9.34 percent. This could have been attained if *all* of the mortgages acquired since 1954 had been VRMs which used as an index the rates on new mortgages.

McKenzie then ran several simulations in which he varied the terms of the rollover mortgage with respect to the maximum allowable change each period and the maximum cumulative change. All of the VRMs had four-year adjustment periods. He also allowed for variations in the proportion of new mortgages that were made as VRMs. He found that under most of the simulations, the average mortgage portfolio yield would be only 10 to 40 basis points higher. Income effects were small because over the period in question, newly issued mortgages grew at a fairly high rate from year to year, especially in the last few years of the simulation. Thus, as McKenzie points out, "an estimated 58.8 percent of the mortgage balances outstanding at the end of 1978 were less than three years old and an estimated 67.5 percent were less than four years old."[63] He concludes that if loan closings are able to grow at a rate of roughly 10 percent per year, then the flow of new mortgages will always be large relative to the stock of old ones. This means that adjustable mortgages with adjustment periods of at least four years will have little effect on the current yield of the mortgage portfolio.

The Graduated-Payment Mortgages

The GPM is not a beneficial mortgage instrument for SLAs with respect to interest rate risk exposure. By lowering the early payments and raising the later payments, a GPM creates a higher duration asset. The increase in the duration over that of an equivalent yielding SFPM would depend upon how low the initial payments were set relative to what the SFPM payment would have been, and how long a period is allowed before the GPM payments stabilize. For most GPMs, the increase in duration over that for an equivalent yielding SFPM is not substantial, but it is nonetheless a move in an inappropriate direction.

The two modified versions of the GPM, namely the PAM and the GPAML, would appear to be much better suited for SLAs than straight GPMs. By incorporating a pledged account into the mortgage arrangement of a PAM, the SLA is acquiring a relatively long-lived liability. The combined cash flows of the pledged account and the mortgage produce cash flows and a duration virtually equivalent to those of an SFPM. If the pledged account is an interest-free escrow account or a passbook account, then the SLA is increasing the yield on the mortgage without increasing its own interest rate risk exposure.

The GPAML functions much more like an adjustable mortgage than a GPM. In other words, depending on the terms in the mortgage contract regarding adjustments in the interest rate, the adjustable feature should reduce the effective maturity of the mortgage to the adjustment period. The duration of the mortgage would be somewhat less than the adjustment period. The duration would not be as low as that of a straight, adjustable mortgage because of the rising pattern of mortgage payments, but it would be substantially less than that of an SFPM.

Balloon mortgages could be considered the same as an unrestricted adjustable mortgage whose adjustment period equals the maturity of the mortgage. It is unlikely that SLAs would ever offer "interest-only" mortgages. The advantage of a partially amortized balloon mortgage over an adjustable mortgage is that in the latter an index is specified and the adjustment in the contract rate is restricted by changes in the index. But the rate on a renewed partially amortized balloon is freely negotiable. It is easy to understand why consumer advocate groups find the balloon mortgages the most objectionable of the AMIs.[64]

The GEHLs will have less interest rate risk exposure than comparable SFPMs. The fact that GEHLs are offered at lower interest rates than comparable SFPMs increases their average duration. However, the fact that they have a steadily rising payment pattern which simply speeds up the repayment of principal reduces their average duration. The latter effect easily dominates the former.

The Profit Sharing Mortgages

The SAM and SEM instruments have serious drawbacks with respect to several types of risk exposure. The foremost drawback is that the price appreciation potential on any piece of real estate is, of course, speculative. Some regions of the country may experience long and sustained periods of price increases, but this nonetheless does not guarantee that these regions will continue to experience such price increases.

The variability of price increases in real estate around the country is demonstrated in Table 4.3.[65] For the period from 1973 to 1980, all parts of the country experienced substantial real estate price increases. But there are large disparities in the amount of increase.[66] For example, the average residence in the San Francisco Standard Consolidated Statistical Area (SCSA) went up 201.2 percent during this period, while the average residence in the Boston SCSA went up only 65.2 percent.[67] Furthermore, an examination of Table 4.3 reveals that many of those communities which had large price increases over the entire period had some years with negligible or even negative price changes. Even within the same SMSA there can be drastic differences in the changes of housing prices. Table 4.4 provides a selection of real estate price changes for the Washington, D.C., SMSA. As in the national market, the different neighborhoods appreciated at different rates, and the rates of appreciation varied dramatically from year to year.

This variability in price increases means that the expected cash flows on SAMs or SEMs are speculative, and thus the expected yield is uncertain. A second drawback to these mortgages is that if an expected duration is computed, it would be larger than that of an equivalent yielding SFPM because a substantial portion of the cash flow has been shifted to the maturity of the mortgage.[68]

SAMs have still other potential problems with regard to expected yield. For example, some home improvements may increase the value of the property by an amount greater than the cost of the improvement. But most improvements generate value increases less than their cost. This means that with an SAM, the lender will be subsidizing all of the cost-ineffective improvements because the computations of the net price appreciation includes a deduction of all home improvements on a cost basis.[69]

A related problem is that even though the associations might have well-developed estimates of the likely different price appreciations in the different local neighborhoods, they would probably offer only one set of terms on the SAMs in order to comply with discrimination laws. It is likely that borrowers would also develop estimates of the relative price appreciation. The result would be that only the buyers in the neighborhoods with the lowest expected price appreciation would opt for the SAMs. Thus, SLAs would have to price SAMs

Table 4.3
National Real Estate Prices, 1973-1980

	1973 Average Sales Price (In Thousands of Dollars)	1980 Average Sales Price (In Thousands of Dollars)	Cumulative Percentage Increase 1973-1980	Percentage Change Over Selected Years			
				1974	1976	1978	1980
National Average	31.5	68.3	116.8	12.7	7.1	14.7	5.4
Atlanta SMSA	37.5	67.2	79.2	16.3	5.2	1.1	12.6
Boston SCSA	42.5	70.2	65.2	0.5	5.7	6.9	18.0
Chicago SCSA	38.4	76.5	99.2	12.8	11.4	11.8	15.0
Denver SMSA	32.3	74.1	129.4	12.4	10.7	15.5	−3.5
Detroit SCSA	33.6	59.6	77.4	9.2	1.2	14.4	11.4
Greensboro SMSA	27.3	50.0	83.2	18.3	−11.2	8.2	9.9
Honolulu SMSA	59.1	121.3	105.2	5.8	−0.7	5.0	21.2
Houston SCSA	36.2	90.3	149.4	26.5	−2.6	12.7	21.2
Los Angeles SCSA	39.6	109.3	176.0	16.2	14.5	17.7	19.8
New York SCSA	47.4	90.2	90.3	11.6	6.0	9.5	17.4
Philadelphia SMSA	32.1	57.6	79.4	14.6	3.5	9.7	11.0
Phoenix SMSA	33.5	82.8	147.2	21.8	9.5	8.8	23.0
Salt Lake City SMSA	32.1	61.4	91.3	2.5	−0.9	14.1	−8.2
San Francisco SCSA	40.1	120.8	201.2	19.2	8.9	21.2	19.0
Tampa SCSA	31.3	54.5	74.1	8.9	−5.7	17.8	20.0
Wash. D.C. SMSA	45.9	96.3	109.8	11.5	4.6	15.2	7.4

SOURCE: Steve Rohde, "Unrestricted Adjustable Rate Mortgages: A Review of the Early Experience and an Analysis of the Implications of Negative Amortization," in *Adjustable Rate Mortgages: Hearings*, p. 134.

based not on the expected average price appreciation in the area, but on the lowest neighborhood price appreciation.[70]

Still another potential problem associated with SAMs and SEMs is that of surveillance and property maintenance. In other words, "the lender is likely to require minimum maintenance standards and to engage in periodic surveillance to see that they are met. If the standards are not maintained, then costly enforcement and legal actions may be necessary."[71]

There may also be a higher default risk on the SAMs. If the price appreciation

Table 4.4
Washington, D.C., Real Estate Prices, 1973-1979

	1973 Average Price	1979 Average Price	Cumulative Percentage Appreciation	Percentage Change over Previous Year					
				1974	1975	1976	1977	1978	1979
Marshall Heights-Benning Heights	21,039	40,526	92.6	5.9	20.4	10.4	9.9	4.4	19.2
Brookland-Woodridge	24,377	55,504	127.6	3.5	34.0	17.6	−3.2	29.4	11.4
Manor Park-Lamond	24,466	56,809	132.2	21.0	12.7	17.5	6.9	15.1	17.9
University Heights-Michigan Park	28,248	58,225	106.1	1.8	31.9	−4.5	39.1	4.1	11.1
American University Park-Friendship	54,219	129,516	138.9	15.8	3.7	23.4	22.8	11.1	16.2
Georgetown	98,111	234,971	139.5	15.5	13.8	11.9	24.7	4.7	24.8

SOURCE: Steve Rohde, "Unrestricted Adjustable Rate Mortgages: A Review of the Early Experience and an Analysis of the Implications of Negative Amortizations," in *Adjustable Rate Mortgages: Hearings,* p. 153.

of the property is substantial, if the increase in the owner's income is not, and if the shared price appreciation is based on appraised value, then the owner may not be able to pay the shared appreciation or to arrange for financing such a payment.[72]

The DPM eliminates many of the noninterest rate risk problems of the SAMs and SEMs. The interest rate risk problem is somewhat larger, however. Increases in interest rates that are induced by increases in inflation should be partially offset by a greater profit on the price of the house with the SAMs and SEMs. Such an opportunity does not exist for DPMs.

The PLAM

It is, unfortunately, not completely clear as to how PLAMs would affect the interest rate risk exposure and the yields of SLAs. Let us discuss the problem of yields first. Earlier in this chapter we reviewed the standard description of a PLAM. The reader should recall that in this description, a borrower was charged the real rate of interest for the first year, and then in each succeeding year the monthly payment and principal outstanding were adjusted for the realized rate of inflation. In the case of stable real and nominal interest rates, this structure produces a lower yield on the PLAM than on an equivalent SFPM.

To illustrate this point, the numbers in the earlier example will be repeated: a 30-year, $60,000 mortgage when the current market rate on a SFPM is 13 percent. If the lender believes that the 13 percent is composed of a 5 percent real rate of return and an 8 percent inflation premium, then under a PLAM the initial contract rate would be 5 percent. We assumed that the *ex post* inflation rate equals the *ex ante* inflation rate over the life of the mortgage. The initial monthly payment would be $322.09, the monthly payment during the thirtieth year would be $3,001.04, and at the end of the thirtieth year the mortgage would be fully amortized. It turns out that this PLAM has an internal rate of return of only 12.4 percent, compared to a 13 percent rate on the SFPM. The internal rate of return is lower on the PLAM because the inflation adjustments are made with a one-year lag and the inflation compensation lost during the first year is never recovered. To make up for this lagged effect, the rate charged during the first year would have to be somewhat higher than the real rate. One possibility is that the rate during the first year could be set equal to the rate on SFPMs of equal maturity, and another possibility is that the first-year rate could be set equal to the real rate plus the realized inflation rate of the previous year.[73] However, this adjustment in the yield has the side-effect of eliminating the supposed advantage to a PLAM, namely the creation of a low first-year mortgage payment.

The interest rate risk of PLAMs is probably less than that of SFPMs, and it may even be equivalent to an adjustable mortgage with a one-year adjustment period. However, it is possible that the duration might actually be longer than that of an SFPM. For example, if we assume a constant expected inflation rate and a constant expected real rate over the life of the PLAM discussed in the previous paragraph, then its duration would be 11.668 years. The duration of a comparable 30-year, $60,000 SFPM with a contract rate of 12.4 percent is 7.39 years. Thus, PLAMs could substantially exacerbate the duration mismatch.

A more likely premise is that real interest rates will fluctuate. Indeed, there is evidence that in recent years the real rate has been rising.[74] This creates the possibility of below-market yields on PLAMs. For example, suppose in the example above that after the mortgage was issued, the real rate of interest increases to 6 percent and the inflation rate falls to 7 percent. The nominal rates on SFPMs would remain at 13 percent, but the effective yield on the PLAM would be about one percentage point less than the 12.4 percent it was previously yielding. Hence with PLAMs, lenders are incurring the risk associated with changes in the *real* interest rate. However, as we have already seen, with SFPMs lenders are incurring the interest rate risk associated with changes in *nominal* interest rates. The key point is that the variance associated with nominal interest rates is probably much larger than the variance associated with real interest rates. This results in the market value of PLAMs adjusting to interest rate changes almost as if they were unrestricted adjustable mortgages.[75]

One of the suggested benefits of the PLAM is that the ratio of the mortgage payment to the borrower's income would remain constant. This, of course, requires that the borrower's income grows at the rate of inflation. In the post-World War II period, however, there have been steady increases in social security taxes and a persistently progressive income tax structure. This combination has required that in order to maintain an inflation-adjusted real income, a person's gross income must have grown at an average rate of one to two percentage points higher than the inflation rate.[76] Since such consistently higher growth rates in gross income are unlikely for a majority of the mortgage borrowers, it is not obvious that the *real* value of the mortgage payments under a PLAM should be expected to be constant.

The initial offering of PLAMs would likely exacerbate any liquidity problem that an SLA might have because of the low payments during the early years of these mortgages. The liquidity problem occurs as long as deposit rates are based on nominal interest rates and the initial mortgage payments in a PLAM are based on real interest rates. It is certainly possible in this circumstance that the interest payments on the deposits used to finance a PLAM would exceed the payments on a PLAM for a period of several years. An already established portfolio of PLAMs would probably be sufficiently balanced with respect to maturity that liquidity might not be as much of a problem. One suggested solution to this liquidity problem is price level adjusted deposits or PLADs. PLADs are similar to PLAMs in that the depositor is promised the real rate of interest plus an *ex post* inflation adjustment.

PLAMs may also expose SLAs to greater foreclosure risk. As was shown in Table 4.3, there are substantial variations in the price appreciation of real estate. It is not obvious that the market value of the property would always increase sufficiently to maintain a satisfactory mortgage to market value ratio under a PLAM mortgage.

The RAM

The RAM is one of the worst possible instruments that could be designed for an SLA. Advocates of RAMs have suggested that they provide an opportunity for SLAs to immunize the investment yield. The following example will illustrate this point.[77] Suppose an SLA provides a three-year, $1,000 SFPM with a 10 percent yield. If we assume annual payments, then the payment each year would be $402.25. Suppose also that the same SLA agrees to a three-year, 10 percent RAM that calls for payments of $402.25 each year beginning at time period zero, and a payback at the end of three years of $1,464.59. The cash flows for the SFPM, the RAM, and the combined portfolio are shown in Table 4.5. The combined portfolio is equivalent to a three-year, zero-coupon bond with a yield of 10 percent.

Although it is true that the combined portfolio is immunized against interest rate changes, it is not true that the owner of this portfolio is immunized. The combined portfolio clearly has a duration of three years and represents an

Table 4.5
Cash Flows for Example SFPM versus RAM

| | Payments at Time Periods (t) | | | | Rate of Yield |
	t_0	t_1	t_2	t_3	%
SFPM	− 1000.00	+ 402.25	+ 402.25	+ 402.25	10
RAM	− 402.25	− 402.25	− 402.25	+ 1464.59	10
Portfolio	− 1402.25	0	0	+ 1866.84	10

SOURCE: Hadi Alwan and Paul Hanchett, "Reverse Mortgages, Estate Planning and the Financing of Real Estate," a paper presented at the April 1981 Midwest Business Administration Association annual meeting in Chicago, Illinois.

investment of $1,402.25. If this $1,402.25 is financed with liabilities (that is, deposits) whose duration is different than three years, then the lender has some interest rate risk exposure.

Another way of viewing this problem is to note that the SFPM has a duration of 1.94 years, and the combined portfolio has a duration of 3.0 years. This means that the RAM must have a duration substantially greater than 3.0 years. In this case the three-year RAM has a duration of 5.65 years. Thus, accepting RAMs would only *increase* the interest rate risk exposure of SLAs, and it would increase that risk dramatically.

RAMs create still another risk problem for SLAs in that the mortgage to property value ratio will likely increase rather than decrease over time. This ratio may reach its peak, and thus the risk of default would also reach its peak, at the maturity of this mortgage rather than at its issuance.

Other Types of Mortgages

Although it is unlikely that SLAs would ever get involved in offering "no-interest" mortgages, such mortgages would be beneficial to them in terms of interest rate risk exposure. The "no-interest" mortgages are effectively SFPMs with maturities of 5 to 10 years rather than 25 to 30 years. This means that their durations would be even shorter. The high downpayment on these mortgages would have the benefit of of reducing default risk.

Second mortgages have the features of both shorter maturities and higher yields than first mortgages. In fact, a recent survey covering second mortgages found the average maturity to be six years.[78] This combination certainly means lower durations and thus less interest rate risk exposure. However, these mortgages could also be expected to have greater default risk, and it appears that they do.[79] One potential problem with second mortgages as sources of income for SLAs is that there is apparently not much opportunity to resell them in the secondary market.[80]

Finally, the "blended" mortgages have the same risk characteristics as the mortgage itself. That is, a "blended" AML has the same risk characteristics as an AML, and a "blended" SFPM has the same risk characteristics as an SFPM. The primary benefits of blended mortgages are that they bring in extra fee income and may facilitate the removal of low interest rate mortgages from the portfolio sooner than would otherwise be the case.

Default Risk on AMIs

It was previously suggested that some of the AMIs may have higher default risk potential than comparable SFPMs. For evidence on this point, James Smith has run some simulations using *The Panel Study of Income Dynamics* (PSID) data for 1968 to 1976. This data base is an ongoing research project of the Survey Research Center of the University of Michigan.[81] Smith assumed in his simulations that people in the study took out an SFPM and a GPM in 1971, such that the initial payment under each totaled 25 percent of the borrower's income. By 1976, a mortgage payment to income ratio greater than 25 percent would have been experienced by 24 percent of the families with the SFPM, compared to 39 percent of the families holding the GPM. Smith then analyzed the characteristics of those families which were best able to handle the increasing payments of the GPM. He found that the best candidates are "families headed by young persons who have above average educations for persons of their age and/or have jobs with high occupation status."[82]

A much broader but similar study has recently been reported by Bruce G. Webb.[83] Webb uses virtually the same data base, namely the PSID for the years 1968 to 1975. He examines a total of six mortgage forms, including the GPM and the SFPM, and he employs four different definitions of probable delinquency. The main conclusion is that "all of the AMI's studied . . . were riskier than the fixed rate mortgage, based on the number of potential delinquencies."[84] The riskiest mortgage is the PLAM.

Webb then examines various characteristics of the probable defaulters under the various AMIs and for the various definitions of default. He finds that a borrower with high risk characteristics will be likely to have a potentially delinquent loan whether or not the mortgage has highly variable payments. However, Webb does find that the severity of potential delinquency is significantly related to several borrower characteristics, primarily nonwhite household heads and older household heads. The severity problem for older household heads is particularly acute under the PLAM.

Many of the AMIs discussed also show a potential problem with regard to collateral protection. In many states, future advances which are optional are not protected in the event they are made after a junior lien has been placed on the property. This problem could be particularly acute in the case of RAMs and any mortgages which incorporate negative amortization. Obligatory advances are more likely to be protected.[85]

BORROWER ATTITUDES TOWARD AMIs AND ACTUAL USAGE

The primary criticisms made of AMIs on behalf of borrowers usually follow one of two lines of argument. The first, mentioned previously, is that it is simply unfair to ask borrowers to bear interest rate risk. The second is that borrowers may not be able to handle the interest rate risk.[86] Little research has been directed toward ascertaining the actual reactions of borrowers. One of the few studies was performed by Kent Colton, Donald Lessard, and Arthur Solomon(CLS).[87]

CLS found that, despite the consumer-oriented criticisms, 80 percent of the respondents in their telephone survey indicated they would prefer to have a choice among mortgage instruments. Even within the subgroup of those who did not like any of the AMIs described, 70 percent indicated a choice should be available. CLS were next able to identify a fairly distinct group that clearly preferred the GPM. As one might have expected, these people included "young renter households . . . especially those in lower-income brackets with expectations of rising incomes."[88] The group of people that preferred the VRM was less well-defined but seemed to include those with special circumstances such as plans to move soon, or those attracted by the supplemental features added to the mortgage such as "a waiver of the prepayment penalty, an open line of credit or the ease of transfer."[89]

CLS also found evidence of distrust of the financial institutions with regard to AMIs. For example, 92 percent of those surveyed felt that lending institutions should be required to offer the SFPM along with any AMI. They also found that when the people in the sample were presented with additional information in a follow-up mail survey, more of them became interested in taking a VRM. Further evidence about consumer ignorance or misunderstanding about VRMs and SFPMs was suggested by the fact that only 28 percent of those surveyed indicated they had a prepayment penalty in their SFPM. Although CLS had no data on how many mortgages actually had prepayment penalties, they felt this number was far too low and indicated that many consumers really did not understand the conditions of their own mortgages. In the more extensive panel surveys, many panelists stated they had no idea about the prepayment feature of their mortgage. In fact, after the panel dialogues, many of the panelists indicated they would have liked a "training session" like the panel survey before they had acquired their mortgage.

It is somewhat ironic that consumer groups criticize the various AMIs despite evidence that such mortgages would increase the rate of home ownership at least in various SMSAs. James Follain and Raymond Struyk found that the use of a modest GPM "could ultimately increase the number of homeowner households inside SMSAs by about 0.8 million."[90] They also find that an SEM, based on a 20 to 25 percent sharing arrangement, would have about twice as large an effect. VRMs would have little effect on tenure patterns, as would PLAMs during periods of low inflationary expectations. But during periods of high inflationary expectations, they found PLAMs to be the most stimulative of the four AMIs considered.

One additional piece of evidence as to consumer acceptance of adjustable mortgages would have to be the growth in their use in the last few years. Recent research on the spread in usage and the evolution in terms of adjustable mortgages provides some indication of the likely future directions of AMIs. One of the most extensive surveys to date was conducted recently by the American Mortgage Insurance Company (AMIC).[91] They selected a represent-ative cross-sample of 400 SLAs, contacted them by telephone, and had a 98 percent response rate. The first discovery was that 9 percent of the SLAs offered both SFPMs and adjustable mortgages, 32 percent offered SFPMs but no ad-justables, 28 percent offered adjustables but no SFPMs, and 31 percent were offering neither SFPMs nor adjustables.[92] Of the 63 percent that were not then offering adjustables, over half indicated they planned to do so by the end of the year.[93] Finally, the AMIC survey showed that little use was really being made of the other AMIs. The survey asked the SLAs whether they currently offered or intended to offer any of the other AMIs by year-end. The affirmative responses were as follows: GPMs—6.1 percent, GPAMLs—8.4 percent, WRAPs—20.8 percent, SAMs—1.8 percent, RAMs—1.5 percent, and PAMs—11.8 percent.

A more modest survey of AMI usage was recently conducted by Beverly Hadaway and covered the Ninth Federal Home Loan Bank District.[94] Of the 616 SLAs in the district, 149 responded to the survey.[95] Of the seven AMIs defined in her survey, only three were offered by the respondents. Among these three, 41 percent of the respondents offered VRMs, 39 percent offered rollover mortgages, and only 3 percent offered GPMs.[96] The few types of mortgages not offered by the respondents included SAMs, DIMs, RAMs, and an equity adjusted mortgage. For comparative purposes, 12 percent of the respondents offered only SFPMs, and 4 percent indicated they offered some other type of mortgage, typically some form of balloon.

An even more recent survey of mortgage usage was conducted by Stephen Zabrenski and Virginia Olin in February 1982. They contacted the 20 largest SLAs in each of the 12 bank districts and found that three-fourths of these large associations offered AMLs and one-half of this group offered them exclu-sively.[97] By comparison, one-half of the respondents offered SFPMs and only one-third offered these exclusively. Furthermore, during the month of January, AMLs accounted for 70 percent of the total number of commitments issued by the respondents.[98]

In addition to the question on the usage of the various types of mortgages offered, these surveys and others have also covered the terms of the adjustable mortgages. One such study, by Byrl Boyce and Keith Johnson, looked at the use of adjustable mortgages by New England thrifts prior to May 1981.[99] Their study used as a sample the 20 thrifts in New England which had the most ARM volume. Of these 20, 17 were mutual savings banks, and all but three of these institutions had started offering some type of adjustable mortgage only after 1974. One of the institutions, however, has been offering them since 1913. A common theme among the thrifts interviewed was a desire to minimize the variations in the instruments offered to the public. An ideal way was to offer only one type of adjustable mortgage. The preferences in terms favored one-year and three-year review periods, as opposed to something as long as five years or as short as quarterly or semiannually. Changes in the effective yields were almost always accommodated through changes in the monthly payment. Many of the institutions that were offering SFPMs along with adjustables were offering the former only because they intended to resell any such offerings in the secondary market.[100]

The AMIC survey found that among those SLAs offering adjustable mortgages, two-thirds used the Federal Home Loan Bank Board mortgage contract rate as the index, and only 12 percent allowed negative amortization.[101] These features probably reflect the requirements by the Federal Home Loan Mortgage Corporation that any adjustable mortgage it purchases have these particular features. The incorporation of negative amortization as a feature, however, was closely related to the size of the lending institution. Virtually all of those allowing negative amortization had assets greater than $1 billion. Over three-quarters of the SLAs in this survey adjust the payments in one- to three-year intervals. About one-fourth place a cap on the percentage of increase in the monthly payment in any one adjustment period, and 40 percent have a maximum percentage increase over the life of the mortgage.[102]

The Hadaway study found that the VRMs offered resembled SFPMs in that 86 percent of the respondents offering VRMs had 30-year maturities,[103] and the most common loan-to-value ratio was 80 percent. The VRMs were typically offered at rates up to 25 basis points less than those on comparable SFPMs. Nearly one-half of the VRM issuers used the FHLBB index as their reference index, and about seven-eighths used 5 percent as the maximum change in the interest rate over the life of the loan. Nearly two-thirds used a one-year frequency of change interval for VRMs, and three-quarters used a three-year frequency for renegotiable mortgages.

The Zabrenski and Olin survey found nearly identical results.[104] Namely, the typical AML was indexed to the FHLBB contract rate, it had an annual adjustment period, and it was a fully amortized, 30-year loan. The primary difference between their survey and Hadaway's was that they found unlimited changes in the interest rate and monthly payment as most common, although the 2 percent limit per adjustment was the next most common.

CONCLUSIONS

The conclusions about the AMIs seem fairly straightforward. The AMLs and the GPAMLs will remove much of the interest rate risk exposure SLAs have had from their duration mismatch. The PLAMs and GEHLs will help the problem somewhat. The other AMIs simply do not contribute much to alleviating the interest rate risk exposure problem, are not particularly attractive to potential borrowers, or are actually counterproductive. This does not mean that these other forms of mortgages are without socially redeeming features. Indeed, some institutions such as pension funds and life insurance companies may actually have a need for financial securities with durations longer than those offered by the traditional SFPMs. For example, James McNulty has quoted Henry Kaufman as saying that "perhaps the greatest threat to the traditional bond investment" is the shared appreciation mortgage.[105]

A cynic might point out that various forms of the adjustables have been around for several years, and the SLAs in 1982 were in their worst condition ever. The response to this is threefold. First, if the AMIs had not been introduced when they were, the SLA industry would be in even worse shape today.

The second response is that the SLAs are suffering from a stock versus flow problem created in part by the high interest rates. Because of the high interest rates rather than the form of mortgage offered, the volume of new mortgage lending is down and the pace of prepayments has slowed considerably. This means the SLAs have had to live longer with the old, low-rate SFPMs in their portfolio (the stock) and have not been able to add a sufficient number of new mortgages (the flow). It follows that once interest rates drop, and the SLAs can incorporate more of the adjustable mortgages into their portfolios, their interest rate risk exposure will be substantially reduced.

The third response to the cynic is that the financial problems of the industry accrue from their inability to forecast accurately the cost of liabilities. Regardless of what mortgage instrument is used, an SLA needs to price a mortgage so that its yield exceeds the average cost of the liabilities used to finance it over the life of the mortgage. Even with adjustable mortgages, SLAs must still make this forecast for the length of the adjustment period. This is not meant to imply that the rapid rise in the cost of liabilities in recent years was predictable. Rather, it was the inability to forecast this rise which created much of the problem and not the type of mortgage instrument used.[106] In fact, it is somewhat ironic that just as the SLAs have begun using these various AMIs which reduce their interest rate risk exposure, they have also received the authority to use financial futures in a way which enables them to transfer to others the task of forecasting changes in interest rates.

NOTES

1. Henry J. Cassidy, "The Changing Home Mortgage Instrument in the United States," *Federal Home Loan Bank Board Journal,* December 1978, p. 11.

2. Ibid.

3. Other restrictions include that any lender offering a VRM is required to offer the borrower an SFPM, and the lenders are restricted in that the majority of their mortgage portfolio cannot be in VRMs. The lender also has to disclose to the borrower what the

mortgage payments would be under the "worst case" scenario in which interest rates rose quickly to the maxiumum and stayed there.

4. For even more details on the VRM, as well as the Renegotiable-Rate Mortgage (RRM) which is discussed next, the reader is referred to Henry J. Cassidy, "Comparison and Analysis of the Consumer Safeguards of Variable Rate and Renegotiable Rate Mortgage Instruments," Research Working Paper No. 95, Office of Policy and Economic Research, Federal Home Loan Bank Board, April 1980.

5. The inflexible maturity on the RRM was designed to make the RRM more viable in the secondary market. See Cassidy, "Comparison and Analysis," p. 2.

6. In addition, there are no portfolio limitations on RRMs, and it is not mandatory that borrowers be offered the choice.

7. When the lender describes the "worst case" scenario to the potential borrower under an RRM, only the effect upon the monthly payment after the first interest rate change need be shown.

8. "Negative amortization" occurs whenever the mortgage payments are insufficient to pay the interest due on the mortgage. The difference between the mortgage payment and the interest is then added to the principal.

9. Additional information on these eight plans can be found in Reynolds Griffith and Zack E. Mason, "The Adjustable Rate Mortgage: Which Index is Best?" a paper presented at the Fall 1982 meeting of the Southwestern Federation of Administrative Disciplines in Dallas, Texas; and Larry E. Wofford and Richard C. Burgess, "Structuring Adjustable Rate Mortgages: Single Asset and Portfolio Considerations," a paper presented at the October 1982 meeting of the Financial Management Association in San Francisco, California.

10. See Joseph A. McKenzie, "A Borrower's Guide to Alternate Mortgage Instruments," *FHLBB Journal,* January 1982, p. 19.

11. "Short-term Mortgage Loans Hot Item in Wisconsin," *Chicago Tribune,* September 28, 1980, Sect. 14, pp. 1, 1D.

12. "U.S. Eases Rules On Reverse Annuity, Balloon Mortgages," *Wall Street Journal,* October 16, 1981. A popular misconception about balloons is that prior to the 1930s, they were the dominant form of mortgage. If they were dominant, however, it was not an overwhelming dominance. Recent evidence suggests that SFPMs constituted roughly 47 percent of all home mortgages in the late 1920s. However, it was primarily the non-SLA lenders that were providing the balloons. These lenders included life insurance companies (90 percent in balloons), mutual savings banks (100 percent in balloons), and commercial banks (90 percent in balloons). SLAs had roughly 95 percent of their mortgages as fully amortized loans and the other 5 percent as nonamortized balloons. See Cassidy, "The Changing Home Mortgage Instrument," p. 13.

13. McKenzie, "A Borrower's Guide," p. 19.

14. Ibid.

15. "Statement of Richard T. Pratt," in *Adjustable Rate Mortgages: Hearings Before the Subcommittee on Financial Institutions Supervision, Regulation and Insurance of the Committee on Banking, Finance and Urban Affairs,* House of Representatives, Ninety-Seventh Congress, First Session, Serial No. 97-34, p. 207.

16. James P. Meagher, "An Office Space Glut . . . More on GEMs," *Barron's,* August 2, 1982, p. 14.

17. James P. Meagher, "Fast-Payoff Mortgages Win a Fan," *Barron's,* July 19, 1982, p. 14.

18. I do not mean to imply that all GEHLs are issued at lower rates. Some are issued at the same rate as SFPMs. In this case, GEHLs would be disadvantageous compared to SFPMs if one assumes the latter has no prepayment penalty. The disadvantage is due to the fact that a GEHL forces the borrower to do what otherwise could be done on a voluntary basis.

19. G. Christian Hill, "Growing-Equity Home Loans are Gaining Popularity because of Quick Repayments," *Wall Street Journal,* October 6, 1982, p. 52.

20. See James Carberry and G. Christian Hill, "Some Mortgage Firms Swap Lower Rates for Share in the Gain When Home is Sold," *Wall Street Journal,* August 22, 1980.

21. For additional details, see Stanley L. Iezman, "The Shared Appreciation Mortgage and the Shared Equity Progam," *Real Estate Review,* Fall 1981, p. 42.

22. Ibid.

23. Ibid., p. 46.

24. Ibid.

25. See Robert Guenther, "Two Mortgage Ideas Fizzle . . . Granny Flats . . . Rental Advice," *Wall Street Journal,* March 31, 1982.

26. See Liza Bercovici, "Shared Equity Mortgages Break New Legal Ground," *Real Estate Review,* Winter 1982, p. 59.

27. Iezman, "The Shared Appreciation Mortgage," p. 47.

28. Bercovici, "Shared Equity Mortgages," p. 59.

29. Ibid., p. 60.

30. This example is drawn from Arnold Kling, "Son of SAM: A Proposal for a Deferred-Payment Mortgage," *Housing Finance Review,* Vol. 1, No. 1 (January 1982), pp. 93-102.

31. The term "PLAM" was first used in Richard Cohn and Stanley Fischer, "An Analysis of Alternative Nonstandard Mortgages," *Mortgage Study Reports,* Report No. 5, December 1974.

32. This example is drawn from George C. Kaufman and Eleanor Erdevig, "Improving Housing Finance in an Inflationary Environment: Alternative Residential Mortgage Instruments," *Economic Perspectives,* Federal Reserve Bank of Chicago, July/August 1981, pp. 1-23.

33. As Kaufman and Erdevig point out in "Improving Housing Finance" (p. 18), the SLA could protect itself from the tilt risk by offering PLADs, or price level adjusted deposits.

34. The numbers in this example are taken from Henry J. Cassidy, "Price Level Adjusted Mortgages versus Other Mortgage Instruments," *FHLBB Journal,* January 1981, p. 5.

35. For a discussion of the tax treatment of a PLAM, see Daniel Holland, "Tax and Regulatory Problems Posed by Alternative Nonstandard Mortgages," *New Mortgage Designs for an Inflationary Environment: Proceedings of a Conference Held at Cambridge, Massachusetts,* January 1975, edited by Franco Modigliani and Donald Lessard.

36. See, for example, Benjamin Wolkowitz, Michael Asay, and Ellen D. Harvey, "The Economics and Regulation of Alternative Home Mortgage Instruments," Research Papers in Banking and Financial Economics, Board of Governors of the Federal Reserve System, March 1979, pp. 15-16.

37. See Hadi Alwan and Paul Hanchatt, "Reverse Mortgages, Estate Planning and the Financing of Real Estate," a paper presented at the April 1981 meeting of the Midwest Business Administration Association in Chicago, Illinois.

38. H. David Raper, "Converting the Elderly Homeowner's Equity into Income," *Real Estate Review,* Summer 1982, p. 125.

39. Daniel C. Draper, "Alternative Mortgage Instruments," *Real Estate Review,* Fall 1981, p. 36.

40. "U.S. Eases Rules on Reverse Annuity, Balloon Mortgages," *Wall Street Journal,* October 16, 1981.

41. "Statement by Richard T. Pratt," *Adjustable Rate Mortgages: Hearings,* p. 209.

42. See Lew Sichelman, " 'No-interest' Loans of Interest to FTC," *Chicago Tribune,* February 21, 1982.

43. The higher purchase price would, of course, create a lower capital gain in the event the real estate is sold at a profit and the proceeds are not reinvested within two years. However, using finance charges as an offset to capital gains which may be several years in the future is usually much less beneficial than using them as a deduction to current income.

44. Sichelman, " 'No-Interest' Loans."

45. See G. Christian Hill, "Lenders Pushing Second Mortgages to Ease Pinch of Long-Term Loans," *Wall Street Journal,* November 4, 1980.

46. See McKenzie, "A Borrower's Guide," p. 20.

47. For an analysis of one such program, see Thomas V. Wright, "Analysis of an Institutional Alternative to Residential Land Contract Sales," *FHLBB Journal,* September 1982, pp. 9-12.

48. Stephen Wermiel, "Mortgage Shift Can Be Blocked, Top Court Rules," *Wall Street Journal,* June 29, 1982, p. 3.

49. James P. Meagher, "Due-on-Sale: A Day in Court," *Barron's,* April 19, 1982.

50. G. Christian Hill and John Andrew, "Power to Call in Mortgages upon Sale of Homes is Seen Being Given All Thrifts," *Wall Street Journal,* June 29, 1982, p. 3.

51. John Andrew, "Assumable-Mortgages Ruling Seen further Hurting Market," *Wall Street Journal,* June 30, 1982, p. 23.

52. Wermiel, "Mortgage Shift Can Be Blocked."

53. Mark Meador, "The Effects on Mortgage Repayments of Restrictions on the Enforcement of Due-on-Sale Clauses: Aggregate and Micro California Results," Research Working Paper No. 107, Office of Policy and Economic Research, Federal Home Loan Bank Board, August 1982, p. 14.

54. Larry Ozanne, "The Financial Stakes in Due-on-Sale: The Case of California's State-Chartered Savings and Loans," Research Working Paper No. 109, Office of Policy and Economic Research, Federal Home Loan Bank Board, July 1982, p. 2.

55. See, for example, "Testimony of Gale Cincotta, Chairperson, NATIONAL PEOPLE'S ACTION" or "Testimony of Jonathan Brown, Staff Attorney, Public Interest Research Group," both in *Adjustable Rate Mortgages: Hearings.*

56. John A. Halloran, "Mortgage Risk in a Portfolio Theory Context," *Journal of the Midwest Finance Association,* 1978, p. 116.

57. See M. Chapman Findlay III and Dennis Capozza, "The Variable-Rate Mortgage and Risk in the Mortgage Market: An Option Theory Perspective," *Journal of Money, Credit and Banking,* May 1977.

58. Ibid., p. 359, fn. 4. This point is also made by George G. Kaufman in "The Questionable Benefit of Variable Rate Mortgages," *Quarterly Review of Economics and Business,* Vol. 13, No. 3 (1973).

59. See Allan M. Grover, "Choosing the Right VRM Index," *FHLBB Journal,* August 1980, pp. 4-7.

60. Ibid., p. 7.

61. Joseph A. McKenzie, "Simulation Analysis of Rollover Mortgage Portfolios," Research Working Paper No. 98, Office of Policy and Economic Research, Federal Home Loan Bank Board, June 1980.

62. Ibid., p. 3.

63. Ibid., p. 9.

64. See Steve Rohde, "Unrestricted Adjustable Rate Mortgages: A Review of the Implications of Negative Amortization,"*Adjustable Rate Mortages: Hearings,* pp. 23-24.

65. Average sales prices are not, of course, an exact measure of the value of the property sold. Such prices are easily distorted by changes in the mix of houses on the market. They are also distorted due to variations in the terms of the contract. For example, a rate may involve a below-market interest rate loan between the seller and lender or the assumption of a below-market interest rate mortgage, which means that the price may overstate the value of the house.

66. The same story of large and variable price increases can be said for real estate prices over the 1960-1970 period. See, for example, James Follain and Raymond Struyk, "Homeownership Effects of Alternative Mortgage Instruments," *American Real Estate and Urban Economics Association Journal,* Spring 1977, p. 14.

67. SCSAs are well-defined geographical areas specified by the Bureau of Census. An SCSA is designated whenever what had previously been two SMSAs ("standard metropolitan statistical areas") had grown together to form one large, homogeneous community.

68. In this case the maturity date refers to the date on which the house is sold or the date at which it is appraised to determine the price appreciation that must be shared. In the latter case, a new mortgage would normally be written at the new market rate to finance the payment of the price appreciation.

69. See Joseph A. McKenzie, "A Comprehensive Look at Shared-Appreciation Mortgages," *FHLBB Journal,* November 1980, p. 14; and Stanley Iezman, "The Shared Appreciation Mortgage," p. 44.

70. This point is developed more fully by Lewis Freiberg, "The Problem with SAM: An Economic and Policy Analysis," *Housing Finance Review,* Vol. 1, No. 1 (January 1982), pp. 73-91.

71. Kaufman and Erdevig, "Improving Housing Finance," p. 20.

72. See McKenzie, "A Comprehensive Look," p. 13; and Iezman, "The Shared Appreciation Mortgage," p. 44.

73. This point is also discussed in Holland, "Tax and Regulatory Problems."

74. Martin Feldstein, "Why Short-Term Interest Rates are High," *Wall Street Journal,* June 8, 1982, p. 26.

75. I would like to thank my colleague Rich Cohn for his insights on this point.

76. See Walt Woerheide, "What Does It Take to Stay Even with Inflation?" *Journal of Institute of Certified Financial Planners,* Vol. 2, No. 4 (Summer 1981), pp. 242-48. Some of the other issues associated with the income tax effects of PLAMs are discussed in Kaufman and Erdevig, "Improving Housing Finance," p. 18.

77. The example is drawn from Alwan and Hanchett, "Reverse Mortgages," p. 3.

78. This statistic is from a survey performed cooperatively by the National Second Mortgage Association and the Credit Research Center at Purdue University for the business year 1978. The results are reported in Richard L. Peterson and Debra A. Drecnik, "Second Mortgage Survey, 1979," Working Paper No. 33, Credit Research Center, Purdue University, West Lafayette Ind., 1980.

102 The Savings and Loan Industry

79. Ibid.

80. Ibid., p. 10.

81. James Smith, "Measuring Economic Strain under Alternative Mortgage Instruments," Invited Working Paper No. 27, Office of Policy and Economic Research, Federal Home Loan Bank Board, September 1979.

82. Ibid., p. 125.

83. Bruce G. Webb, "Borrower Risk under Alternative Mortgage Instruments," *Journal of Finance,* Vol. 37, No. 1 (March 1982), pp. 169-83.

84. Ibid., p. 181.

85. For a more extensive discussion of this issue, see Draper, "Alternative Mortgage Instruments."

86. See, for example, Jandhyala L. Sharma, "Creative Financing Techniques Will Not Save the S&Ls," *Real Estate Review,* Fall 1981.

87. The study by Kent Colton, Donald Lessard, and Arthur Solomon is "Borrower Attitudes toward Alternative Mortgage Instruments," Invited Research Working Paper No. 31, Office of Policy and Economic Research, Federal Home Loan Bank Board, January 1980. Another study on this topic was Gerald Albaum and George Kaufman, "Variable Rate Residential Mortgage: Implications for Borrowers," *Alternative Mortgage Instrument Research Study,* Vol. 1, Federal Home Loan Bank Board, Washington, D.C., January 1978.

88. Colton et al., "Borrower Attitudes," p. 33.

89. Ibid., p. 33.

90. Follain and Struyk, "Homeownership Effects of Alternative Mortgage Instruments," p. 5.

91. "Survey of Savings and Loan Associations' Adustable Mortgages," American Mortgage Insurance Company, Raleigh, N.C., September 1981.

92. Ibid., p. 2.

93. A subsequent survey in March 1982 found that only one-half of the SLAs were offering either adjustables only or adustables and SFPMs. This was below the expected level because of uncertainty about the economy and resistance from home buyers. See "More S&Ls Offer AMLs," *Chicago Tribune,* April 11, 1982.

94. The Ninth District includes New Mexico, Texas, Arkansas, Mississippi, and Louisiana.

95. Beverly Hadaway, "Alternative Mortgage Activity in the Ninth Federal Home Loan Bank District," *FHLBB Journal,* August 1982, p. 6.

96. The results of the survey are not as precise as they may initially appear because the definitions offered in the survey for VRMs and rollover mortgages are not very distinctive.

97. Stephen T. Zabrenski and Virginia K. Olin, "Characteristics of Adjustable Mortgage Loans by Large Associations," *FHLBB Journal,* August 1982, p. 21.

98. Ibid.

99. Byrl N. Boyce and Keith B. Johnson, "Adjustable Rate Mortgages: The Experience in New England Thrifts prior to May 1981," a paper presented at the 1981 meeting of the Eastern Finance Association in Newport, Rhode Island.

100. This same intention was noted in some survey results reported by Steve Rohde in "Unrestricted Adjustable Rate Mortgages."

101. Again, the survey results by Rohde support the fact that a majority of the lenders are not incorporating negative amortization. However, he also reports "a substantial number" do use negative amortization combined with the more volatile Treasury bill rates as index numbers. See Rohde, "Unrestricted Adjustable Rate Mortgages."

102. The survey results by Rohde, "Unrestricted Adjustable Rate Mortgages," support this point as he reports that that the majority have no ceiling on interest rate increases.

103. Hadaway, "Alternative Mortgage Activity," p. 10.

104. Zabrenski and Olin, "Characteristics," p. 21.

105. James E. McNulty, "Real Estate Financing," *Real Estate Review,* Winter 1982, p. 14.

106. This point about VRMs was made nearly ten years ago by George Kaufman in "The Questionable Benefit."

5

Financial Futures and Forward Commitments

A financial instrument which has grown in popularity and sophistication in recent years and may be of substantial benefit to SLAs is the financial futures contract. Some SLAs have been dealing in forward contracts for years. Financial futures and forward contracts are both agreements made today for a transaction to be made in the future. They differ in that financial futures are contracts traded on organized exchanges with brokers acting on behalf of clients, and the contracts have standardized terms. A forward contract is negotiated between a buyer and seller, and the terms of the contract are tailored to their specific needs and desires. Because of aspects such as liquidity and monitoring costs, financial futures offer SLAs better opportunities to reduce their own interest rate risk exposure than do forward contracts. This advantage to SLAs has been recognized by the FHLBB, as indicated by their recent regulations on futures and options.

THE FINANCIAL FUTURES CONTRACT

A substantial number of financial futures contracts are currently traded on various exchanges. The more important ones for the thrift institutions are the Government National Mortgage Association (GNMA), Treasury bond (T-bond), Treasury note (T-note), and Treasury bill (T-bill) contracts.[1] There are actually two GNMA contracts. One is the GNMA CDR or Collateralized Depository Receipt and the other is the CD GNMA or Certificate Delivery GNMA. The larger volume occurs in the GNMA CDR contract.[2] Because the needs of institutions such as SLAs are best served in the markets with the largest volume, all subsequent discussion about GNMA contracts will concern the GNMA CDR contract. The CDR is a "document prepared, signed and dated by the Depository—an authorized bank—to verify that the Originator has placed in safekeeping $100,000 principal balance of GNMA 8s or the equivalent, on the date indicated."[3,4]

A financial futures contract calls for delivery of the agreed upon principal value amount of a specified financial instrument at an agreed upon delivery date. As an example, a seller of a December GNMA CDR contract agrees to make delivery in December of a depository receipt for $100,000 worth of GNMA certificates which have an 8 percent coupon rate. The buyer of this contract agrees to take delivery and make payment at that time.

The Clearing House

One of the features about futures contracts which novices to futures trading sometimes find difficult to understand is that delivery rarely occurs. A seller avoids making delivery by simply buying a contract with the identical terms as the one originally sold. A buyer avoids taking delivery by simply selling the contract which had been previously purchased.

Avoiding delivery is so simple due to the existence of a clearing house associated with the futures market. Although the buyer and seller of a contract will set a price for the trade, the clearing house intervenes such that the buyer and seller each have legally binding contracts with the clearing house rather than with each other. Thus, the seller of the futures contract is agreeing to make delivery to the clearing house, and the buyer of the contract is agreeing to take delivery from the clearing house. Thus, if the seller (buyer) of a contract wishes not to make (take) delivery, then buying (selling) a contract for the same security and with the same delivery date in effect cancels the contractual agreement with the clearing house.

The clearing house guarantees the integrity of the contract in two ways. The first is the one just described in which it facilitates the cancellation by any party of that party's contractual obligation. The second is that buyers and sellers need not concern themselves with the creditworthiness of the other party to the transaction, but only with the creditworthiness of the clearing house. The creditworthiness of clearing houses has heretofore not been an issue, and is not likely to be an issue anytime soon.

The Concept of Forward Rates

For people accustomed to spot transactions in financial instruments (that is, trades in which cash is paid in exchange for the immediate delivery of a financial instrument), the trading of a financial future may seem like needless speculation.[5] However, the purchase of almost any financial instrument involves a similar form of speculation. For example, suppose an investor wishes to buy T-bills and has an intended holding period of six months. At least two investment choices are available. The first is an obvious one in which the investor buys six-month T-bills. A second choice might be that the investor buys three-month T-bills and then at maturity reinvests the proceeds in more three-month T-bills.

In the above example, let three months represent one time period, and assume the investor has $1 million to invest. If the yield-to-maturity on six-month T-bills is currently $_0r_2$, then the terminal value of the first investment choice could be represented as

$$T_1 = \$1,000,000(1 + {_0r_2})^2$$

where T_1 = terminal value of the first investment strategy, and

$_0r_2$ = the yield-to-maturity today on T-bills which mature in two time periods (six months).

Similarly, the terminal value of the second investment strategy in which three-month T-bills are purchased twice could be represented as

$$T_2 = \$1,000,000(1 + {_0r_1})(1 + {_1r_2})$$

where T_2 = terminal value of the second investment strategy,

$_0r_1$ = the yield-to-maturity today on three-month T-bills which mature in one time period (three months), and

$_1r_2$ = the yield-to-maturity on three-month T-bills which would be purchased one period from now and held to the end of the second period.

The selection of an investment strategy depends on the relationship between $(1 + {_0r_2})^2$ and $(1 + {_0r_1})(1 + {_1r_2})$. The yields-to-maturity for six-month T-bills $(_0r_2)$ and three-month T-bills $(_0r_1)$ at time zero are always observable. Unfortunately, the yield three months into the future on three-month T-bills is not observable. Therefore, in selecting an investment strategy in this example, the investor is necessarily speculating on the yield on three-month T-bills, three months from today $(_1r_2)$. This particular yield is referred to as a forward rate, which is implicit in any set of yields for different maturities. This speculation on forward rates is conceptually identical to the trading of futures contracts.

Hedgers and Speculators

In order to understand the futures markets, it is useful to classify buyers and sellers into the two broad categories of speculators and hedgers.[6] A speculator is a person who hopes to make a profit on changes in the price of the contract and whose trades are based only on his expectation of future price changes. The decision to speculate in a particular contract is made without regard to any other assets or liabilities the speculator has or expects to have. Thus, a "short speculator" sells a futures contract with the expectation of buying it back later at a lower price, and a "long speculator" buys a futures contract with the expectation of selling it later at a higher price.

A hedger buys or sells a futures contract in order to offset some of his price risk exposure in other assets or liabilities he has or expects to have. A short hedger, for example, would be one who owns mortgages as assets and sells one or more GNMA futures contracts.[7] If interest rates rise, the market value of the mortgages drops, but the futures position becomes profitable. Thus, the losses on the mortgages are hedged by gains on the futures contract.

An example of a long hedger would be one who plans to acquire some mortgages in the future and based on that expectation buys a GNMA futures contract today.[8,9] If interest rates drop between the date on which the decision was made to acquire the mortgages and the actual date of purchase, the long hedger would end up acquiring mortgages with a lower than anticipated yield but would have a profit on his futures position. If interest rates rose over the same period, the long hedger would be able to acquire the mortgages at a higher yield but would have a loss on the futures position. As in the case of the short hedger, improvement or deterioration in the yield on the mortgages will be offset or hedged by gains or losses on the futures contract.

The point of the previous examples is that a hedger is one who has two positions, one of which is in a futures contract. If properly constructed, the gain or loss in one position due to interest rate changes will be offset by the loss or gain in the other position.

The offset is not perfect, however. Hedges are typically imperfect in the sense that the gain or loss on one position is rarely exactly equal in magnitude to the loss or gain on the other position. This lack of a perfect hedge is a crucial aspect to the use of futures contracts and requires still more explanation. To facilitate this explanation, actual market quotations as they appeared in the *Chicago Tribune* on May 24, 1983 are reproduced in Table 5.1.

The first set of numbers in Table 5.1 are for GNMA futures contracts which are traded on the Chicago Board of Trade (CBT). The first contract listed is the one which requires delivery of GNMA CDRs in June of 1983. The first price shown is the price at which the contract started trading. In this example, the opening trade is at 69-06. The second number in the quote represents the fractional part of the price and is expressed in terms of 32nds. Thus, 69-06 means 69-6/32, which converts to 69.187. In terms of dollars and cents, this represents a price of 69.187 percent of the $100,000 principle, or $69,187.50. The next two prices, 69-22 and 69-03, represent the highest and lowest prices at which the contract traded that day. The last price, 69-21, is the "settle," which is related to the closing or last price at which the contract is traded. In fact, the settle price and the closing price may be the same. The settle price is set by members of the exchange and is used for determining margin calls, which will be discussed shortly. For our purposes, we can treat the settle price as the closing price. The next column gives the change in the settle price from the previous day. In this case, the settle price is 3/32 lower than it was on the previous day. The last two columns show the highest and lowest prices at which this contract has ever traded. These are 73 and 54-28/32, respectively.

Basis Risk

To illustrate why a hedge will not be perfect, let us return to the example of the short hedge. Let us say that on May 24 an investor buys GNMA 8 percent certificates and simultaneously sells the September GNMA futures contract at the settlement price of 68-30. It is likely that the GNMA 8 percent certificates, which were purchased in the cash market, were obtained at a price of about 80-20.[10] The difference between the cash market price and the futures market price is referred to as the "basis." A perfect short hedge would require that the basis be constant. However, the basis is not constant over time. In this example, if the certificates purchased in the cash market are deliverable, then the basis will

Table 5.1
Financial Futures Quotations from the Chicago Tribune, *May 24, 1983*

	Open	High	Low	Settle	Net Chg	Contract High	Low
GNMA							
$100,000 prin; pts & 32nds of 100 pct.							
Jun	69-06	69-22	69-03	69-21	− 03	73-00	54-28
Sep	68-18	68-30	68-12	68-30	− 03	72-15	54-30
Dec	67-25	68-09	67-23	68-08	− 04	71-14	54-29
Mar 84	67-10	67-23	67-09	67-22	− 04	70-26	54-28
Jun	66-20	67-10	66-20	67-07	− 04	70-09	54-29
Sep	66-18	66-28	66-18	66-26	− 04	69-24	55-16
Dec	66-04	66-17	66-03	66-15	− 04	69-14	55-18
Mar 85				66-06	− 04	68-29	57-05
Jun	65-29	65-30	65-29	65-30	− 04	69-05	57-17
Sep				65-23	− 04	68-20	65-03
Dec	65-17	65-17	65-17	65-17	− 04	68-13	64-27

Prev. sales 8,914.
Prev. day's open int. 44,236, up 475.

	Open	High	Low	Settle	Net Chg	Contract High	Low
U.S. TREASURY BONDS							
8 pct. $100,000; pts. & 32nds of 100 pct.							
Jun	75-22	76-11	75-20	76-08	− 02	80-00	57-28
Sep	75-01	75-23	75-01	75-20	− 03	79-12	58-05
Dec	74-19	75-06	74-18	75-04	− 02	78-27	58-10
Mar 84	74-03	74-23	74-03	74-22	− 02	78-12	58-20
Jun	73-27	74-10	73-24	74-10	− 01	77-28	58-28
Sep	73-15	73-31	73-15	73-31	− 01	77-19	59-03
Dec	73-06	73-22	73-06	73-22	− 01	77-19	59-10
Mar 85	72-31	73-14	72-31	73-14	− 01	77-15	63-24
Jun	72-21	73-07	72-21	73-07	− 01	77-15	70-04
Sep				73-01	− 01	76-02	70-00
Dec				72-28	− 01	76-05	72-28

Prev. sales 85,796.
Prev. day's open int. 137,760 up 1,008.

Table 5.1 (continued)

	Open	High	Low	Settle	Net Chg	Contract High	Contract Low
U.S. TREASURY BILLS $1 million; pts. of 100 pct.							
Jun	91.53	91.58	91.46	91.55	−.11	92.40	85.83
Sep	91.29	91.31	91.21	91.28	−.17	92.18	85.85
Dec	91.10	91.11	91.00	91.08	−.15	91.91	85.85
Mar 84	90.90	90.91	90.83	90.87	−.16	91.68	86.45
Jun	90.67	90.72	90.67	90.69	−.17	91.47	86.50
Sep	90.56	90.56	90.50	90.51	−.17	91.29	88.52
Dec	90.36	90.36	90.36	90.33	−.16	91.11	90.01

Prev. sales 13,486.
Prev. day's open int. 43, 046, up 89.

SOURCES: Chicago Mercantile Exchange (U.S. Treasury Bills statistics); *Chicago Tribune,* Tuesday, May 24, 1983, Section 3, page 18. GNMA and U.S. Treasury Bonds futures quotations courtesy of the Chicago Board of Trade.

converge to zero on the delivery date from its current level of 11-22[(80-20)-(68-30)].

Changes in the basis create what is referred to as basis risk. An investor who sets up a short hedge is transferring the price risk on the asset being hedged to the buyer of the futures contract and is replacing this with basis risk.[11] In order for hedging to be a risk-reducing activity, it is necessary that the basis risk be less than the price risk of the asset being hedged. In the case of our short hedge example, that is almost certainly the case because the GNMA certificates purchased in the cash market are virtually identical to the commodity specified in the contract. Furthermore, events which affect current interest rates and thus the cash price of GNMA certificates will likely have a similar effect on the expected yield on certificates which would be delivered a few months in the future. As the asset owned in the short hedge becomes dissimilar to the commodity specified in the contract, it becomes less beneficial to substitute basis risk for price risk.[12]

Margin and Price Limits

Two aspects of futures trading which often create confusion are the treatment of margin and the daily price limits. Futures contracts differ from other securities in that the buyers and sellers are only agreeing to make a trade at a future date and at an agreed upon price which will be paid at the time of delivery. At the time of the trade the buyer and seller only put up initial margin. The initial margin is simply a good-faith deposit to guarantee that the buyer and seller will be available and ready on the delivery date to conduct the transaction.[13] For GNMAs, the initial margin is $2,000 per contract.[14] An important feature of these margin requirements is that they may be posted in the form of T-bills. Thus, the buyer and seller can receive interest from their margin money.

After posting the initial margin, the buyers and sellers are subject to maintenance margins. On GNMAs, the maintenance margin is $1,500 per contract.[15] This means that the equity value in any GNMA contract position for any one person who is long or short will always equal or exceed $1,500. The equity value of a contract for the buyer (that is, the person who is long) is the initial margin plus any margin adjustments, plus the difference between the current price and the purchase price. For the seller (that is, the person who is short) it is the initial margin plus any margin adjustments, plus the difference between the price at which the contract was sold and the current price. If the price of the contract moves down, or against the buyer, the buyer must deposit additional margin. If the price of the contract moves up, or against the seller, he would be the one to deposit additional margin.

One benefit of these margin postings is that if the price moves in one's favor, then margin is returned to the one who has benefited by the price moves. In effect, the money is moved from the account of the one who has lost to the one who has gained. Thus, if the price of the contract moves up, or in favor of the buyer, he receives the excess margin. Similarly, if the price moves down, or in favor of the seller, he also is given back excess margin. These margin adjustments are made on a daily basis and are referred to as "marking-to-market."

One way to view this posting or returning of margins each day is that the value of the contract is reset to zero.[16] In other words, after the margins have been made, a person holding a position could liquidate that position with no *additional* gains or losses.

For a hedger, adverse margin adjustments can be a problem. For example, if interest rates were falling, a short hedger in GNMAs would enjoy an increase in the market value of his GNMA certificates but would also suffer a rise in the value of the futures contracts he has sold and would be subject to margin calls on the futures position. Since the increase in the value of the GNMA certificates will not be realized until they are sold, the short hedger must use other assets to meet the margin calls. The point here is that even if the hedge is perfect, daily margins calls could create a cash-flow problem.

In order to restrict the magnitude of margin calls in any one day, daily price limits are set for each contract. For GNMAs, the daily price limit is 64/32s, or two points.[17] In the September GNMA contract discussed earlier which had a settlement price of 68-30, all trading in the contract the next day would have to be between 70-30 and 66-30. If no one wished to trade within this range, then no trading would take place, and the settlement price would be set at the appropriate limit.

Sometimes, no trading occurs in a particular contract because no buyer and seller wish to trade that contract on that day. Such was the case for the GNMA contracts of March and September 1985 as shown in Table 5.1. As in the case of limit days, a settlement price is determined in order to make margin adjustments. The settlement price is set to be consistent with the changes in the settlement prices of contracts which did trade that day.

POTENTIAL BENEFITS TO SLAs FROM FINANCIAL FUTURES

The actual use of financial futures by SLAs is, of course, limited by regulations, and these regulations will be discussed in the next section. In the meantime, let us explore the ways in which SLAs might use futures and how these uses would affect their risk exposure.

First, it should be pointed out that a duration statistic cannot be computed for a futures contract. The reason is that there is no price paid at the time a position is established.[18] As mentioned before, both buyer and seller only put up earnest money; they do not pay and receive the price of the contract. Thus, the initial value of the contract is zero, and after each margin adjustment the value is reset to zero. However, although duration statistics cannot be computed per se, it is possible to talk about how positions in financial futures alter the effective durations of the other assets and liabilities held by an SLA.

An SLA, like any other investor, theoretically could enter the financial futures market as either a speculator or a hedger.[19] As a speculator, an SLA could buy or sell futures contracts depending on its management's expectations of price changes in these contracts. Other than regulatory restrictions, the main problem with SLAs speculating in financial futures is that some positions would exacerbate rather than ameliorate their interest rate risk exposure.

For example, if a typical SLA were to buy a GNMA futures contract, then it would probably be widening its duration mismatch. This is because any changes in the value of the futures contract from a change in interest rates would likely be in the same direction as changes in the market value of its mortgages from changes in interest rates. In effect, the purchase of GNMA futures contracts would serve to lengthen the duration of the asset portfolio.

It is much more likely that SLAs would use futures markets to create hedges. There are two obvious hedges. The foremost would be the mortgage short hedge, and the other would be a money market certificate short hedge. Each of these is discussed below.

The Mortgage Short Hedge

The mortgage short hedge would largely follow the short hedge example given earlier in the chapter. The crucial issues are how much to hedge and which contracts should be used for hedging. Unfortunately, there are no exact answers to these questions. However, a few observations can be made.

The quantity to hedge depends upon management's expectations about interest rate movements. If the SLA management strongly believed that interest rates were going to drop, then it would be prudent not to engage in any short hedging. If the SLA management strongly believed interest rates were going to rise, then it would want to short hedge a large portion of its portfolio. However, management would not want to be "fully hedged" all of the time because hedging involves current and potential costs such as brokerage commissions, the opportunity cost of the assets pledged as margin, and the uncertainties of future margin calls. So a permanently hedged portfolio should not be as profitable as one which is selectively hedged.

One constraint on the amount of the portfolio to be hedged is that some of the assets an SLA owns do not have the necessary attributes to use as part of a beneficial hedge. Recall that hedging is the substitution of basis risk for price risk, and that basis risk depends on the similarity of the asset being hedged to the deliverable commodity. Short hedges with GNMA certificates owned by an SLA would work quite well. Short hedges with newly issued conventional mortgages would probably work almost as well, although there is certainly not universal agreement on this point. Ken Thygerson has suggested that the correlation between GNMA yields and conventional mortgage yields may be sufficiently low so that potential hedgers "could actually increase their risk exposure by hedging."[20] Most other writers have argued that there is little doubt that SLAs would benefit from hedging conventional mortgages.[21] Whatever the resolution of the issue of the short hedge protection for newly issued conventional mortgages, the protection provided by short hedges against seasoned conventional mortgages is certainly questionable.[22] The first problem is that there is no real market for mortgages that have been outstanding for several years and thus no readily observable set of market values. This means that it is not obvious what the basis is, and the basis risk is thus unknowable. Furthermore, it is not at all clear how much in futures contracts should be sold to hedge optimally a given amount of seasoned mortgages.

The second issue mentioned earlier is that of the choice of futures contracts to be used for the short hedge. From Table 5.1 it is apparent that 11 different GNMA contracts were available on that date for a short hedge. One observation which would indicate it is more appropriate to use the nearer contracts is that the open interest positions are substantially larger on the nearer contracts.[23] The open interest position at the close of each day for each contract represents the number of deliveries that would occur if that were the last possible delivery date for that contract. The open interest position in the nearest-term one or two contracts is invariably high relative to the open interest in the longer-term delivery date contracts. The open interest in the longest-term GNMA contracts is usually no more than a few hundred, while the near-term contracts regularly have an open interest of 15,000 to 20,000 contracts.

The open interest position is important because trading volume is proportional to the open interest.[24] The larger the open interest position and the greater the volume, the easier it is for any one trader to buy or sell without influencing the market price, and the greater the likelihood that the current price fully reflects all publicly available information. The disadvantage of using the nearer-term contracts is that hedges for long holding periods would have to be reestablished each time a delivery date rolled around, which means increased commission costs.

The point here is that the strategy and value of a mortgage short hedge is really an empirical issue with minimal theoretical direction. However, experimentation with several short hedge strategies permits some estimates of the effects of mortgage short hedging.

Let us begin with the assumption that an SLA is writing $100,000 in new mortgages at the start of every calendar quarter. Then arbitrarily assume that the SLA is interested in hedging these mortgages for two years. Three hedging strategies will be utilized. The first is to sell a two-year GNMA futures contract on the first business day of the quarter, and then buy back the contract on the first day of the delivery month, two years later. The second hedging strategy is to sell a one-year futures contract on the first day of the calendar quarter, buy back this contract one year later on the first day of the delivery month, and sell another one-year futures contract at the same time, and then buy the second contract back on the first day of its delivery month. The third strategy is similar to the second except that six-month contracts are used. Thus, over the two-year hedging period, the SLA would have sold and bought back a total of four contracts. The dates of trade, prices, and gains and losses associated with strategy one are shown in Table 5.2.

Now that the three hedging strategies have been defined, it is crucial to understand what it is that is being hedged. In this case, it is the "theoretical change" in the market value of the conventional mortgage after two years, a change which is "theoretical" because there is no active secondary market for two-year-old mortgages. The theoretical change in market value is defined as the difference between the price for which the mortgage might be sold if a secondary market existed and the book value of the mortgage after two years. In order to determine what each mortgage might be sold for, first assume that each mortgage has a contract rate equal to the index rates published by the FHLBB for the month in which the mortgage is issued. The index series used is the average effective interest rate on loans closed, assuming prepayment at the end of ten years. The index numbers are shown in Table 5.3. Then we must compute the market value two years later by using the effective index number on new mortgages on the later date.[25] It is the difference between the remaining book value and the market value which is being hedged.

For the 13 quarters examined, the average book value of the mortgages two years after they were issued is $98,780. The average "theoretical" market value is $85,682. In economic terms, the SLA has sustained an average loss on these

Table 5.2
Gains or Losses on Short Hedge Strategy #1

Time Period	Date Hedge Established	Price at Which Contract was Sold*	Date Hedge Lifted	Price at Which Contract Purchased*	Gain (Loss)
1	Jan. 3, 1977	95-07	Dec. 1, 1978	89-28	5-11
2	April 1, 1977	92-24	Mar. 1, 1979	87-26	4-30
3	July 1, 1977	94-05	June 1, 1979	87-00	7-05
4	Oct. 3, 1977	95-28	Sept. 4, 1979	85-02	10-26
5	Jan. 3, 1978	93-17	Dec. 1, 1979	78-30	14-19
6	April 3, 1978	91-13	Mar. 3, 1980	68-16	22-29
7	July 3, 1978	87-17	June 2, 1980	77-03	10-14
8	Oct. 2, 1978	90-03	Sept. 2, 1980	72-05	17-30
9	Jan. 2, 1979	87-21	Dec. 1, 1980	67-15	20-06
10	April 2, 1979	87-21	Mar. 2, 1981	65-01	22-20
11	July 2, 1979	87-15	June 1, 1981	63-22	23-25
12	Oct. 1, 1979	81-08	Sept. 1, 1981	56-27	24-13
13	Jan. 2, 1980	78-09	Dec. 1, 1981	64-13	13-28

* SOURCE: *Statistical Annual,* Chicago Board of Trade, for the years 1977-1981.

mortgages of $13,098 (see Table 5.4). Had strategy one been followed, the SLA would have had an average profit of $15,308 on the 13 hedges. The correlation coefficient between the "theoretical" losses on the mortgages and the gains from the short hedges is .849. Under strategy two, the average gain is $16,079, and the correlation coefficient is .867. Under strategy three, the average gain is $17,067, and the correlation coefficient is .875.

The numbers in the foregoing exercise are not intended to imply that strategy three would always be superior to the other two. Nor are they meant to imply that the profit from the hedging action will always exceed any loss in the market value of the mortgages held by the SLA. Rather, they suggest that (1) none of the short hedge strategies is perfect for newly issued conventional mortgages in the sense that the magnitude of the losses on one equaled the gains on the other; (2) in terms of profits and losses, there is not an overwhelming difference as to which strategy to use if the hedger intends to maintain the hedge for a relatively long period of time such as two years; and (3) short hedge strategies are appropriate and beneficial activities for SLAs.

Table 5.3
Assumed Contract Rates, 1977-1981

Month	Year				
	1977	1978	1979	1980	1981
January	9.05	9.15	10.18	11.87	13.26
February	8.99	9.18	10.20	11.93	13.54
March	8.95	9.26	10.30	12.62	14.02
April	8.94	9.30	10.36	13.03	14.15
May	8.96	9.37	10.47	13.68	14.10
June	8.98	9.46	10.66	12.66	14.54
July	9.00	9.57	10.78	12.51	14.72
August	9.02	9.70	11.01	12.25	15.27
September	9.04	9.73	11.02	12.35	15.29
October	9.07	9.83	11.21	12.60	15.65
November	9.07	9.87	11.37	13.04	16.38
December	9.09	10.02	11.64	13.28	15.87

SOURCE: *Federal Reserve Bulletin*, Washington, D.C., 1977-1982, various issues.

Table 5.4
Summary Statistics for the Various Short Hedging Strategies

Variable	Mean	Standard Deviation
Market value of mortgages after two years	$85,682	$3,989
Difference between market value and book value after two years	− $13,098	$4,158
Gains from Strategy One	+ $15,308	$6,885
Gains from Strategy Two	+ $16,079	$7,267
Gains from Strategy Three	+ $17,067	$7,889

The Money Market Certificate Short Hedge

Earlier in this section, it was mentioned that there are two obvious hedges for SLAs. The mortgage short hedge was one, and the other was a money market certificate (MMC) short hedge. The introduction of the MMC has allowed the SLAs to replace the problem of disintermediation with the problem of an uncertain cost of deposits. Because the rate on the MMC was tied to the rate on six-month Treasury securities, the SLAs have been able to offer competitive rates. However, they can only guess as to the changes in these rates over future time periods. By utilizing short hedges, SLAs can substantially reduce the volatility in the cost of MMCs.

As in the case of the mortgage short hedge, there is no perfect MMC hedge available because there is no futures contract on six-month Treasury securities. There is, however, a futures contract on 90-day T-bills which should work fairly well.

As in the case of mortgage short hedges, there are no clear-cut rules about how much to hedge and when to hedge. At one extreme, an SLA could hedge all of its MMCs for as far into the future as possible. In Table 5.1 we note that there are seven T-bill contracts listed. The most distant contract could be for two years into the future. Thus, the SLA could sell a full strip of T-bill contracts.[26] That is, it could sell all seven contracts, and then as each hedge is lifted during the maturing month of the contract, replace it with a short hedge of the next contract to be introduced. This strategy could be referred to as a full, continuous hedge. At the other extreme, an SLA could place a short hedge in the nearest term contract whenever it felt that money market rates were going to rise substantially.

The relative magnitude of benefits from the various hedging strategies is really an empirical question. As in the previous discussion on mortgage short hedges, there is some empirical evidence available. Specifically, Terry Maness and A. J. Senchack examined the benefits of various short hedge strategies over the period from November 30, 1978 to October 29, 1981.[27] They looked first at what they referred to as continuous hedges. The continuous hedges were established at periods ranging from one week to 26 weeks prior to the issuance of MMCs. In the case of the 26 week hedges, they found that "if a hedge ratio of . . . two (2) had been used then the average effective cost of the MMCs over that period of time would have been 65.76 basis points *less* than the bench-mark cost of MMCs."[28] The bench-mark cost is defined as "the six-month Treasury bill average auction rate at the time the hedge position is placed."[29] They note that over the same period, a nonhedged strategy would have produced an average cost "106.9 basis points *above* the bench-mark cost."[30] In other words, the bench-mark rate represents a naive forecast of what the MMC rate would be when the hedge is lifted.

Maness and Senchack then enumerated six possible selective hedge strategies that an SLA might follow if it were attempting to optimize its timing in the placing and lifting of hedges. They found that over the sample period used, none of the selective strategies performed as well as the continuous hedge, but all of them performed better than an unhedged strategy.

The implications of this study would seem to be similar to the implications of the mortgage short hedge. Namely, there are substantial benefits to such hedging, but there are no hard and fast rules as to how much hedging should be done, when such hedges should be used, and what contracts to use for the hedges. The major benefit to hedging the MMCs is that the combination of the short futures position and the MMCs will give the MMCs the appearance of longer-term, fixed-rate certificates. In other words, the effective duration of the MMCs is increased.

FHLBB REGULATIONS ON FUTURES CONTRACTS

The FHLBB passed a major overhaul of its regulations concerning futures transactions on July 2, 1981, which became effective July 10.[31] The intent of the changes was to broaden the ability of SLAs to protect themselves from interest rate risk through the use of financial futures.

Under the old regulations, SLAs were restricted to dealing only in GNMA futures and only where such transactions could be matched directly against firm commitments or anticipated reinvestments. The new regulations permit transactions that would reduce the net interest rate risk exposure. These include, but are not limited to, short futures positions used:[32]

1. to protect the risk resulting from forward commitments to originate or purchase mortgages or mortgage-related securities;
2. to protect the value of mortgage loans or other investments held in the portfolio;
3. to fix liability costs; and
4. to protect against other risks resulting from a maturity imbalance between assets and liabilities.

In other words, there is virtually no restriction to the SLA establishing a short position in an interest rate futures contract.

The Board continues to look askance at the establishment of a long position. They recognize, however, that those SLAs that act like mortgage bankers may indeed have a legitimate need to establish a long position in a futures contract. Accordingly, they will permit a long position "only to the extent that an institution's short forward commitments exceed 10 percent of long-term assets."[33] The latter are defined as all fixed-rate assets with a current maturity of at least five years. At the current time, the Board sees no interest rate risk reduction associated with spreading and accordingly disallows any long positions associated with spreading.[34]

Previously, the Board had required that SLAs meet certain financial standards before they were allowed to engage in trading futures. The new regulations have removed all requirements with the appropriate rationale that since futures provide risk reduction capability, those SLAs that failed to meet the eligibility requirements were really the ones that should have been hedging with futures contracts.

The new regulations permit the SLAs to trade any "interest-rate futures contract that is designated by the Commodity Futures Trading Commission and is based upon a security in which the institution is authorized to invest."[35] This means that the SLAs can currently trade the futures contracts for GNMAs, T-notes, T-bonds, and T-bills. The regulation is written to allow for the possibility that new and appropriate instruments might be introduced and that it would be preferable not to have to rewrite the regulations each time a new instrument appears.

The Board also repealed all regulations regarding limits on positions by SLAs. This removal may have been unwise because it is certainly possible for an SLA to sell so many contracts that it ceases to be a short hedger and has become a bearish speculator. The spirit of the decision to leave the position limit to the SLA's board of directors is to be applauded; but in the next few years, one would expect at least one SLA to over-hedge and suffer the consequences. In lieu of regulatory limits, the Bank Board has substituted detailed requirements as to how the board of directors at each SLA must monitor their positions in any futures transactions. In addition, the Bank Board has established fairly rigorous bookkeeping requirements for recording all transactions in futures contracts.

In conjunction with trading futures contracts, the Bank Board has allowed the SLAs to use what is referred to as hedge or deferral accounting. Hedge accounting means that "gains or losses on the futures contracts shall be deferred and amortized over the expected life of the corresponding assets or liabilities rather than recognized immediately."[36] As a form of income smoothing, hedge accounting deals better with the economic realities of hedging than do traditional accounting procedures. Traditional accounting procedures would incorporate any losses on futures contracts into current net income and defer any gains (that is, show all accrued losses but defer showing any accrued gains on positions in futures contracts). The mortgages or MMCs being hedged would be shown at book value. Thus, if interest rates fall, traditional accounting would prohibit SLAs from showing the increase in the value of their mortgages and require that they show the loss in the value of the futures contract, thus penalizing current earnings and net worth. If interest rates rose, the SLAs could show neither the loss in the value of the mortgages nor the gains in the value of the futures contract. Economic reality would best be represented if the change in the market value of all interest-rate-sensitive assets could be shown. Hedge accounting is an excellent step in this direction.

At the time of this writing, the FHLBB is considering amendments to its rules on forward commitments and financial options trading.[37] Most important, the intent of the regulatory changes is to allow SLAs to buy put options on financial futures and to sell or write call options. The simultaneous purchase of a put option and sale of a call option is conceptually equivalent to the sale of a futures contract. This construction of what might be termed an "artificial" short futures position would have several advantages, the most important of which is that there would be no requirement to mark-to-market for the purpose of margin calls. This lack of potential margin calls would substantially facilitate cash-flow planning by any SLA using these tools.

By itself, the writing of call options on an interest-rate-sensitive security is risky if that security is not owned.[38] In the case of GNMA call options, the SLA could write covered calls against conventional mortgages. This would be somewhat riskier than classical covered writing because changes in the value of conventional mortgages may not mirror perfectly all changes in the value of GNMA certificates. However, such writing is substantially less risky than naked writing. It is also less risky than holding long-term mortgages. The reason is that in covered writing, although the SLA gives up the value of the appreciation of the mortgage in the event that interest rates decline in exchange for a fixed premium, its losses in the value of its mortgages are reduced by the amount of the premium in the event that interest rates rise. In effect, covered writing reduces the magnitude of both the potential gains and losses of holding mortgages. This reduction in magnitude is by definition a reduction in risk.

The writing of call options by SLAs would provide less risk reduction than the writing of an artificial short futures position or actually taking a short hedge position in futures contracts. The reason is that the writing of a covered call option provides only the limited gain of the premium income if interest rates rise. At the same time, there is a large potential loss of value in the mortgage portfolio from a rise in interest rates. Taking a short position in a futures contract or establishing an artificial short futures position would more closely match potential gains in the option or futures contract to the potential losses on the mortgage portfolio resulting from interest rate increases.

However, this limited risk reduction capability from writing call options may also be matched with the prospect of higher expected yields than that provided by the full hedges. The writing of a call option produces premium income. If there is no change in interest rates, this income is additional profit. The construction of an artificial short futures position provides less income because the purchase of the put option uses a substantial portion of the premium income from the sale of the call option. If there is no change in interest rates, the difference in premiums between the call option that was sold and the put option that was purchased becomes added profit. Taking a short futures position provides no income, except that provided on the securities pledged as collateral, which the SLA would have had anyway. Thus, if there is no change in interest rates, there is also no added income.

The purchase of a long position in put options would also serve to reduce the interest rate risk exposure of SLAs engaged in mortgage banking operations.

Institutions with firm forward commitments to originate mortgages could purchase a put option to protect themselves against interest rate increases until such time as the money is lent. As in the previous discussion, the sale of an interest rate futures contract would provide more risk reduction.

SLAs with standby forward commitments to originate mortgages would find the purchase of a put option the ideal instrument for transferring interest rate risk. The standby commitments will certainly be utilized if interest rates rise since the value of the put option increases with increases in interest rates. In this case, the potential loss on the standby commitment is matched by potential gains in the value of the put option.

It would seem clear that interest rate options would be of substantial benefit to the SLA industry. As instruments for the transfer of interest rate risk, they would provide the industry with more choices and strategies than are now available, and create several strategies which have the effect of decreasing the duration mismatch from which SLAs suffer.

THE FORWARD COMMITMENT MARKET

The forward commitment market has several similarities to and some differences from the financial futures market. The forward market, as mentioned at the start of this chapter, is a negotiated market. Its most common transaction involving SLAs currently is for a mortgage banker to arrange through a dealer a forward commitment from an SLA. The forward commitment may be either a standby or a firm commitment.

The seller of the commitment (that is, the mortgage banker) pays a fee to the buyer (that is, the SLA) at the time the contract is signed. Prior to the regulations passed on June 1, 1979, the SLAs were able to incorporate all of the fee into current income.[39] The payment of the fee is substantially different than the posting of margin by both the buyer and seller of a futures contract.

The second key difference is that with a forward commitment there are no margin calls and no active trading market. This means that if interest rates rise and the SLA's commitment turns into a sure loss in terms of market value, such a loss requires no special action until delivery date. In the futures market, the SLA would be forced to meet margin calls regularly and thus to deal with losses in market value as they accrue.

This traditional role of buyer in the forward market has actually increased the SLAs' interest rate risk exposure. Rather than buying mortgages at the current time, they are agreeing to buy mortgages at a future date, thus increasing the effective maturity and the duration of these assets. The benefit from such participation is the fee income. The relevant issue is whether the fee income is sufficient to offset the additional interest rate risk exposure. The large losses experienced by many financial institutions in this market suggest that at least heretofore such was not the case.[40]

CONCLUSION

The purpose of this chapter has been twofold. The first was to make a strong case that interest rate futures contracts and interest rate options can be extremely beneficial to savings and loans in helping them reduce their interest rate risk exposure. The second was to demonstrate that although we know such instruments are beneficial, we can not give any quantitative dimensions to the value of their contribution.

The reader will recall the indication that duration values could not be computed for futures contracts. It was further demonstrated in the mortgage and MMC short hedge examples that it would not be possible to compute the duration statistic for combinations of futures positions and mortgages or MMCs. So this results in the awkward position of saying that interest rate futures and options are beneficial, but we are not sure how beneficial.

The topic of the next chapter, consumer lending authority, will lead us to the opposite conclusion. That is, we can measure fairly precisely the effect of consumer loans upon the duration mismatch of SLAs, but it appears that the consumer lending authority is not going to be particularly beneficial to the industry in reducing its interest rate risk exposure.

NOTES

1. The GNMA is an agency which guarantees the payment of interest and principal on the mortgages underlying the certificates it guarantees. For a more detailed description of these certificates, see David S. Kidwell and Richard Peterson, *Financial Institutions, Markets, and Money,* Dryden Press, Hinsdale, Ill., 1981, pp. 494-95.

2. In fact, the CD GNMA contract is nearly "dead." This contract calls for delivery of actual GNMA certificates with coupon rates at or below what is referred to as "the current GNMA production rate." The production rate is 50 basis points below whatever the current FHA/VA ceiling rate is.

3. *Understanding the Delivery Process,* The Board of Trade of the City of Chicago, 1980, p. 18.

4. GNMA 8s are certificates supported by mortgages, all of which have 8 percent coupon rates.

5. A cash transaction can either be a spot transaction or a forward transaction. As noted in the text, a spot transaction is a payment of cash for immediate delivery, but a forward transaction is an agreement to pay cash for a future delivery.

6. A thorough discussion of the categories of buyers and sellers would show that there are really several categories and that the categories' distinctions are dubious. However, for explanatory purposes we will assume that there are only two categories and that these are well defined.

7. This description of a short hedge is also referred to as a cash hedge. See Charles T. Frankle and Andrew J. Senchack, Jr., "Economic Considerations in the Use of Interest Rate Futures," *The Journal of Futures Markets,* Spring 1982, p. 107.

8. Another name for this activity is anticipatory hedging. See Frankle and Senchack, "Economic Considerations," p. 107.

9. An example of a long hedge in the SLA industry would be an association agreeing today to provide mortgage money at a future date at the future market rates.

10. Price quotations for GNMA certificates in the cash market are provided daily in the *Wall Street Journal*. This particular quote of 80-20 was noted in the May 25, 1983 edition of the *Journal*.

11. This statement assumes that the person buying the contract is a speculator. If the buyer is a long hedger, then one could say that both parties have substituted basis risk for price risk and in the process eliminated price risk.

12. See the discussion by Robert Kolb, John Corgel, and Raymond Chiang, "Effective Hedging of Mortgage Interest Rate Risk," *Housing Finance Review*, April 1982, pp. 136-37.

13. Susan M. Phillips and Paula A. Tosini, "A Comparison of Margin Requirements for Options and Futures," *Financial Analysts Journal*, November/December 1982, pp. 54-58.

14. *1981 Statistical Annual Interest Rate and Metals Futures*, Chicago Board of Trade, 1981, p. 61. Margins are subject to change and may be different for different member firms.

15. See previous footnote.

16. Myron S. Scholes, "The Economics of Hedging and Spreading in Futures Markets," *The Journal of Futures Markets*, Summer 1981, p. 267.

17. If a contract closes up-limit or down-limit for three consecutive days, then the limits are increased for the next trading day.

18. See Robert W. Kolb and Gerald D. Gay, "Immunizing Bond Portfolios with Interest Rate Futures," *Financial Management*, Vol. 11, No. 2 (Summer 1982), pp. 81-89.

19. As will be pointed out in the next section, SLAs are fairly restricted with respect to their ability to speculate in the futures market.

20. Kenneth Thygerson, "Futures, Options, and the Savings and Loan Business," *Savings and Loan Asset Management under Deregulation: Proceedings of the Sixth Annual Conference*, Federal Home Loan Bank of San Francisco, 1980, p. 141.

21. See, for example, Dale P. Riordan and Jerry Hartzog, "The Impact of the Deregulation Act on Policy Choices of the Federal Home Loan Bank Board," *Savings and Loan Asset Management under Deregulation: Proceedings of the Sixth Annual Conference*, Federal Home Loan Bank of San Francisco, 1980, pp. 33-58; Robert L. Losey and Susan Kelsey, "Interest Rate, Default, and Basis Risk in Hedging Fixed Rate Conventional Mortgages, *Federal Home Loan Bank Board Journal*, November 1981, pp. 10-12; and Dwight M. Jaffee, "Interest Rate Hedging Strategies for Savings and Loan Associations," *Managing Interest Rate Risk in the Thrift Industry: Proceedings of the Seventh Annual Conference*, Federal Home Loan Bank of San Francisco, 1981, pp. 83-106.

22. See Frankle and Senchack, "Economic Considerations," p. 109.

23. The open interest positions are not shown in Table 5.1, but are listed on a daily basis in publications such as the *Wall Street Journal*.

24. The reader may confirm this point by looking at any issue of the *Statistical Annual* published by the Chicago Board of Trade.

25. The use of the same index rate implies an assumption that these two-year-old mortgages would be prepaid after ten years, which is admittedly inconsistent with the previous assumption that the newly issued mortgages would also be prepaid after ten

years. This inconsistency is necessary in view of the lack of a mortgage interest rate series for two-year-old mortgages.

26. A strip is the establishment of the same position over a series of contracts with consecutive maturities.

27. Terry S. Maness and A. J. Senchack, "Hedging the Cost of Money Market Certificates by Savings and Loan Associations," a paper presented at the March 1982 Southwestern Federation of Administrative Disciplines meeting in Dallas, Texas.

28. Maness and Senchack, "Hedging the Cost," p. 11, fn. 2. The "hedge ratio" is defined as the ratio of the dollar value of the principal value of a futures contract to the dollar value of the asset or liability being hedged.

29. Ibid.

30. Ibid., p. 13.

31. The material in this section is based on Memo Number 81-380 dated July 2, 1981, published by the FHLBB and entitled "Futures Transactions." The actual changes are reported in 12 CFR Parts 545, 563, 571.

32. Ibid., p. 3.

33. Ibid., p. 4.

34. Spreading refers to the simultaneous purchase and sale of contracts with different delivery dates. A long spread (the purchase of the near-term delivery date and the sale of the longer-term delivery date) is made with the expectation that the price differential or spread between the two contracts will widen. A short spread (the sale of the near-term contract and the simultaneous purchase of the longer-term one) is made with the expectation that the price differential will narrow. Spreading is speculating on the change in the spread between two pairs of futures contracts. An example would be a "butterfly spread" which would be the purchase of one futures position combined with the sale of two positions of the next maturity and the purchase of one position in the subsequent maturity.

35. Memo No. 81-380.

36. Ibid., p. 8.

37. See Memo Number 8-135 by the FHLBB, entitled "Amendments on Forward Commitments, Financial Options Trading, and Financial Futures Trading," dated February 25, 1982. Final approval to trade financial options was granted on August 11, 1982.

38. The sale or writing of a call option without owning the underlying asset is referred to as "naked writing." Ownership of the underlying security when the option is sold is called "covered writing."

39. See James E. McNulty and William E. Chalker, "The Forward Commitment Market for Mortgage-Backed Securities," *Federal Home Loan Bank Board Journal*, June 1980, pp. 13-14.

40. Steven S. Anreder, "Built on Stilts: Overspeculation, Thin Margins Shake the Market for Ginnie Maes," *Barron's*, November 12, 1979. I do not mean to imply that it was clear *ex ante* that the fee income was insufficient for the risk involved.

6

Consumer Lending

One of the features of the Depository Institutions Deregulation and Monetary Control Act (DIDMCA) was the expansion of the consumer lending authority granted to SLAs. Consumer lending authority is simply the privilege to provide nonmortgage loans to individuals. This expanded authority, which was enhanced further in late 1982, has long been advocated by many groups and individuals, including Irwin Friend, in his edited collection, *Study of the Savings and Loan Industry;* Leo Grebler, in his *The Future of Thrift Institutions;* the *Report of the President's Commission on Financial Structures and Regulations;* the United States Savings and Loan League; the National Commission on Consumer Finance; and the Office of Economic Research at the FHLBB. Although all the groups have supported consumer lending authority, they have differed as to the reasons.

The earlier arguments in favor of the expanded lending authority centered on two premises. The first was that the expanded authority would increase the profitability of SLAs and thus make them financially stronger institutions. The second was that consumer loans would provide extra liquidity because they had such short maturities that the consumer loan portfolio could be relatively quickly reinvested in other assets such as mortgages should such a need arise.[1] In other words, they supplement the liquidity position of the thrift associations.

Recent research suggests that these two premises are probably not valid but that two other reasons can be mustered to support the contention that the expanded lending authority would be beneficial for the industry. The first is that as short-term loans, consumer loans have a low duration and thus would reduce the interest rate risk exposure of the savings and loans. The second is that consumer loans are highly likely to lead to greater mortgage loan demand and higher deposit growth rates, both of which should serve to increase profits. Loan demand and deposits would increase because many of the individuals acquiring consumer loans at SLAs are presumed to return to the SLA with their deposits and mortgage applications.

Table 6.1
Investment in Consumer Lending
by SLAs as a Percentage of Total Assets for Selected Years

Category	12/31/77	12/31/80	12/31/81
Mobile Home Loans	.6	.4	.6
Home Improvement Loans	.8	.9	.9
Loans on Savings Accounts	.6	1.1	.8
Education Loans	.1	.2	.2
Other Consumer Loans	.1	.3	.4
Investment in Service Corporations	.3	.5	.6
Total	2.5	3.4	3.5

SOURCE: *Savings and Loan Sourcebook,* United States League of Savings Associations, 1978, 1981, and 1982.

DEFINITION OF CONSUMER LENDING AUTHORITY

With the attention given to the consumer lending authority associated with the DIDMCA, it would be easy to forget that some SLAs have long had broad authority to make consumer loans and all SLAs have recently had some authority. In Texas, Massachusetts, Maine, and Connecticut, the state-chartered associations have had fairly broad consumer lending powers. The most notable case is that of Texas where the state-chartered associations may invest nearly all of their assets in consumer loans, although they are restricted to a loan limit of $10,000 per borrower.[2]

Prior to the DIDMCA, the consumer lending activity of federally chartered SLAs was restricted to the following:[3]

1. loans with deposits pledged as collateral,
2. mobile home chattel paper,[4]
3. home improvement loans,
4. education loans, and
5. consumer loans made through service corporations.[5]

Although pledged-account loans had no percentage of assets limitation, mobile home paper was restricted to 10 percent of assets, home improvement loans to 20 percent of assets, education loans to 5 percent of assets, and the investment in service corporations to 1 percent of total assets.[6] As can be seen in Table 6.1, although these asset limitation restrictions totaled 36 percent, SLAs had probably no more than 3.4 percent of their assets invested in consumer loans as of December 31, 1980. This 3.4 percent figure is based on the assumption that consumer loans by service corporations equal the investment in the service corporations by the SLAs. It should be noted, however, that the investment in consumer loans as a percentage of assets grew at a rate of roughly 11 percent per year between 1977 and 1980.

The DIDMCA expanded this consumer lending authority in three ways.[7] First, it permitted SLAs to allocate up to 20 percent of their assets to consumer loans, which are defined to include overdrafts, and to assets such as commercial paper and corporate debt. Second, it granted SLAs the authority to offer credit card services and access to remote service units. Third, it granted authority to make second mortgages, and it lifted geographic restrictions on residential mortgages which were not more than 90 percent of the appraised value.

In the fall of 1982, Congress expanded and broadened the consumer lending powers it had granted. Specifically, SLAs could now put "10 percent of their assets in commercial loans, 10 percent in leases and 30 percent in consumer loans."[8] These changes followed authorization by the FHLBB in the spring of 1982 for SLAs to enter the brokerage business,[9] final entry into which was delayed by legal challenges from the Securities Industry Association.[10]

THE EFFECT OF CONSUMER LENDING ON THE PROFITABILITY AND RISK EXPOSURE OF SLAs

As can be seen from the previous section, the description of consumer lending authority includes some fairly diverse types of loans. Most of the analysis of the potential benefits of consumer lending for SLAs has concentrated on the installment loan variety, which is one of the loans approved under the DIDMCA. The important question, however, is how will consumer lending affect the net profitability and the riskiness of a thrift operation? The net profitability issue is best approached by an examination of the gross yields and expenses associated with installment loans.

Net Profitability of Installment Loans

Traditionally, interest rates on consumer loans are among the highest that are legally charged in this country. Small, short-term consumer loans provided by finance companies can have interest rates in excess of 20 percent. Consumer loans provided by credit unions and commercial banks tend to have gross yields 200 to 300 basis points above the gross yields on mortgage loans. The relatively large gross yield is easily understood when one examines the deductions from the gross yield.

The two expenses associated with consumer lending are operating expenses and loan losses. Consistent, uniform data on these two variables are difficult to identify, but some indication can be taken from various published statistics. For example, over the last three years, SLAs have had a ratio of operating expenses to total assets of slightly less than 1.4 percent.[11] This statistic would include loan losses. In addition, the ratio of salaries to gross income in 1981 was approximately 6.5 percent. Since SLAs still have approximately 80 percent of their assets in mortgages, these numbers may be indicative of the expenses associated with mortgage lending.

In contrast, credit unions, which engage primarily in consumer installment lending, have an operating expense ratio in excess of 3.0 percent, a salaries-to-gross-income ratio of 11.6 percent, and a loans-to-employee ratio of about $633,000.[12] Based on the Federal Reserve System's 1978 *Functional Cost Analysis* for mortgage loans, commercial banks had an operating expense ratio (before losses) of slightly more than .8 percent, a loss ratio of about .06 percent, and a mortgages-serviced-to-employee ratio of about $4 million. For installment credit, the expense ratio (before losses) averaged about 2.7 percent and the loss ratio averaged about .45 percent.[13] Furthermore, based on functional cost data for commercial banks for the years 1974 to 1978, there is on average little difference in the net yields between installment credit and mortgage loans.[14] All of these statistics suggest that the operating expenses associated with consumer lending are higher than those associated with mortgage lending, and the default ratio on consumer loans is substantially higher. They also suggest that the higher operating expenses of consumer loans are primarily because of their being a more labor-intensive asset.

The fact that consumer loans have higher gross yields and higher costs creates the possibility that on a net yield basis they are no more profitable than other forms of loans. This is the conclusion reached by John Crockett and A. Thomas King based on an analysis of asset and liability yields at various Texas SLAs.[15] Crockett and King first compared the average profitability of federally chartered mutual SLAs in Texas with that of state-chartered stock association and state-chartered mutuals. They found that the state stock associations had the highest average profitability, followed by the state mutuals and the federal mutuals, and that the two types of mutuals were quite close in their profitability.[16] Since these results are consistent with our earlier observations about the profitability of stocks and mutuals (see Chapter 2), it is not clear that the differences in profitability are due to the differences in their consumer lending authority.

In the same study, Crockett and King attempted to measure the net profitability of various assets and the full cost of various liabilities by estimating for 427 chartered stock associations the regression

$$\Pi_{BT} = \sum_{i=1}^{N} a_i A_i - \sum_{j=1}^{M} b_j L_j + e$$

where Π_{BT} = before-tax profit,

a_i = the net yield of the ith asset,

A_i = the dollar value of the ith asset,

N = the number of assets,

b_j = the full cost of the jth liability,

L_j = the dollar value of the jth liability,

M = the number of liabilities, and

e = a random error term.[17]

Although some of the computed coefficients are plainly implausible, most would seem consistent with reasonable *a priori* expectations. The authors find that consumer loans tend to have a higher net yield than conventional mortgage loans, but they are quick to point out that this most likely only reflects the more current coupon levels associated with the short-term consumer loans over the older and lower coupon levels of the long-term mortgages. They offer as part of their conclusions the observations that "financial markets are competitive, and one should not expect that some assets would provide consistently higher returns than others after adjusting for risk."[18]

A similar conclusion about the net profitability argument can be inferred from a study by Robert Eisenbeis and Myron L. Kwast.[19] They compare a sample of 254 commercial banks which specialized in real estate lending with a sample of commercial banks that did not engage in real estate lending and a sample of savings and loans. The real-estate-specialized banks were defined as those for which during seven of the ten years from 1970 to 1979 held at least 65 percent of their total loans as real estate loans.[20] The basic argument for this comparison is that these real-estate-specialized banks would be a reasonable approximation of how SLAs with expanded asset power in areas such as consumer loans might act.

The first point Eisenbeis and Kwast make is that the specialized banks tended to be the most profitable of the group.[21] The authors then analyze the determinants of profitability and suggest that the superior performance of the real-estate-specialized banks relative to SLAs is due not to differences in tax laws or leverage but to differences in operating costs and portfolio composition.[22] The differences in operating costs are then traced to higher interest expenses at SLAs. These higher interest expenses more than offset the apparently lower wages and employee benefits offered by the savings and loans. (The higher wages and benefits at banks could be expected in view of their greater involvement in labor-intensive activities such as consumer loans.) The authors conclude that diversification of thrift liability authority may be more important than diversification asset authority.[23] It can be inferred from this that on a net basis, consumer loans are no more profitable than other types of loans.

Consumer Loans and Risk

We are now ready to address the question posed earlier of how consumer lending would affect the riskiness of an SLA. There are several aspects to this question. These include the effect of consumer loans on the volume of deposits and other loans an SLA holds, on the interest rate risk exposure of an SLA, and on the liquidity needs of an SLA.

It has already been suggested that consumer loans appear to be no more profitable on a net basis than mortgage loans. Rather, the common belief today is that the major benefit of consumer lending is that it will enable an SLA to attract more deposits and to have a slightly greater loan demand.[24] The higher growth rates in deposits and loan demand are supposed to occur because of the convenience and acquaintanceship with the institution provided to consumer loan borrowers, which shall be referred to as the convenience and acquaintanceship hypothesis.

Although this hypothesis has much intuitive appeal, it greatly lacks empirical support. The only such tests of this argument have been provided by Shelby Smith and Ken Thygerson.[25] Smith compared the state-chartered SLAs in Texas which had consumer lending authority to the federally chartered associations which did not. Choosing a sample of 30 matched pairs of SLAs to conduct various tests, he found no statistically significant difference in the deposit or mortgage loan growth rates between the two types of charters. Thygerson simply computed the arithmetic mean of the annual growth rates in the total assets and the total deposits at state-chartered and federally chartered institutions for the period from 1960 to 1972. Although he finds that the state associations had asset and deposit growth rates of 15.4 and 15.0 percent, respectively, compared to rates of 10.1 and 10.0 percent for federal associations, his results are not conclusive because they are not adjusted for changes in the number of associations. During this period, several federal associations converted to state charters, and many more *de novo* state charters were granted than were federal charters.

One possible explanation for Smith's result is that the benefits from consumer lending occur primarily at the time that a consumer loan program is started, but such benefits do not continue to compound. Smith investigated this possibility by selecting another sample of eight matched pairs of SLAs. One of each pair converted from a federal to a state charter during the period between January 1967 and October 1975, and the other was a federally chartered association similar in operations, but which did not convert. This time Smith did find that the converting associations had statistically significantly higher growth rates in both deposits and mortgage loans.

There are so many problems with these tests that, as Smith himself points out, one should not be too quick to draw any inferences. For example, the real motives for the conversions are not known, and it is possible that the conversions occurred for reasons other than acquiring consumer lending authority. Also, no statistics are presented to show the amount of consumer lending undertaken after the conversions occurred. It is possible there was no significant increase in consumer lending by the converting associations and that the conversions were part of strategic moves by associations headed by aggressive managers who achieved the higher growth rates without the benefit of consumer lending.

In still another test of the convenience and acquaintanceship hypothesis, Smith asked a large, state-chartered association to provide information about its personal loan customers. He found that the consumer borrower who also had deposits at the SLA was much more likely to have a mortgage with the SLA than the borrower who did not have deposits at the institution. In other words, customers who utilized the SLA for two services (consumer loans and deposits) were more likely to use the SLA for a third service (mortgage loans) than those who used only the one service of consumer loans.[26] This is weak empirical support for the convenience and acquaintanceship hypothesis, and its value is dubious because Smith's study does not make apparent how much additional deposit and mortgage loan business an SLA will attract if it enters the field of consumer lending. The few numbers he provides are not overwhelming in terms of their magnitude, and the numbers in Thygerson's study are not useful in this particular regard.

We are now ready to examine the effect of consumer lending on the interest rate risk exposure and the liquidity of an SLA. The duration statistic for a consumer installment loan is going to be relatively small for three reasons. The first is that the maturity for this type of loan is usually no more than about four or five years and frequently only two to three years. The second is that the payments, like those for mortgages, are level and include principal and interest. The third is that, also like mortgages, there is a high propensity for borrowers to prepay on their loans.[27] The prepayments reduce the actual average maturity on these loans to 15 or 16 months.[28] Hence it is obvious that any investment in consumer installment loans will have substantially less interest rate risk exposure than would a comparable investment in most types of mortgages.[29]

The Effect on Liquidity

The short duration nature of consumer loans has led several writers on the topic to argue that consumer loans would provide thrift associations the added benefit of a secondary source of liquidity. The liquidity benefit argument usually takes one of two forms. One is that during periods of rising interest rates when deposit growth is lower than normal, the steady stream of repayments from consumer loans could be used to fund new mortgages. Then, presumably, when interest rates start to drop and the deposit growth rate returns to normal, the consumer loan portfolio could be rebuilt. In other words, the treatment of consumer loans as a source of liquidity means that its cash flows would be subjugated to the needs of the mortgage portfolio as a contracyclical tool. The other argument about the liquidity benefit of consumer loans is that because of the rapid turnover in these loans, the average yield can adjust more quickly to market rates. This means the added profits during periods of rising interest rates can be used to pay higher yields on the various liabilities, enabling the SLA to avoid or reduce the problem of disintermediation.[30] Both of these arguments, however, are weak at best.

The problem with the contracyclical cash flow benefit is that it would not occur as a practical matter. Consumer lending operations cannot be turned on and off because to do so would hinder the ability to attract profitable customers and would harm the morale and efficiency of the department. A reduction in consumer loans to support mortgages means that some borrowers will be turned down who would otherwise be granted loans. Once rejected, many of these borrowers will go elsewhere for their loans and will have a propensity not to return. Thus, while the SLA would find it easy to slow the growth of consumer loans, they would likely find it quite expensive to revive that growth. In fact, empirical evidence suggests that commercial banks that restrict consumer credit during tight monetary periods have below-average and even negative changes in deposit levels.[31]

The second drawback to an on-off operation is that the good employees will become discouraged during the slack periods and will probably leave. It is unlikely that they could be effectively shifted from consumer loans to mortgage loans at such times for two reasons. One is that, as noted earlier, an average employee supports a substantially higher volume of mortgages than of consumer loans. The other is that it is not apparent that consumer lending skills can be easily translated into mortgage lending skills or vice versa.

The other liquidity benefit argument described earlier is that consumer loans facilitate faster adjustments in portfolio yield, which in turn facilitate faster adjustments in deposit rates. There are two problems with this argument. First, consumer loan rates have historically been quite sticky. Rather than change the explicit rate charged, commercial banks initially change their credit standards and their aggressiveness in soliciting business.[32] Eventually, these responses lead to changes in the net yield on consumer loans, but the benefits from improvements in such things as the default rate do not provide higher yields initially. Nonetheless, it is true that the average yields on consumer loan portfolios adjust somewhat more quickly than the average yields on mortgage loan portfolios.[33] However, the differences are not all that dramatic.

Another problem with the second liquidity argument is that no one expects consumer loans to become a significant part of the SLA's loan portfolio.[34] Even the largest estimates project consumer loans as little more than 10 percent of total assets, and it is difficult to envision such a small portion of the asset portfolio as providing the rapid yield changes necessary to adjust all the deposit rates to market rates.

In fairness to the liquidity benefit arguments, it should be noted that both Thygerson and Smith found that the state-chartered associations in Texas had less liquid assets as a percentage of total assets than did the federal associations.[35] One should not infer, however, that this means that consumer loans serve as a form of liquid assets. It is quite possible that both the lower liquidity ratios and the use of consumer loans reflected more aggressive managerial attitudes rather than one serving as a substitute for the other. As Smith notes, "the State charters are *acting* [italics mine] as if less liquidity is needed."[36] Another issue associated with consumer lending authority is its effect on the stability of the flow of funds to the mortgage market. Some evidence on this point has been provided in the previously described study by Eisenbeis and Kwast.[37] They compare the coefficients of variation of net changes per year in assets for their three categories of financial institutions. They conclude that the real-estate-specialized banks were more stable over the sample period than either the regular commercial banks or the SLAs.[38] They argue that this implies that real-estate-specialized lenders with consumer lending authority would likely be a steady source of real estate finance.[39]

Other Types of Consumer Loans

The discussion about consumer loans so far has been limited to installment loans. There are, of course, other types of consumer loans, and each of these will be discussed briefly. Perhaps the most prominent alternative is bank credit cards. However, there are several institutional factors which would suggest that SLAs would be unlikely to do well in the bank credit card business. For example, extremely large fixed costs are associated with such an operation, and the loan losses are higher than on any other type of consumer loan. In fact, only the largest commercial banks actually seem to make money on the credit card business.[40] The smaller institutions appear to be in the business more to provide an extra service that helps them keep their customers. Still another problem with the credit card operation is that cash flows would likely be procyclical. For example, during periods of rising interest rates and disintermediation when SLAs would be trying to limit loans, consumers would be making greater use of their credit cards and thus increasing their outstanding loans.[41]

Another form of consumer credit is auto loans. For SLAs, however, direct auto loans are not a very profitable line of business because many banks and credit unions use cheap auto loans as a way of attracting other types of business.[42] Indirect auto loans are similarly not very profitable, but banks provide them in order to attract other merchant business, including merchant deposits.[43] Although SLAs were granted authority to put up to 10 percent of their assets in commercial loans in late 1982, it is doubtful that they would generate enough business as a result of indirect auto loans to make this a worthwhile activity.

PRELIMINARY AND EXPECTED DEVELOPMENTS AS SLAs ENTER THE FIELD OF CONSUMER LENDING

Since mobile home lending is a form of consumer lending, it is possible that evidence about the potential performance of SLAs as they enter the broader field of consumer lending can be gleaned from their performance record when they entered the field of mobile home lending. If this is the case, then one could infer that the expanded lending authority will be a very good deal for consumers and not particularly beneficial for the thrift industry.

The benefit to the consumer is based on the fact that the SLAs offered at least as good terms as other mobile home lenders and in some cases better terms. For example, SLAs had a tendency to offer longer maturities and accept lower downpayments than their competitors, namely, the finance companies and commercial banks.[44] Although there is no direct evidence on actual rates charged, some evidence has been presented on changes in rates. Smith examined some of the data published by the Manufactured Housing Institute and found SLAs acted about the same as their competitors in their tendencies either to raise or lower their rates.[45,46]

An additional bit of evidence as to the industry's generosity upon entering the mobile home loan business is that their delinquency rate was roughly double that of their competitors.[47] One reason for this higher default is that SLAs apparently had mistakenly assumed that mobile home lending was more like traditional home mortgage lending than consumer lending. But mobile homes at that time tended to be poorly made and thus suffered from rapid deterioration and short lives.[48] The SLAs were used to making loans which had as collateral reasonably built, long-lived property which appreciated in value. Perhaps not suprisingly, many mobile home borrowers found themselves in a position where the balance due on their loans exceeded the value of the property, a prime condition for increased defaults. Furthermore, since many of the homes were poorly made, homeowner squabbles with dealers and with bankrupt producers frequently led to delinquency problems.

David Walker made some analysis of the preliminary moves by SLAs into the field of consumer lending. Walker found that as of June 30, 1981, 15 months after passage of the DIDMCA, the increase in SLA participation in the consumer loan market is negligible. This conclusion is also supported in Table 6.1, which shows that the increase in the maximum amount of assets allocated to consumer loans in 1981 by all SLAs was only one-tenth of one percent.

A more detailed breakdown of assets for the Texas SLAs as of year-end 1981 has been provided by Crockett and King and is reproduced in Table 6.2. Not unexpectedly, the state associations have the larger investment in consumer loans because of their long-lived authority to make these types of loans. But the differences between the state and federal associations are underwhelming and suggest that there will be no major moves by SLAs into consumer lending.

Walker also found, not unexpectedly, that the allocations of assets to consumer loans was not uniform. His statistically significant results showed that the ratio of consumer loans to total assets was a positive function of the deposit-to-total-assets ratio and a positive function of the total assets of the association. Since a high deposits-to-total-assets ratio is equivalent to a low net-worth-to-total-asset ratio, Walker argues that "it is apparent that the largest S&Ls . . . [and] associations in the weakest financial position are most active in the consumer loan markets."[49] Walker speculates that these weak SLAs are trying to use consumer loans to improve their financial position. Unfortunately, as we have seen earlier, if this is the case then these associations are likely to be disappointed.

It should be noted that there is some reason to believe that many of the thrifts will find entry into the consumer lending field quite expensive. There

Table 6.2
Asset Compositions of Various Texas SLAs, 12-31-81
(Percentage of Assets)

	Federal Mutuals	State Stocks	State Mutuals
Mortgages	80.57	77.16	80.32
Mortgage-Backed Securities	2.54	2.63	1.93
Loans on Savings Accounts	1.04	1.14	1.37
Home Improvement Loans	3.12	1.95	1.56
Education Loans	.04	.02	.00
Consumer Auto Loans	.05	.20	.21
Other Closed-End Consumer Loans	.17	1.67	.88
Credit Cards, Open-End Consumer Loans	.00	.01	.16
Unsecured Construction Loans	.00	.01	.02
Mobile Home Loans	.17	.48	.26
Other Non-Consumer Loans	.02	.21	.72
Accrued Interest Receivable	.03	.05	.07
Real Estate Owned (Default)	.13	.46	.45
Real Estate Owned for Development	.02	1.59	.76
Cash and Investment Securities	9.06	9.51	8.66
Fixed Assets	1.29	1.30	1.22
Other Assets	1.80	1.96	1.82

SOURCE: John Crockett and A. Thomas King, "The Contribution of New Asset Powers to S&L Earnings: A Comparison of Federal- and State-Chartered Associations in Texas," Research Working Paper No. 110, Office of Policy and Economic Research, Federal Home Loan Bank Board, July 1982, p. 10.

would, of course, be the normal startup costs. But these costs may be larger than anticipated for two reasons. One is that with many of the thrifts simultaneously starting consumer lending divisions, they will find themselves paying large premiums to attract capable managers from the current pool of experienced consumer loan officers. The other is that these high salaries for the new consumer loan officers will likely demoralize the staff in the more traditional mortgage loan division.[50] This demoralization will presumably lead to higher costs in the form of a higher employee turnover rate and lower rates of productivity.

Some estimates have been developed as to the likely extent of SLA participation in the consumer loan market. For example, Brian Maris envisions these loans growing to about 9.6 percent of total assets by 1986, at which time they will likely level out relative to total assets.[51] Richard Marcis and Dale Riordan do not evision quite as much growth. They see consumer loans accounting for about 6.5 percent of total assets by 1986 and moving to only 7.5 percent of total assets by 1988.[52] The projections by Marcis and Riordan are part of a set of forecasts of the industry balance sheet under different interest rate scenarios. Although they project parts of the rest of the asset mix to be dependent upon the sequence of future interest rates, they see the percentage of assets in consumer loans as independent of interest rate scenarios.

CONCLUSIONS

Although the thrift industry has received substantially expanded consumer lending authority in the last few years, it would appear that such authority is of relatively little value for most of the industry. While it is true that consumer loans have higher gross yields, they also are costly to provide and have higher default rates. On a net yield basis, they are apparently no more profitable than other types of loans. They also do not provide a secondary source of liquidity.

They do offer the opportunity of an extra service that SLAs can offer consumers in the competition between thrifts and commercial banks for a loyal customer base. They also have the attractive feature of having a quite low duration. Therefore, it is likely that some of the larger SLAs who can afford the fixed cost of a consumer loan operation will make good use of the consumer lending authority. Nevertheless, most of the industry will find itself better served by not entering the consumer loan field. In fact, the previously mentioned forecasts by Maris and by Marcis and Riordan are perhaps both overly optimistic as to the involvement of the thrift industry with consumer loans.

NOTES

1. See, for example, Leo Grebler, *The Future of Thrift Institutions in the United States,* Joint Savings and Loan and Mutual Savings Banks Exchange Groups, Danville, Ill., 1969; and Kenneth Thygerson, "The Case for Savings and Loan Participation in the Consumer Credit Market," Working Paper No. 4, United States Savings and Loan League, Chicago, 1973.

2. Shelby J. Smith, "Texas S&Ls: Implications for Consumer Lending," Invited Research Working Paper No. 13, Office of Economic Research, Federal Home Loan Bank Board, June 1976, p. 27.

3. Ibid., pp. 26-27.

4. A chattel mortgage is one with personal property, as opposed to real estate, as collateral.

5. A service corporation is a "regulated business organization wholly owned by one or more associations, which may engage in specified business activities that the parent cannot or does not want to engage in." *'82 Savings and Loan Sourcebook,* U.S. League of Savings Associations, Chicago, p. 59.

6. The authority for education loans and investment in service corporations was granted under the Housing Act of 1964, along with an increase in the limit on home improvement loans from 15 to 20 percent. See E.M. Mortlock, "New Housing Law Benefits Savings and Loan Associations," *Commercial and Financial Chronical,* September 1964, p. 1048.

7. See David A. Walker, "Effects of Financial Deregulation on Bank and Thrift Institution Competition," a paper presented at the November 1981 Southern Finance Association meeting in New Orleans, Louisiana.

8. John Andrew, "S&Ls Wary about Flexing New Muscles in the Riskier Commercial-Loan Arena," *Wall Street Journal,* October 5, 1982, p. 18.

9. Timothy D. Schellhardt, "Thrifts Cleared to Enter Securities Field by Bank Board; Legal Challenges Likely," *Wall Street Journal,* May 7, 1982.

10. "Plan to Let 3 S&Ls Enter Brokerage Field is Assailed by SIA," *Wall Street Journal,* May 14, 1982, p. 33.

11. *'82 Sourcebook,* p. 41.

12. Richard L. Peterson, "Consumer Lending by S&Ls," *Savings and Loan Asset Management under Deregulation: Proceedings of the Sixth Annual Conference,* Federal Home Loan Bank of San Francisco, p. 181.

13. Ibid., pp. 182-83.

14. Brian Maris, "Savings and Loans and Consumer Credit: An Assessment," Research Working Paper No. 94, Office of Policy and Economic Research, Federal Home Loan Bank Board, April 1980, p. 11.

15. John Crockett and A. Thomas King, "The Contribution of New Asset Powers to S&L Earnings: A Comparison of Federal- and State-Chartered Associations in Texas," Research Working Paper No. 110, Office of Policy and Economic Research, Federal Home Loan Bank Board, July 1982, pp. 20-21.

16. Ibid., p. 3.

17. Ibid., p. 14.

18. Ibid., p. 22.

19. Robert A. Eisenbeis and Myron L. Kwast, "The Implications of Expanded Portfolio Powers on S&L Institution Performance," a paper presented at the October 1982 Financial Management Association meeting in San Francisco, California.

20. Ibid., p. 3.

21. Ibid., p. 5.

22. Ibid., p. 9.

23. Ibid., p. 17.

24. See, for example, Peterson, "Consumer Lending"; Maris, "Consumer Credit"; Thygerson, "The Case"; Smith, "Texas S&Ls"; and James L. Kichline, "Prospects for Institutional Reforms of the Major Depository Intermediaries," in Board of Governors of the Federal Reserve System, *Ways to Moderate Fluctuations in Housing Construction,* Washington, D.C., 1972, pp. 282-300.

25. Smith, "Texas S&Ls"; and Thygerson, "The Case."

26. Smith, "Texas S&Ls," p. 74.

27. Peterson, "Consumer Lending," p. 184.

28. Ibid.
29. This is the same conclusion reached by Crockett and King, "New Asset Powers," p. 23.
30. See, for example, Thygerson, "The Case," p. 13.
31. See Paul Smith, "Response of Consumer Loans to General Credit Conditions," *American Economic Review*, September 1958, pp. 649-55.
32. Maris, "Consumer Credit," p. 19.
33. Maris, "Consumer Credit," p. 4; and Peterson, "Consumer Lending," p. 194.
34. We will look at the projected growth rates in SLA consumer lending later in the chapter.
35. Thygerson, "The Case," p. 29; and Smith, "Texas S&Ls," p. 43.
36. Smith, "Texas S&Ls," p. 43.
37. Eisenbeis and Kwast, "Expanded Portfolio Powers."
38. Ibid., p. 15.
39. Ibid., p. 17.
40. Peterson, "Consumer Lending," p. 190.
41. Maris, "Consumer Credit," p. 16.
42. Peterson, "Consumer Lending," p. 198.
43. An indirect auto loan is one in which the bank will provide financing through the auto dealer rather than directly to the auto buyer.
44. See Thygerson, "The Case," pp. 17-19.
45. Smith, "Texas S&Ls," p. 85.
46. Thygerson had earlier looked at the data on rate changes and had concluded that SLAs were more prone to lower their rates and less prone to raise them. It is difficult, however, to see how he reaches this conclusion based on the data he provides. See Thygerson, "The Case," p. 20.
47. Smith, "Texas S&Ls," pp. 89-90.
48. Peterson, "Consumer Lending," p. 178.
49. Walker, "Effects of Financial Deregulation," p. 14.
50. Jody Long, "Florida S&Ls, Expecting Deregulation to Step Up Competition, Grid for Battle," *Wall Street Journal,* April 28, 1983, p. 54.
51. Brian Maris, "Consumer Lending by S&Ls: The Prospects," *FHLBB Journal,* May 1980, pp. 20-26.
52. Richard G. Marcis and Dale Riordan, "The Savings and Loan Industry in the 1980's," *FHLBB Journal,* May 1980, pp. 2-15.

7

The Elimination of Interest Rate Ceilings

The revolution in the liability structure of the SLA industry which began during the seventies has accelerated during the first half of the eighties. This acceleration has occurred in part because of the inclusion in the Depository Institutions Deregulation and Monetary Control Act of the provisions that require interest rate ceilings be phased out by 1986 and all SLAs be given the authority to offer negotiable order of withdrawal or NOW accounts beginning January 1, 1981. As part of the phaseout process, several new types of accounts, such as the money market deposit account and the "Super NOW" account, have been authorized for SLAs. These two events will greatly affect the interest rate risk exposure and profitability of the thrift institutions.

THE CREATION OF INTEREST RATE CEILINGS

Most of the aspects of the actual history of interest rate ceilings in the SLA industry were provided in Chapter 1, so it will be unnecessary to repeat all of that material here. However, it will be appropriate to start the discussion by reviewing briefly the history of ceilings in the banking industry.

Although interest rate ceilings were not imposed on the thrift industry until 1966, they were established for the commercial banking industry in 1933. Ostensibly, the banking ceilings were established to eliminate the "cut-throat" competition among commercial banks which was supposedly one of the causes of the banking collapse in that period.[1] As a practical matter, Congress gave ceilings to the banking industry as compensation for getting it to accept federal deposit insurance.[2] Compensation was needed because in 1933, the premiums associated with deposit insurance were viewed by many in the banking industry as too expensive.

This imposition of ceilings was not an economically significant event because from 1933 until 1956, market interest rates (defined here as the yield on three-month Treasury bills) were continually and substantially below ceiling rates. In 1957 and 1962, the ceilings were raised as market rates approached the ceilings.

There were temporary periods in the late fifties when market rates moved above the ceilings, but the ceilings became really constraining for extended periods of time starting only in late 1965.[3] Hence it is inappropriate to argue that the first 32 years of ceilings in the banking industry was either beneficial or detrimental to the operation of the industry. In other words, there are no economic lessons to be learned from the existence of ceilings prior to 1965.

Three reasons were cited for the imposition and retention of interest rate ceilings for the SLA industry.[4] The first was, as in the case of banks, to protect the industry from "cut-throat" competition between SLAs. In actuality, the competition was a regional one. The SLAs in the western states, primarily California, were paying much higher rates than the eastern SLAs during the early sixties and thus were attracting deposit money that otherwise would have gone into the eastern institutions. The western associations could be so aggressive because they did not hold large portfolios of older and thus lower-yielding mortgages.[5] As a result, when the ceilings were first imposed on SLAs in September 1966, they were binding only on the western associations.

The second reason for the ceilings was to protect the SLA industry from competition with the banking industry so that there would be a steady flow of funds for mortgages.[6] This was accomplished by setting higher ceilings for SLAs than for commercial banks, which created what is referred to as the interest rate differential. The rationale was that SLAs were the main source of money for mortgages, and a steady flow of mortgage money was necessary to maintain a steady growth in the housing construction industry. The third reason for the ceilings was that changes in the ceilings would help control credit and monetary aggregates.

THE CONSEQUENCES OF INTEREST RATE CEILINGS

From the beginning, there have been critics of the ceilings. The criticisms fall into two categories.[7] The first is that ceilings discriminate against the small saver. Low-income households have been shown to hold their investment assets in the form of demand deposits, savings accounts, and U.S. Savings Bonds,[8] probably because they lack the minimum amounts frequently necessary to buy investments which are not subject to ceilings, and they may lack the necessary sophistication.[9] In any case, all three of these investment vehicles have been restricted to below-market rates because of interest rate ceilings.

The second criticism is that the ceilings are extremely inefficient as macroeconomic tools.[10] Changes in ceilings do not always produce the expected results, and any results could probably be achieved more quickly and less expensively with other tools. In addition, ceilings have several unfortunate side-effects with respect to macroeconomic policy. One is that they tend to make household savers become procyclical with their deposits, resulting in the adoption by SLAs of more cautious policies such as lower mortgage-deposit ratios. Also, the cyclical vulnerability creates greater incentives for innovation to by-pass the regulations and strengthens the competitive positions of nonregulated financial instruments and institutions. Finally, the cyclical nature of deposit flows leads to inefficient, nonprice competition. Since this last criticism has some rather major implications, let us look at each of its components separately.

The argument that the ceilings restrict the flow of funds to the thrift institutions implies that they lead to higher mortgage rates because the SLAs have less money to lend and ration it by charging the higher rates.[11] That the ceilings restricted the flow of funds in the early 1970s has been documented by Neil Murphy at least in the case of cooperative banks in Massachusetts.[12] Murphy found that quite a few of the cooperative banks in Massachusetts left the FHLBS and its attendant ceilings because they were still able to have their deposits insured by the Co-operative Central Bank without the restriction of deposit rate ceilings. By comparing the growth rates in deposits between banks that left the FHLBS and similar banks that did not during a period when the ceilings were generally binding, Murphy found that the former group had statistically significant higher growth rates.

In contrast, proponents of the ceilings have argued that they produced *lower* mortgage rates.[13] Their reasoning is usually based on the assumption that the thrifts compute the mortgage rates they charge by using the markup method. That is, because the ceilings enabled SLAs to acquire deposits more cheaply than they otherwise would have, their average cost of funds is lower than it would otherwise be. Since the markup method of pricing involves adding a fixed profit margin to the cost-of-funds number, a lower average cost of funds produces a lower mortgage rate. The critics of ceilings, however, contend that this argument is wrong on two accounts: that the ceilings raise rather than lower the average cost of funds and that SLAs use what is referred to as a competitive pricing strategy rather than a markup pricing strategy.[14]

The argument that ceilings raise rather than lower the average cost of funds is predicated on the assumption that it is always more expensive for SLAs to borrow money than to acquire deposits.[15] If ceilings are effective, then by definition the SLAs offer below-market rates on deposits. As a result, they attract fewer deposits than they otherwise would have and must make up the difference between actual and desired deposits by borrowing in the capital markets. The higher cost of this borrowed money results in a higher rather than a lower average cost of funds.

Probably the most significant support for the markup model has been two sets of regressions developed by Jaffee and Rosen.[16] Although there are minor differences in the formulations of the two models, they are similar enough to be treated as if they were the same. The essence of the regression is that the SLA mortgage rate on new homes is the dependent variable, and the independent variables include the SLA mortgage rate on new homes lagged one period and the effective interest rate on deposits, as well as several other variables. Jaffee and Rosen find that the deposit rate has a positive and statistically significant coefficient and conclude that this supports the markup strategy.

However, there has been substantial and well-documented criticism of the Jaffee-Rosen work, and some additional research tends to support the competitive strategy. For example, David Pyle points out that a good case could be made that the average deposit rate in the Jaffee-Rosen model is really a surrogate for some other variable. Specifically, Pyle breaks down the average deposit rate into a time trend and variations around that trend, and he finds that "the relationship between mortgage interest rates and the effective deposit interest rate reported by Jaffee and Rosen is not significantly different from the relationship between mortgage interest rates and a simple time trend."[17]

Jaffee and Rosen attribute Pyle's result "simply to a quirk in the data that were available over the sample between 1965 and 1978."[18] They reran both their model and Pyle's version using additional data subsequent to their original sample and found that their model produced a better fit than Pyle's. They argued that their original results still held.

Still other problems with the Jaffee-Rosen work have been identified by Tom King.[19] King notes that multicollinearity is a rather serious problem in the Jaffee-Rosen study, as "simple correlations among the explanatory variables are as high as .80."[20] Although multicollinearity does not bias the coefficients per se, it does make them quite sensitive to the model specification. In addition, King points out that the simple correlations between the mortgage rate and the deposit rate lagged one period is .99, and the coefficient of determination for the regression without the lagged mortgage rate is .95. In other words, it is highly likely that the estimated coefficients do not correctly sort out the influence of each independent variable on the dependent variable.[21] Still another problem is that Jaffee and Rosen use as their mortgage rate series the FHLBB series based on mortgages closed each month. King points out that the terms on these mortgages were probably set several months earlier, meaning that the regression may actually be measuring mortgage rates as a function of future variables. Finally, King observes that the mortgage rate series is somewhat biased in that it incorporates the rates on mortgages in states where binding usury ceilings may be in effect.

King reran the Jaffee-Rosen tests with some minor technical changes based on his criticisms, and he found that in one case the coefficient for the deposit rate becomes negative and statistically significant, but in another he obtains the same result that Jaffee and Rosen did. King concludes that a direct regression test of the markup and competitive strategies is simply not informative, and he provides some alternative tests. Specifically, he runs the same regressions as before but uses as dependent variables the term-to-maturity and the loan-to-value ratios on mortgage loans. Finding that the coefficient for the rate on deposits is positive and statistically significant in both of these regressions, he argues that even if SLAs do raise the mortgage rates when deposit rates rise, they also increase the term of the loan and decrease the downpayment. These latter two adjustments may easily offset the first such that mortgage loans become more attractive to potential borrowers. King then argues that these adjustments in the combination of terms support the competitive strategy rather than a simple markup strategy.

Some additional evidence which supports the competitive strategy over the markup has been developed by R. Alton Gilbert. He looks at the spread between the average cost of funds and the mortgage rate for SLAs over the period from 1966 to 1981 and notes that the spread has ranged from 165 to 386 basis points.[22] Hence, if a markup strategy is in effect, it is certainly not very stable. Over this same period, Gilbert next looks at the standard deviations of the spread between mortgage rates and ten-year Treasury bonds and the spread between mortgage rates and the average cost of funds. The former has a standard deviation of 27 basis points, and the latter has a standard deviation of 59 basis points.[23] Again emerges simple but rather impressive evidence for the competitive strategy.

Finally, support for the competitive theory has also been derived from simulations performed by Robert Taggert, Jr., involving Massachusetts savings banks.[24] These banks are unique in that they did not become subject to interest rate ceilings until 1970. Using two-stage least squares regressions, Taggert develops a set of simultaneous equations describing various financial ratios for the savings banks. He develops his model with data covering the period from 1948 to 1969. Projections of what the performance of the savings banks would have been in 1970-1975 without ceilings show that the gross income would have been slightly *less* than the observed gross income with ceilings. This suggests that whatever economic profits the banks were receiving from the ceilings were not being passed on to the borrowers in the form of below-market mortgage rates, and thus the model supports the competitive strategy of mortgage pricing.

The second criticism against the ceilings—that they are inefficient macro-economic tools—had a further component to it, namely, that the ceilings led to inefficient nonprice competition. To better understand this criticism, we need first to discuss the magnitude of the economic profits generated by the ceilings. Despite the fact that ceilings that are constraining reduce the level of deposits an SLA would have, the deposits that remain will unquestionably be cheaper than they otherwise would have been. By simulating what the deposit rates might have been without ceilings, David Pyle estimates that for the years of 1968, 1969, and 1970, savers at SLAs lost a total of $1.59 billion.[25] Based on simulations involving mutual savings banks in Massachusetts and Connecticut, Taggert and Woglom estimate that in those two states, over the 1970-1975 period, savers lost $708 million in interest. In a nationwide projection, they estimate lost interest income to have been $20 billion over the entire period.[26] Clotfelter and Liberman estimate lost interest income at $830.9 million, $1,962.9 million, and $1,455.0 million for the years 1968 to 1970, respectively.[27] If these amounts are reasonable estimates of the lost interest the depositors are incurring, then these are also estimates of money that the thrifts saved over this period. Moreover, if these economic profits were not given to borrowers through below-market mortgage rates, then what happened to this money?

Fortunately, virtually all of the studies on this question agree about what happened, although as one might expect there is some disagreement as to the magnitudes and motives. The money has apparently been dissipated primarily in the form of higher operating expenses, and the rest has gone to pay taxes and to augment reserves. Lewis Spellman, for example, estimates what he describes as the "implicit deposit rate" which results from the imposition of effective ceilings.[28] The "implicit deposit rate" is the nonpecuniary yield provided on deposits and is paid in the form of financial services and goods. Not surprisingly, he finds that the implicit rate varies directly with the net revenue per deposit dollar. He also estimates that the implicit deposit rates "amounted to between 13 and 27 percent of observed average cost."[29]

The study by Taggert which has previously been described contains several estimates of how the money was dispersed. For example, Taggert finds that the Massachusetts savings banks had opened 90 more branches by 1975 than they probably would have in the absence of ceilings.[30] This result is consistent with the study by Chase, who found that by 1972 there were 36 percent more branches than would have existed without Regulation Q.[31] The problem with the branches, as has been documented by Cassidy,[32] is that for any given size measured in total assets, more branches produce a higher average cost of operations. In other words, the below-market cost of the deposits has induced the thrifts to invest more than they otherwise would have in fixed assets in the form of branches in order to attract these deposits. It would be erroneous to assume, however, that the lifting of the ceilings would render all of the branches superfluous. Many of these branches would have been established even without ceilings. In fact, in high-income areas, branches provide a very high, tax-free, nonpecuniary yield.[33] The branches in low-income areas would more likely be the ones phased out when ceilings are lifted.

Taggert also finds that "the largest gaps between hypothetical and actual values, in both absolute and percentage terms, come in the form of wages. . . ."[34] It is not completely clear as to why there is such a large increase in wages. Taggert suggests that the extra branches accounted for approximately one-half of this extra expense. But the remainder could be accounted for by either managerial decisions to use a more labor-intensive operation or to what is referred to as managerial expense-preference behavior. In this case, the expense-preference behavior might be to pay higher than necessary wages because the money is available to do so.

Taggert also estimates the excess expenses as a percentage of the interest lost to savers. He finds that for the years from 1970 to 1973, the excess expenses ranged from 6.3 to 15.9 percent of the interest lost, while in 1974 and 1975, this percentage figure was well over one-third of the interest lost.

In view of all the criticism of the ceilings, one might easily wonder why they were put into place and then maintained. It would appear that the ceilings are

Table 7.1
Deposits at Insured Associations as of September 30, 1981
(Dollar Amounts in Millions)

Type of Account	Amount	Percentage
Passbook	98,390	19.5
90-day Notice	2,699	.5
Six-month MMC	204,261	40.4
30-month Market Rate Certificate	76,335	15.1
Four-year Market Rate Certificate	3,071	.6
Special Purpose Certificate	6,563	1.3
Other Certificates of Less than $100,000	67,628	13.4
$100,000-minimum Certificates	46,207	9.1
	505,156	100.0

SOURCE: *'82 Savings and Loan Sourcebook,* United States League of Savings Associations, p. 20.

a result of a policy trade-off.[35] Most of the criticisms of ceilings have little to do with the reasons for which they were adopted. Recall that they were conceived to protect the industry from regional and commercial bank competition. The imposition of ceilings is really a political choice of whether these results were worth the consequences described above. Regardless of the ill effects of the ceilings, they have resulted in the reduction of regional and commercial bank competition.

THE CONSEQUENCES OF REMOVING THE CEILINGS

The eventual removal of the ceilings is certainly not a matter of debate. In fact, one could argue that the ceilings have for the most part already been removed by the introduction of the various certificates whose yields are tied to market rates. Table 7.1 shows the breakdown of deposits at insured associations as of September 30, 1981. The deposits issued at market rates include the six-month money market certificates, the 30-month market rate certificates, the four-year market rate certificates and the $100,000-minimum certificates. These account for 65.2 percent of deposits on that date. Thus, when we talk about the removal of ceilings today, we are really talking about ceilings that affect no more than one-third of industry deposits. Nonetheless, the timing of the removal and its ultimate consequences are still important issues.

Probably the most extensively published simulations covering the removal of the ceilings was developed by Dwight Jaffee in 1973.[36] Although somewhat dated, other empirical evidence would suggest the results are no less valid today. Jaffee used what was then known as the "Federal Reserve-M.I.T.-Penn" model as his basis for the econometric projections of what could have happened in the years 1969, 1970, and 1971 had there been no ceilings. He looked at three scenarios. The first is that ceilings were removed for SLAs but retained for commercial banks. Jaffee found that deposits and mortgages at SLAs would have increased by $42 billion and $38 billion, respectively, over what they were. More important, he found that transfers to reserves would have *increased* by approximately one-third of a billion dollars over this period. The increase in profits occurs despite a decrease in the spread between the yield on new mortgages and deposits because of the increase in the volume of mortgage transactions.

The second scenario involved the removal of ceilings from both the banks and SLAs. The rates offered by the two institutions were not constrained so that the rate computed for the banks followed its traditional pattern of being lower than the rate for the SLAs. Jaffee again found that deposits and mortgages would have grown more rapidly but in this case only by $4.9 and $5.8 billion, respectively. More importantly, the transfer to reserves and surplus declined by an average of two-thirds of a billion dollars over each year in the simulation. Jaffee pointed out that "the actual magnitude of transfer would remain positive even after the ceilings are removed from all institutions."[37] In other words, the industry as a whole would still have had profits left over after payment of interest expenses.

In the final scenario, Jaffee adds the constraint that commercial banks offer the same deposit rate as SLAs. In this case, deposits and mortgages would have declined by $30.8 and $34.9 billion, repectively, from what actually occurred. Furthermore, the transfer to reserves would have declined by a total of $4.5 billion over this period relative to actual results. This loss would have eliminated the reserves and surplus of the industry. In view of this last scenario and the competitive battle for deposits during this period, it would appear that the ceilings combined with the interest rate differential may have saved the SLA industry from disastrous competition with the banking industry.

It is clear from the foregoing scenarios that two important issues in the lifting of ceilings are what type of yield the SLAs will offer on passbook accounts and what type of interest rate differential will evolve. With respect to the type of yield offered, it has been noted that during the 1971 to 1972 period when the Regulation Q ceilings were not binding on the banks, the rates at commercial banks closely approximated those of six-month T-bills.[38] However, it has also been pointed out that over the 1961 to 1964 period, there was a high degree of geographical variation in SLA deposit rates which was attributed to differences in local market conditions such as the degree of competition and income levels.[39]

With regard to the second issue of what type of interest rate differential might evolve between yields on deposits at SLAs and those at commercial banks, it would appear that commercial bank rates have historically been at least 50 basis points below those of thrifts.[40] However, banks have become more aggressive since 1966 in setting deposit rates. They have pushed for elimination of the differential whenever possible as new types of deposit instruments have been introduced in the seventies. But the banks have not been as aggressive as the SLAs in seeking the NOW account deposits. It is probable that the banking industry as a whole will set their deposit rates below those of the SLA industry but at a much smaller spread than existed prior to the ceilings becoming effective.

Some additional evidence regarding the aggressiveness of banks following the lifting of interest rate ceilings can be gleaned from what occurred during the "wild card" experiment. This experiment, as the reader may recall from Chapter 1, occurred in 1973 when ceilings were lifted at banks and SLAs on certificates of $1,000 or more which had a maturity of four years or more. The experiment was somewhat tainted in that shortly after it started, the regulatory bodies limited the amount of such certificates that could be acquired to five percent of total deposits, and the experiment was terminated in November. There has been some debate about how much in deposits were lost by SLAs to commercial banks during the experiment. Edward Kane has argued that the loss in deposits from elimination of the differential was only about one billion dollars.[41] Kane's estimate has been recently reinforced in work by Hartzog, Losey, and Woerheide.[42] Hartzog et al. developed two regression models to identify the gross savings receipts and the withdrawals at SLAs during the period from May 1971 to December 1977. Based on the coefficients of the two models, they estimated that "from July to October 1973, SLAs lost $1.5 billion due to the loss of the differential, $2.6 billion due to the competition from Treasury bills, and $1.9 billion due to normal seasonal variations."[43] These numbers would suggest that while SLAs would lose some deposits to banks because of elimination of the differential, the magnitude of the loss would not be too severe.

One problem with the foregoing industry simulations is that there is no indication in the reported results of any allowance for the ability of the SLAs to adjust their operating costs. There is some evidence that SLAs do have that ability. It has already been noted that Spellman found that changes in the implicit interest rate moved in line with changes on the net yield on deposits.[44] It has also been mentioned that Taggert found evidence of a sharply accelerating rate of excess expenses.

These two examples are well supported in recent work by Thomas Kilcollin and Gerald Hanweck involving the banking industry. Their argument was that the economic profit associated with deposits covered by ceilings would cause the banks to find ways involving nonprice competition to acquire those deposits. Furthermore, the magnitude of the competition would depend on the spread between market rates and the ceilings. In their empirical tests, Kilcollin and Hanweck divided the banks in their sample into four groups based on total assets because the larger banks tend to have a smaller percentage of their liabilities subject to Regulation Q. They concluded that changes in the spread between market rates and ceiling rates

has historically resulted in significant changes in interest income and non-interest expense for all banks even within a one-year time frame. While these changes have largely been offsetting for large banks, they have not been for small banks. The result is that smaller banks' net operating income has varied positively with the restrictiveness of Regulation Q on an annual basis.[45]

The authors go on to argue that, at least in the case of commercial banks, long-run profitability will not be hampered when the ceilings are lifted. They do acknowledge that a drag on short-term profits would most likely result from such an action. However, they find no evidence that the short-term losses would be sufficient to eliminate the capital of any particular bank, at least as things stood in 1979.[46]

If we assume that these results would also hold true for the SLA industry, then they suggest that the SLAs will suffer some immediate losses when the ceilings are eliminated, provided that commercial banks do not attempt to match the deposit rate of the SLAs. However, within one or two years, the thrift industry should be able to reorient its operations sufficiently to convert much of what had been implicit interest to explicit interest. The fact that, as pointed out earlier with Table 7.1, roughly two-thirds of current SLA deposits are already issued at market rates would suggest that most associations should not be hurt too badly by the final removal of ceilings.

One indirect piece of evidence as to the impact that the lifting of ceilings would have on SLAs has been offered recently by Larry Dann and Christopher James.[47] Dann and James evaluated the performance of a portfolio of 34 SLA stocks around three dates on which an increase in interest rate ceilings occurred. The first date was May 16, 1973, when ceilings were suspended on CDs of $100,000 or more and maturities of 90 days or more. The second date was July 5, 1973, when the wild-card experiment started, and the third date was May 11, 1978, when the six-month MMC was introduced. The authors found that for a period from ten days before the introduction of the MMCs to ten days afterward, the portfolio declined 8.74 percent. It declined 2.66 percent when the wild-card experiment was announced, and it *increased* in value by 2.18 percent when the ceilings were removed on large CDs. This suggests that the introduction of the MMCs and the associated lifting of ceilings were viewed as having rather serious consequences for the industry. The other two events were apparently viewed as being far less serious. Thus while the lifting of ceilings may have some serious consequences for the industry, it would probably not be viewed as a total disaster.

Several writers view the introduction of such instruments as the six-month MMC as harmful to the interest rate risk exposure of the SLAs. Kaplan and

Smith note that with the MMC's introduction "the dilemma of funding long-term assets with short-term deposits was exacerbated."[48] However, such a description misses part of the point of these certificates. Money that is placed in an MMC at an SLA is much more likely to remain on deposit at the association and to be cheaper over time than deposits subject to ceilings. A certificate with a longer maturity than the six-month MMC, but which is also at a below-market rate due to ceilings, is much more likely to be withdrawn at maturity. This means that any assets financed with this longer-term certificate will likely have to be refinanced with borrowed money. It is still valid to assume that borrowed money is more expensive than deposit money, if for no other reason than that the former is not insured by the FSLIC and the latter is.[49] In fact, simulations reported by Jaffee and Rosen indicate that were it not for the MMCs in 1979, the SLAs would have had a disintermediation of roughly $24 billion rather than the net inflow of $38 billion they actually received.[50]

CONCLUSIONS

As pointed out earlier, the debate about the removal of ceilings is not as significant today as it would have been ten years ago. The reason is the much smaller percentages of deposits that are actually subject to the ceilings. The imposition of ceilings may have been one of the more politically feasible policy choices available back in 1966. Unfortunately, they have had consequences which, while rational from an economic perspective, have been economically inefficient. That is, the SLAs have competed for deposits on a nonprice basis. There is also some evidence they may have engaged in expense-preference behavior in the form of larger salaries and more branches. The probable consequences of these actions is that many SLAs are not going to be in a competitive position when ceilings are lifted. Indeed, some SLAs may well become bankruptcies or supervisory merger candidates. There is evidence, however, that the industry as a whole should be able to eliminate or phase out the implicit interest expenses within the relatively short time of a few years. They may also be forced to eliminate their expense-preference behavior as they are forced to compete with market rates for all of their deposits.

The elimination of the ceilings should then mean that SLAs will be less subject to the disintermediation crises they have repeatedly suffered over the last 15 years. Although the elimination will mean the loss of some economic profit, it should lead to fewer problems because of interest rate risk exposure and a more profitable, healthier industry.

NOTES

1. George Kaufman, Larry Mote, and Harvey Rosenblum, "Implications of Deregulation for Product Lines and Geographical Markets of Financial Institutions," a paper

presented at the Eighteenth Conference on Bank Structure and Competition, Federal Reserve Bank of Chicago, April 1982.

2. Frank Morris, "The Test of Price Control in Banking," *New England Economic Review*, May/June 1979, Federal Reserve Bank of Boston, p. 50.

3. See R. Alton Gilbert, "Will the Removal of Regulation Q Raise Mortgage Interest Rates?" *Federal Reserve Bank of St. Louis Review*, December 1981, p. 4.

4. Scott Winningham and Donald G. Hagan, "Regulation Q: A Historical Perspective," *Economic Review*, April 1980, Federal Reserve Bank of Kansas City, pp. 10-16.

5. Dwight Jaffee, "Eliminating Deposit Rate Ceilings," *Federal Home Loan Bank Board Journal*, August 1973, p. 6.

6. Kenneth T. Rosen, "Deposit Deregulation and Risk Management in an Era of Transition," in *Managing Interest Rate Risk in the Thrift Industry: Proceedings of the Seventh Annual Conference*, Federal Home Loan Bank of San Francisco, 1981, pp. 15-34.

7. Jaffee, "Rate Ceilings," p. 7.

8. Edward J. Kane, "Short-Changing the Small Saver: Federal Government Discrimination against Small Savers during the Vietnam War," *Journal of Money, Credit and Banking*, November 1970, pp. 513-22.

9. Robert Bleiberg, "Forgotten Man No Longer: The Saver of Modest Means May Finally Get His Due," *Barron's*, May 28, 1979, pp. 7-8, 10.

10. Jaffee, "Rate Ceilings," p. 7.

11. Dwight Jaffee and Kenneth Rosen, "The Changing Liability Structure of Savings and Loan Associations," *Journal of the American Real Estate and Urban Economics Association*, Spring 1980, p. 39.

12. Neil B. Murphy, "Testing the Effect of Thrift Institution Escape from Federal Deposit Interest Ceilings: The Case of Co-operative Banks in Massachusetts," a paper presented at the 1975 Midwest Finance Association meeting in Chicago, Illinois.

13. See, for example, Kane, "Short Changing," p. 518; and Jaffee and Rosen, "Changing Liability Structure," p. 39.

14. A "competive pricing strategy" is one in which the mortgage rate charged is the same as whatever rate the competitors are charging. In other words, the mortgage rate is set at whatever the market will bear. This rate is thus independent of the average cost of funds.

15. See Thomas Meyer and Harold Nathan, "Mortgage Rates and Regulation Q," Working Paper Series No. 171, Department of Economics, University of California-Davis, July 1981.

16. Dwight Jaffee and Kenneth Rosen, "Mortgage Credit Availability and Residential Construction," *Brookings Papers on Economic Activity*, No. 2, 1979, pp. 333-76; and D. Jaffee and K. Rosen, "A Monthly Forecasting Model of Deposits, Mortgages, Advances, and Housing," a paper presented at the mid-year meeting of the American Real Estate and Urban Economics Association, May 1978.

17. David H. Pyle, "Deposit Costs and Mortgage Rates," *Housing Finance Review*, Vol. 1, No. 1 (January 1982), p. 45.

18. Dwight M. Jaffee and Kenneth T. Rosen, "Deposit Costs and Mortgage Rates: Reply," *Housing Finance Review,*Vol. 1, No. 1 (January 1982), p. 50.

19. A. Thomas King, "The Deposit Rate and the Mortgage Rate: Does Regulation Q Promote Homeownership?" Research Working Paper No. 85, Office of Economic Research, Federal Home Loan Bank Board, September 1979.

20. King, "Deposit Rate," p. 11.

21. Ibid.

22. Gilbert, "Removal of Regulation Q," p. 9.

23. Ibid.

24. Robert A. Taggert, Jr., "Effects of Deposit Rate Ceilings: The Evidence from Massachusetts Savings Banks," *Journal of Money, Credit and Banking,* May 1978, pp. 139-57. A less technical but otherwise identical version of the paper is provided in Robert A. Taggert, Jr., and Geoffry Woglom, "Savings Bank Reactions to Rate Ceilings and Rising Market Rates," *New England Economic Review,* Federal Reserve Bank of Boston, September/October 1978, pp. 17-31.

25. David H. Pyle, "The Losses on Savings Deposits from Interest Rate Regulation," *The Bell Journal of Economics and Management Science,* Autumn 1979, pp. 614-22.

26. Taggert and Woglom, "Savings Bank Reactions," p. 18.

27. Charles Clotfelter and Charles Liberman, "On the Redistribution Impact of Federal Interest Rate Ceilings," *Journal of Finance,* March 1978, pp. 199-213. For other estimates of what savers have lost, see Bruce W. Morgan, "Ceilings on Deposit Interest Rates, the Saving Public and Housing Finance," *Equity for the Small Saver,* Hearings on S. Con. Res. 5 before the Subcommittee on Financial Institutions, Senate Committee on Banking, Housing, and Urban Affairs, 96 Cong. 1 Sess (GPO, 1979), p. 175; David H. Pyle, "Interest Rate Ceilings and Net Worth Losses by Savers," in Kenneth E. Boulding and Thomas Frederick Wilson (eds.), *Redistribution through the Financial System,* Praeger, New York, 1978, pp. 87-101.

28. Lewis J. Spellman, "Deposit Ceilings and the Efficiency of Financial Intermediation," *Journal of Finance,* March 1980, pp. 129-36.

29. Ibid., p. 134.

30. Taggert, "Effects," p. 148.

31. Kristine Chase, "Interest Rate Deregulation, Branching, and Competition in the Savings and Loan Industry," *Federal Home Loan Bank Board Journal,* November 1981, p. 3. Additional evidence of the use of branches for nonprice competition can be found in Lawrence J. White, "Price Regulation and Quality Rivalry in a Profit-Maximizing Model: The Cost of Bank Branching," *Journal of Money, Credit and Banking,* February 1976, pp. 97-106; William M. Peterson, "The Effects of Interest Rate Ceilings on the Number of Banking Offices in the United States," Research Paper No. 8103, Federal Reserve Bank of New York, 1981; and Walt J. Woerheide, "S&L Operating Expenses— A Historical Record," *FHLBB Journal,* October 1979, pp. 16-21.

32. Henry Cassidy, "S&L Branching and Operating Costs," Research Working Paper No. 75, Office of Economic Research, Federal Home Loan Bank Board, 1978.

33. See Edward J. Kane, "S&Ls and Interest-Rate Reregulation: The FSLIC as an In-Place-Bailout Program," *Housing Finance Review,* Vol. 1, No. 3 (July 1982) p. 237.

34. Taggert, "Effects," p. 148.

35. Jaffee, "Rate Ceilings," pp. 7-8.

36. Jaffee, "Rate Ceilings."

37. Ibid., p. 11.

38. Thomas Eric Kilcollin and Gerald A. Hanweck, "Regulation Q and Commercial Bank Profitability," Research Papers in Banking and Financial Economics, Federal Reserve System, March 1981, p. 10.

39. John S. Lapp, "The Determination of Savings and Loan Association Deposit Rates

in the Absence of Rate Ceilings: A Cross-Section Approach," *Journal of Finance,* March 1978, pp. 215-30.

40. Jaffee, "Rate Ceilings," p. 12.

41. Edward J. Kane, "Getting Along without Regulation Q: Testing the Standard View of Deposit Rate Competition during the 'Wild-Card Experience,'" *Journal of Finance,* Vol. 33, No. 3 (June 1978), pp. 921-32.

42. B. G. Hartzog, Jr., Robert Losey, and Walt Woerheide, "The Effect of the 'Wild Card' Experiment on Savings Flows at SLAs," a paper presented at the 1979 Southern Finance Association meeting in Atlanta, Georgia.

43. Ibid., p. 2.

44. The implicit rate, as the reader may recall, is defined as the nonpecuniary yield paid on deposits which is provided in the form of financial services and goods.

45. Kilcollin and Hanweck, "Regulation Q," p. 13.

46. Ibid., p. 19.

47. Larry Dann and Christopher James, "An Analysis of the Impact of Deposit Rate Ceilings on the Market Values of Thrift Institutions," *Journal of Finance,* December 1982, pp. 1259-75.

48. Donald M. Kaplan and David L. Smith, "The Role of Short-Term Debt in Savings and Loan Liability Management," *New Sources of Capital for the Savings and Loan Industry: Proceedings of the Fifth Annual Conference,* Federal Home Loan Bank of San Francisco, 1979, p. 162.

49. However, deposit money is subject, of course, to account size limitations.

50. Jaffee and Rosen, "The Changing Liability Structure" pp. 44-45.

8

The Introduction of NOW Accounts

The prohibition of interest payments on demand deposits was established in 1933 at the same time and for the same reasons as the creation of interest rate ceilings for the commercial banking industry. This prohibition can be viewed as setting the interest rate ceiling on checking accounts at zero. Savings and loans were not at that time authorized to issue demand deposits. As described in Chapter 1, the first thrift NOW account was offered by the Consumer Savings Bank in Worcester, Massachusetts in 1972. This offering represented a successful attempt to by-pass one aspect of the regulatory control of the industry. The idea for the NOW account had originated in 1970. Savings banks in Massachusetts were already then allowed to waive the 30-day withdrawal notice for regular savings accounts and could give withdrawals in the form of counterchecks made payable to a third party. The Worcester bank only proposed changing the site of the creations of the third party draft. It was not until two years later that the Massachusetts Supreme Judicial Court decided that the Consumer Savings Bank had a valid point.[1] The initial spreading of the NOW account to commercial banks in Massachusetts, to the rest of the New England states, and then to New York and New Jersey was a regulatory-controlled evolvement. The spreading of NOW accounts to the rest of the country was accomplished in one quick jump through Title III of the DIDMCA which was called the Consumer Checking Account Equity Act. The final, full authorization for NOW accounts was given as part of the compensation to the SLA industry for the phasing out of the interest rate differential that was implicit in the interest rate ceilings.[2] By the time of this writing, the NOW accounts have become an extremely widespread deposit offering.

As with their many other new powers, the relevant questions concerning the NOW accounts are how will they affect the risk exposure and the profitability of the SLA industry? The fact that NOW accounts have been utilized in the New England area for several years and nationwide for over two years permits examination of their effect on the SLA industry and allows us to draw some conclusions with respect to the above-mentioned questions.

THE NEW ENGLAND EXPERIENCE AND THE EARLY
NATIONWIDE EXPERIENCE

Although the New England experience with NOW accounts started in 1972, it did not become fully widespread until 1977.[3] This is based on the fact that by 1977, nearly all of the SLAs offering NOW accounts for the first time were "small" associations, which in this case have less than $50 million in total assets.

Not unexpectedly, the penetration rate of the NOW accounts in the various New England states has grown at different speeds. In this case, the penetration rate could be defined as the number of NOW accounts per 100 households. It appears, however, that differences in these rates follow fairly normal economic considerations and can be quite well explained. Specifically, the penetration rate increases as the percentage of institutions offering NOW accounts increases, as the number offering them absolutely free increases, and as the average minimum balance requirements for those that require them decreases. These three factors explain 80 to 90 percent of the variance in the penetration rates.[4]

Additional evidence about penetration rates has been provided in two studies, the first by Lewis Mandell and Neil Murphy and the second by David Walker. Both of these studies look at penetration rates on a state-by-state basis after the nationwide introduction of NOW accounts. Mandell and Murphy first note the relatively rapid speed of the nationwide penetration of NOW accounts. They point out that for all of the New England banks combined, at the end of the first quarter of 1981, the ratio of NOWs to individual, partnership, and corporation (IPC) Demand and Savings Deposits was 14.8 percent. For all of the remaining states, where NOW accounts were only three months old, this ratio was already up to 11.3 percent.

Using the latter group as a sample, Mandell and Murphy ran an ordinary least squares regression in which the dependent variable was "the natural logarithm of the total NOW balances in the state at the end of the first quarter of 1981."[5] They found that with six variables they could explain almost 67 percent of the variance in NOW deposits. Oddly enough, they also found that the logarithm of total deposits was statistically insignificant. They suggested that this might be due to the high correlation of this variable with the logarithm of the level of automatic transfer (AT) accounts at year-end 1980.[6] This second variable proved to be the most significant of the independent variables, and the authors suggested it represented a measure of prior exposure to an interest-bearing transaction account. The next most statistically significant variable was a dummy variable which was set equal to one whenever more than 50 percent of all deposits were located in SMSAs. Mandell and Murphy suggested that this was consistent with the results of an unpublished study which found that "larger institutions tended to offer NOWs on more advantageous terms and hence result in a higher level of NOWs."[7] Finally, the authors found that the existence of statewide branching was negatively and significantly related to the level of NOW accounts, but they could offer no explanation for this result.

The testing methodology used by Walker is similar to that of Mandell and Murphy. Walker defined his penetration rate as the ratio of NOW deposits to total deposits and used ordinary least squares regression. He differs in that he uses all 50 states and the District of Columbia as his sample; uses the data for June 30, 1981, six months after the introduction of nationwide NOW accounts; and provides three regressions rather than one. His first regression uses the ratio of NOW deposits at commercial banks to the total of NOW deposits at banks and SLAs within each state. He finds that "banks are more dominant in state NOW account markets if the banks have less capital [meaning more in deposits], pay higher interest on deposits, and make a larger share of the consumer loans in the market."[8] He also finds that the banks' share of NOW deposits increases when SLAs have higher ratios of net income to total assets.[9] These results suggest that states in which banks already compete aggressively for consumer business (as measured by consumer loans and the cost of deposits) are also the ones in which banks compete most heavily for the NOW deposits which would complement their consumer business.

In his second regression, Walker uses the ratio of NOW deposits at commercial banks to total deposits at the banks. He finds that the percentage of NOW deposits is a positive function of the ratio of total deposits to total assets and a negative function of both total assets and the ratio of interest expense to total assets. He argues that since smaller banks have higher deposit-to-total-asset ratios, these results really suggest that it is the larger banks with higher interest expenses that are not aggressively seeking NOW deposits. It should be further noted that the banks with higher nondeposit sources of funds are the ones which will have higher interest expenses. All together, this suggests that the large banks which prefer to deal with corporate customers will have little interest in NOW deposits. This result reinforces the previous observation that those states in which banks actively seek consumer business will be the ones in which the banks obtain a larger share of NOWs.

For his final regression, Walker uses the ratio of NOW deposits at SLAs to total deposits at SLAs. He finds the percentage of deposits in NOW accounts to be a positive function of total assets as well as the ratios of nonmortgage loans to total assets, noninterest expense to total assets, and total deposits to total assets. It is negatively related to the ratios of interest expense to total assets and net income to total assets. The positive relationship with total assets reconfirms the earlier observation that it is the larger associations which tend to offer NOW accounts. The positive relationship with the noninterest expense ratio contradicts Mandell and Murphy's finding that statewide branching is associated with fewer NOW accounts. However, the use of branches to attract NOW accounts would explain the positive effect of the ratio of deposits to total assets and the negative effect of the ratio of interest expenses to total assets. Implicit in this argument are the assumptions that branches are used to attract more deposits and that the convenience of branches serves as an implicit form of interest. The validity of this latter assumption has already been discussed.

The conflict between Mandell and Murphy's result and that of Walker over the effect of branching on NOW accounts may be partially resolved by more recent work by Morgan and Becker on the pricing of NOW accounts.[10] In this regard, Morgan and Becker surveyed a total of 100 banks in Texas, Illinois, California, and Massachusetts. If we assume an inverse relationship between price and penetration rates, then we could say that Morgan and Becker were consistent with the other studies in that size of the bank was inversely related to cost of the NOW account and thus would be directly related to penetration rates. More importantly, they found more expensive pricing schemes in states where branching was prohibited. This would support the implicit evidence in Walker's study that statewide branching would be associated with higher penetration rates. Two of the main conclusions from the Morgan and Becker study are that financial institutions did learn something from the early New England experience with NOW accounts and that pricing policies are highly influenced by various institutional characteristics within each state. The first conclusion is based on the observation that most institutions initially offered conditionally free NOW accounts rather than absolutely free accounts.

An issue related to penetration rates of NOW accounts is that of which characteristics distinguish early offerers of NOW accounts from later offerers. Two studies shed light on this question. The first one, by Donald Basch, provides a statistical analysis of 121 mutual savings banks in Massachusetts following initial offering in May 1972.[11] As with penetration rates, he finds that the savings banks with larger total deposits tend to be the ones which introduced the NOW accounts earlier.[12] He also finds higher loans-to-total-asset ratios, higher advertising-to-total-deposit ratios, and higher proportions of total deposits in larger accounts all to be statistically significant and indicative of an earlier introduction of NOW accounts. Basch attributes the size factor to the fact that only the larger institutions can afford the earlier, and likely higher, startup costs. He suggests the loans-to-total-assets ratio reflects the bank's need for additional deposits. If the deposits in larger accounts are assumed to be more interest rate sensitive, then those banks with larger amounts of interest-sensitive deposits would be more concerned about attracting the less-interest-sensitive NOW accounts. Finally, he suggests the advertising ratio may well be a surrogate for the relative level of aggressiveness of a particular bank's management in attracting deposits. Altogether, he finds that these features explain approximately 50 percent of the variation in the timing of the introduction of NOW accounts by savings banks.

The results by Basch are in close conformity with results reported by Rose and Riener.[13] In a comparison of banks offering NOW accounts with those not offering NOW accounts, the authors find that "NOW banks as a group tended to be more consumer oriented, and willing to take on more risk than non-NOW banks of comparable size, location and age."[14] Rose and Riener did find that the NOW banks had also been less profitable than the non-NOW banks in the period immediately prior to the offering of the NOW account. This lack of profitability was accompanied by greater losses on assets and higher growth rates in total assets and deposits.

At least one survey of actual NOW offerings by SLAs has been published, although the information provided is fairly minimal. The survey sample only included SLAs in the Ninth FHLB District. The primary conclusion of the survey is that all of the large SLAs which responded to the survey offered NOWs, but this percentage declined to 83 percent among the smallest thrifts.[15]

THE PROFITABILITY AND RISKINESS OF NOW ACCOUNTS

Concurrent with the introduction of NOW accounts has been a rather heavy debate about the pricing and profitability of these accounts. The primary fuel for the debate has been the fact that SLAs have consistently offered NOW accounts at cheaper prices than have commercial banks. This relationship was pointed out in the New England experience, it was well anticipated in the southeastern area of the country, and it has been noted in surveys covering such diverse areas as FHLB District Three and Federal Reserve District Twelve.[16] The cheaper prices take the form that more SLAs than banks offer absolutely free accounts and the average minimum balance of the SLAs that do have minimum balances is substantially lower than the comparable figure for banks.

The essence of the debate on pricing and profitablility is that bankers argue that the SLA industry simply doesn't understand the total costs involved in offering NOW accounts, and the defense for the thrift industry is that the NOW accounts are temporarily serving as a loss-leader in order to attract other deposits and other business.[17] The key factor in explaining differences in pricing strategies is the change in demand deposit balances caused by a change in NOW account balances.[18] Specifically, as banks offer NOW accounts, some of the demand deposits will likely shift to the NOWs. Thrifts, however, have no demand deposits to lose. In other words, all of the NOW deposits at thrifts would represent new money and could be aggressively sought. The banks, however, would be substituting some more expensive deposits for less expensive ones and thus would tend to set higher prices (that is, service charges) to discourage some of this conversion. The introduction of passbook savings accounts as a source of funds weakens this normative model. However, the point is still valid provided one assumes that *most* of the money for NOW accounts comes from demand deposits rather than passbook savings accounts.

Before examining the empirical evidence regarding the impact of NOW accounts on industry profitability, it would be beneficial to review briefly the factors which influence the profitability of these accounts. Donald G. Simonson and Peter C. Marks have put together a model which identifies the breakeven average credited balance for a NOW account and provides an analysis of the sensitivity of the breakeven balance to changes in the various parameters.[19] The model simply states that

$$\bar{X}_B = \frac{FC}{(1 - RF)y - r}$$

where FC = fixed costs, including check processing costs per month, account maintenance and other service costs,[20]

$\bar{X}_B$ = breakeven average credited balance,

RF = reserve requirement and float factor,

r = monthly rate paid on transactions accounts, and

y = monthly yield from investing the average balance, where $y > r$.

Simonson and Marks point out that the profitability of an account depends on the *average* credited balance during a month, yet balance requirements are invariably cited in terms of minimum balance during the month. While the latter may be a useful marketing tool, it makes little financial sense. These authors do note some studies which would suggest that average balances appear to be two to three times the minimum required balances, but the relationship is not a highly stable one.

Based on this model, Simonson and Marks show that the average breakeven balance depends not only on each of the variables in the model, but increases at exponential rates in response to increases in the reserve requirement factor, increases in the rate paid on the NOW accounts, and decreases in the investment yield on the funds. In view of the regulatory trend in lifting interest rate ceilings, the rate paid on the NOW accounts may quickly become the most crucial variable affecting the profitability of these accounts in the next few years.

Simonson and Marks also point out that there is another factor to consider in NOW accounts and that is their effect on the cost of equity capital. If acquiring NOW accounts simply increases the financial leverage of an institution, then this would likely increase the required return on equity.[21] However, if they represent a replacement of interest-sensitive savings deposits by less-interest-sensitive transaction deposits, and thus reduce the interest rate risk exposure of an institution, then they may actually reduce the cost of equity capital. We shall return to this point later.

Before we look at the empirical evidence on how NOW accounts affect SLA profitability, there are some lessons to be learned from an examination of their impact on commercial bank profitability. There have been several estimates of this impact with regard to the New England experiment. Unfortunately, there is rather wide disparity in their conclusions.

For example, John Paulus used some simplified assumptions about the shifting of deposits in New England due to the introduction of NOW accounts, and he concluded that they caused about one-fourth of the 28 percent decline in commercial bank earnings during 1975.[22] P.W. Boltz looks at the same data and concludes that NOW accounts had little effect on bank earnings and that the substantial decline was due primarily to a severe recession that occurred in New England during this period.[23] As Michael Asay points out, however, there are severe methodological limitations to both of these studies which cast substantial doubt on their conclusions.[24] Asay and Kilcollin deal with many of these limitations by using a regression model which incorporates lagged values of earnings and divides earnings into permanent and transitory components.[25] They conclude that of the 28 percent drop in commercial bank earnings in 1975, 17 percent was attributable to the introduction of NOW accounts and the remaining 11 percent to economic conditions. This is a substantially higher estimate than that provided by either Paulus or Boltz.

Asay and Kilcollin carry their empirical study one step farther and look at bank profitability as a function of size. They find "that it is exclusively the smaller Massachusetts and New Hampshire commercial banks (under $100 million in assets) that are hurt by NOW accounts, and the smaller mutual savings banks that are beneficiaries of NOW accounts."[26] The authors suggest that the larger banks are able to adjust their operations fairly quickly to the introduction of NOW accounts. This means that whereas previously they had to devote resources in order to offer implicit yields on savings accounts along with explicit yields, the larger banks could more quickly eliminate the resources used to provide an implicit yield and convert these resources to the payment of higher explicit yields. Many of the smaller banks, however, may have operated in geographic areas where they enjoyed a monopoly on transaction accounts before the NOW accounts were introduced. Thus, these smaller banks may have had a more difficult time adjusting their operations to substitute explicit for implicit interest, and they may have lost some monopolistic profits with the advent of NOW accounts at thrift institutions.

Despite the minor harm that NOWs imposed on banks, there is some evidence that they have not harmed the SLA industry. Before examining this evidence, let us first look at the differences between the SLAs that opted to offer NOW accounts and those that did not. Such a comparison was developed by Richard Marcis and Jerry Hartzog. They use as their sample 31 thrift institutions in Massachusetts and New Hampshire which at the end of 1975 had NOW account balances in excess of 1 percent of total assets, and 29 additional firms which had no NOW accounts.[27] Marcis and Hartzog find that the NOW account thrifts had lower ratios of cash to total assets, borrowing to total assets, and net worth to total assets. They also had a higher ratio of fixed assets to total assets. None of the other ratios analyzed, including two net income ratios, showed any statistically significant differences. Marcis and Hartzog conclude that it is the more aggressive managements with the large branch office system which are getting into NOW accounts. The problem with this analysis, as they point out, is that it does not identify how the introduction of NOW accounts influenced the various ratios.

So Hartzog computes the same financial ratios for 1972 as for 1975 with the same sample and then looks at the differences in the changes in the ratios for NOW thrifts and non-NOW thrifts.[28] He finds that the NOW thrifts had a statistically significantly larger change in the ratio of cash to total assets and significantly smaller changes in the ratios of securities to total assets, net worth to total assets, and gross income to net assets. He also finds that the NOW thrifts have significantly higher growth rates for deposits and total assets. He concludes that the *introduction* of NOW accounts creates a larger need for cash on hand, and this cash comes from reductions in the holdings of securities. This reduction in securities is likely responsible for the reduction in the gross income ratio. Finally, the rapid growth in total assets by the NOW thrifts probably explains their relative decline in the net-worth-to-total-assets ratio. Hartzog points out that the excess growth in the deposits of NOW thrifts cannot be attributed solely to the additional NOW deposits. In other words, the NOW deposits apparently brought in other types of deposits.

These additional tests by Hartzog are also noteworthy in terms of the comparisons that were not statistically significant, that is, as before, the two ratios which incorporated net income. This would suggest that by 1975 the NOW accounts did not significantly increase the operating expenses of the offering firms.

The empirical result that NOW deposits also increase the growth rates of other deposits is consistent with consumer selection tests performed by Lorman Lundsten and Lewis Mandell.[29] These authors found that "knowledge of the location of a consumer's checking account supplies the most information about the location of his savings account."[30] They also point out that the only other useful knowledge in identifying the location of a savings account is physical attributes which facilitate consumer convenience. These would include such features as drive-in facilities. The only attribute, other than knowledge of other services used, that is useful in identifying the location of a checking account is the distance to the consumer's residence or place of work. The authors concluded from their study, which was done in the pre-NOW days, that the convenience of "one-stop shopping" at banks was more beneficial in attracting deposits than was the interest rate differential enjoyed by the thrifts. They suggest that the extension and the elimination of the differential would mean that distance alone would become the dominant factor in the selection of a financial institution.

A consideration as important as profitability is how NOW accounts will affect the interest rate risk exposure. More specifically, how does the effective duration of a NOW account compare to that of other deposits? There is some disagreement among industry observers. For example, Rose and Riener suggest that "these accounts are likely to be more interest-sensitive than ordinary checking accounts."[31] However, the more common and probably more correct argument is suggested by Basch, for example: "NOWs, more apt to be used as a transaction account and less sensitive to high open-market rates, may be a particularly attractive addition to such banks' array of deposit attracting strategies."[32] The point here is that NOW accounts are really more of a transaction account than a savings account. As such, they are relatively interest rate insensitive.[33] This point has been empirically supported by Frodin and Startz, who conclude their work with the observation that "we have demonstrated statistically that the demand for money does respond to the payment of interest, but that that response is fairly inelastic."[34]

Even though any one actual deposit into a NOW account may have a fairly short life, what matters to the institution is the average balance of a NOW account. If the average balance is stable over time, then for all practical purposes, the NOW account may have a fairly long *de facto* maturity. As a long-lived, interest-insensitive deposit, NOW accounts would have a large effective duration. NOW accounts, then, may make a fairly large contribution to reducing the interest rate risk exposure of SLAs.

CONCLUSIONS

The empirical evidence about NOWs suggests that they will be highly beneficial to the SLA industry. They are the crucial element in attracting other types of business. There is no indication that they have hurt the profitability of the SLAs which have offered them and some indication they may have helped their profitability. It should be noted, however, that not all thrifts have offered NOWs at the first available opportunity. Presumably, the smaller, less aggressive thrifts will be the last ones to offer them.

The NOW accounts should be extremely beneficial in terms of reducing the interest rate risk exposure of SLAs. Although NOW accounts, like passbook accounts, technically have an instant maturity and thus a zero duration, average balances for NOW accounts are highly stable and relatively interest insensitive. This means that the effective duration will be substantially larger than zero. So whereas passbook accounts are prone to periods of disintermediation, NOW accounts are not.

NOTES

1. Joanne H. Frodin and Richard Startz, "The NOW Account Experiment and the Demand for Money," Working Paper No. 11-79, Rodney F. White Center for Financial Research, University of Pennsylvania, 1979, p. 3.

2. See B. G. Hartzog, Jr., "Nationwide NOW Accounts: Questions and Answers," *Federal Home Loan Bank Board Journal,* January 1980, pp. 2-5.

3. Ralph C. Kimball, "The Maturing of the NOW Account in New England," *New England Economic Review,* July/August 1978, p. 27.

4. Ralph C. Kimball, "Variations in the New England NOW Account Experiment," *New England Economic Review,* November/December 1980, p. 25.

5. Lewis Mandell and Neil B. Murphy, "NOW Accounts: The First Decade," a paper presented at the 1981 Financial Management Association meeting in Cincinnati, Ohio, p. 9.

6. An AT account is one in which customers may automatically transfer deposits from their savings accounts to their checking accounts.

7. Mandell and Murphy, "NOW accounts," p. 10.

8. David A. Walker, "Effects of Financial Deregulation on Bank and Thrift Institution Competition," a paper presented at the November 1981 Southern Finance Association meeting in New Orleans, Louisiana, p. 9.

9. These two relationships are not totally clear as the mathematical results presented by Walker are the exact opposite of his description of his results. I have interpreted his results with the assumption that he used one incorrect word rather than four incorrect signs.

10. George Emir Morgan and Susan M. Becker, "Environmental Factors in Pricing NOW Accounts in 1981," *Journal of Bank Research,* Autumn 1982, pp. 168-78.

11. Donald L. Basch, "Circumvention Innovations: The Case of NOW Accounts in Massachusetts, 1972-77," *Journal of Bank Research,* Autumn 1982, pp. 160-67.

12. Ibid., p. 165.

13. Peter S. Rose and Kenneth D. Riener, "Competing for Consumer Dollars with NOW Accounts," *Business Horizons,* October 1980, pp. 74-78.

14. Ibid., p. 78.

15. Beverly Hadaway, "Alternative Mortgage Activity in the Ninth Federal Home Loan Bank District," *FHLBB Journal,* August 1982, p. 11. The reader may recall that the Ninth District includes New Mexico, Texas, Louisiana, Arkansas, and Mississippi.

16. See, for example, Kimball, "Maturing," p. 35; William N. Cox, "NOW Pricing: Perspectives and Objectives," *Economic Review of the Federal Reserve Bank of Atlanta,* February 1981, pp. 22-25; Don Holdren, "NOW Accounts: A Comment on Competitive Pricing," a paper presented at the 1981 Financial Management Association meeting in Cincinnati, Ohio; and James R. Booth, "NOW Accounts: Competition in Western States," a paper presented at the 1981 Financial Management Association meeting in Cincinnati, Ohio.

17. B.G. Hartzog, Jr., "The Impact of NOW Accounts on Savings and Loan Behavior and Performance," *Quarterly Review of Economics and Business,* Autumn 1979, p. 98.

18. Ibid., p. 106.

19. Donald G. Simonson and Peter C. Marks, "Breakeven Balances on NOW Accounts: Perils in Pricing," *Journal of Bank Research,* Autumn 1980, pp. 187-91. This same material is presented in a less technical manner in Donald G. Simonson and Peter C. Marks, "Pricing NOW Accounts and the Cost of Bank Funds, Part One: Break Even Analysis of NOW Accounts," *The Magazine of Bank Administration,* November 1980, pp. 28-31; and "Pricing NOW Accounts and the Cost of Bank Funds, Part Two: NOWs and the Cost of Funds," *The Magazine of Bank Adminstration,* December 1980, pp. 21-24.

20. It is not obvious that all of these costs are truly fixed in nature. However, Simonson and Marks argue that these costs are either fixed within the relevant range, or it is a reasonable simplification to assume that they are fixed.

21. Of course, the increase in leverage may well reduce the weighted average cost of capital, depending on where the firm is relative to the optimal capital structure.

22. John D. Paulus, "Effects of 'NOW' Accounts on Costs and Earnings of Commercial Banks in 1974-5," Staff Economic Study No. 88, Board of Governors of the Federal Reserve System, 1976.

23. P.W. Boltz, "Commercial Banking under Coordinated Ceiling Rates Payable by Banks and Thrift Institutions," Working Paper, Board of Governors of the Federal Reserve System, April 1978.

24. Michael R. Asay, "Effects of NOW Accounts on Earnings and Competition in Commercial Banking: A Review of Theory and Evidence," Working Paper No. 26, Financial Studies Section, Board of Governors of the Federal Reserve System, April 1979.

25. Michael R. Asay and Thomas Eric Kilcollin, "The Competitive Effects of NOW

Accounts on Financial Institutions in New England," Working Paper No. 35, Financial Studies Section, Board of Governors of the Federal Reserve System, April 1980.

26. Ibid., p. 21.

27. Richard G. Marcis and Jerry Hartzog, "NOW Accounts: Significant Advantages for New England," *Federal Home Loan Bank Board Journal,* June 1978, pp. 2-6, 38.

28. See Hartzog, "Impact of NOW Accounts."

29. Lorman Lundsten and Lewis Mandell, "Consumer Selection of Banking Space—Effects of Distance, Services, and Interest Rate Differentials," *Proceedings of a Conference on Bank Structure and Competition,* Federal Reserve Bank of Chicago, April 28-29, 1977, pp. 260-86.

30. Ibid., p. 267.

31. Rose and Riener, "Competing for Consumer Dollars," p. 78.

32. Basch, "Circumventive Innovations," p. 164.

33. See, for example, Henry Cassidy, "The Role of the Savings and Loan Associations in the 1980s," in "The Savings and Loan Industry in the 1980s," Research Working Paper No. 100, Office of Policy and Economic Research, Federal Home Loan Bank Board, December 1980.

34. Joanna Frodin and Richard Startz, "The NOW Account Experiment and the Demand for Money," *Journal of Banking and Finance,* June 1982, p. 193.

9

Mergers and Conversions

Along with all of their financial problems in recent years, the SLA industry has been undergoing a rather steady structural change accomplished through mergers and conversions. In 1981, there were 217 mergers involving FHLBB member associations. This is up substantially from the total of 108 mergers in 1980 and the 37 mergers in 1979.[1] Mergers can be classified as voluntary or involuntary. Conversions involve either a change in the charter (federal to state or vice versa) or a change in legal structure (mutual to stock). The economic consequences of these structural changes can be analyzed by examining the empirical evidence as regards voluntary mergers, the issues involved in involuntary mergers, and the issue of why conversions occur and who benefits from them.

VOLUNTARY MERGERS: THE EMPIRICAL EVIDENCE

Ostensibly, a corporation enters into a merger because management believes the owners' wealth will be increased in some way.[2] Owners' wealth can be increased through increases in expected income and decreases in the level of risk of that income. The primary benefit usually attributed to mergers is that of synergy. Synergy occurs whenever the value of the whole is greater than the value of the parts individually. In the case of SLAs, synergy would most likely take the form of either economies of scale which lead to increases in expected income, or an efficient management team taking over a less efficient association.

These types of motivation can easily be read into the responses obtained in a survey of acquiring SLAs in mergers. The top four responses were that they absorbed other SLAs in order to:

1. become larger (able to make larger loans and improve service to the area),
2. gain a new branch with trained personnel at low cost,
3. grow or obtain a location for growth in a growing community, and
4. gain additional strength through increased size and additional reserves.[3]

The top four reasons given by managers of acquired SLAs also fit fairly well into the general motive of wealth maximization achieved through synergy. These SLAs allowed themselves to be absorbed because they were:

1. weak institutions, too small to compete;
2. in need of better management, younger personnel, improved service;
3. faced with the retirement or death of a manager; and
4. able to obtain other various benefits from combination with larger associations.[4]

With the theoretical and empirical motives for voluntary mergers in mind, we can now turn to the empirical evidence of what actually seems to occur in mergers. Three types of comparisons have been made that have proved useful. The first is a comparison of the financial characteristics of an acquiring (ACG) SLA with those of an acquired (ACD) SLA. The second is a comparison of ACG SLAs to a set of nonmerging (NM) SLAs that were similar at the time of the merger. The third is a comparison of the ACG and NM SLAs several years after the merger.

Comparisons of Acquiring and Acquired Thrifts

The purpose of comparing ACG and ACD SLAs is to identify the empirical evidence which supports or refutes the suggested motives for the mergers. Probably the most extensive recent comparison of ACG and ACD SLAs is that by William Bradford.[5] Bradford's study sample consists of 510 voluntary mergers of FSLIC-insured SLAs which occurred during the period from 1969 to 1974. Perhaps the most telling statistic of the study is the fact that the mean of the total deposits of the ACG associations was $72,526,000 and the mean for the ACD associations was $12,916,000. In other words, the average ACG association was roughly 5.5 times larger than the average ACD association when measured by deposit size. A similar statistic is provided by Rochester and Neely in their survey of 74 SLA mergers during 1976. They reported the ACG associations had a mean asset size of $197,500,000 and the ACD associations had a mean of $25,600,000, a ratio of 7.7 to 1.[6]

Bradford computed the means of 32 ratios for both the ACG and ACD firms and tested them for statistical differences. He found that on the asset side of the balance sheet, the ACG firms had a higher ratio of single-family mortgages to total mortgages, a lower ratio of insured mortgages to total mortgages, a higher average mortgage balance, and higher percentages of liquid assets and fixed assets to total assets.[7] On the liability side of the balance sheet, he found that the ACG SLAs had a higher ratio of advances to total assets and a lower ratio of deposits to total assets, although the ratios of the sum of deposits and advances to total assets were not significantly different. Bradford also found the ACG association had a larger average deposit and a larger percentage of accounts with balances above the insurance limitation.[8] With respect to the income statement, Bradford finds that the ACG association had a lower ratio of operating expenses to operating income, a lower ratio of personnel expenses and directors' fees to total deposits, a higher ratio of advertising expenses to operating income, a higher mortgage portfolio yield, a lower average deposit yield, and higher net income ratios.[9] Finally, Bradford points out that when the ACG and ACD firms are compared according to charter types, the least number of differences occur in financial characteristics when state stock associations acquire other state stock associations.[10]

Bradford's results thus seem to support what one might intuitively have suspected about mergers: aggressive and efficient organizations take over less aggressive and less efficient organizations. Unfortunately, these results tell us much less than initially appears. Note that nearly all of the characteristics that distinguish the ACG firms from the ACD firms are also the same features that distinguish "large" SLAs from "small" SLAs. So all that the results really say is that large SLAs take over small SLAs. In fact, Bradford points out that the ACD associations had financial characteristics typical for their asset size.[11] This suggests that there is nothing of note in the financial statements of the ACD firms which would explain why they, rather than other SLAs of the same size, were the acquired organizations. In other words, we cannot infer from the data why an ACG SLA would pick one particular small SLA over another, but we can infer why it would pick a small SLA. The reason is that the ACG firm believes it can use the ACD's assets more profitably and run the ACD's operation more efficiently.

Comparisons of Acquiring and Nonmerging Thrifts

The second useful comparison of mergers is that of ACG associations with NM associations. The important issue is what distinguishes SLAs which voluntarily undertake a merger from those which are similar in terms of size and location and elect not to engage in a merger. For this comparison, Bradford used a sample of 83 SLAs from his sample of ACG associations which entered into a merger during the period from 1969 to 1971, and matched each of these with a similar, nonmerging association.[12] He used the following criteria to select his comparable SLAs:

1. both home offices must be in the same SMSA;
2. the assets of the NM association must differ from the ACG firm's by no more that 15 percent;
3. each NM association must not have had a merger within the period starting five years before the ACG firm's merger and ending three years after that date; and
4. both must have the same charter type and legal structure.[13]

After all of this careful matching, Bradford finds that the few statistically significant differences between the NM and the ACG firms are paradoxical in their implications. The NM associations had a higher percentage of assets in multifamily and insured mortgages, a higher ratio of real estate owned to total mortgages, and more liquid assets. These features suggest that the NM firms are simultaneously more aggressive and more conservative than the ACG firms. For our purposes, these results are extremely disappointing because they suggest that there are no characteristics apparent in the financial statements which would reveal why some firms undertake mergers and others do not. Hence, all we can still really say about mergers is that typical, large SLAs merge with typical, small SLAs.

A Comparison of Merged and Nonmerged Thrifts

A final comparison for analyzing voluntary mergers is an evaluation of the subsequent performance of the merged association with a NM association. The purpose is to identify empirically what the merger seemed to accomplish. For this issue, there are two recent empirical studies which unfortunately conflict in their results. Bradford used his same sample of 83 matched pairs of firms and compared the means and changes in the means of various ratios for the ACQ and NM firms at both two years and three years after the merger date. At three years after the merger date, Bradford found no significant difference of note between the two groups in terms of asset structure, liability structure, operating expenses, and profitability; he found acceptable the hypothesis that there are no synergistic benefits produced by mergers.[14]

At two years after the merger, the only difference of note was that the ACG firms had a larger proportion of liabilities in the form of advances and other borrowings than did the NMs. Since this difference had disappeared by the third year, Bradford infers that the ACG firms used borrowed money to finance the merger and eventually returned to more normal levels of borrowings.[15] Finally, Bradford found that although the ACG firms had slightly higher growth rates in deposits after the merger than the NM firms, the differences were not significantly different.

Although Bradford's research is impressive, his results conflict with more recent research by Rochester and Neely (RN). RN use as their sample 74 associations which entered into a merger in 1976. As in Bradford's work, the supervisory or nonvoluntary mergers were excluded. Each ACQ firm was then matched with an NM firm using criteria similar to Bradford's. Specifically, RN used the criteria that the NM firm must:

1. have a home office in the same city, county, or metropolitan area within the home state as the ACG firm;
2. be approximately the same age;
3. be of the same asset size; and
4. not have engaged in a merger during the 1973 to 1979 period.[16]

As in Bradford's work, RN then compared 31 ratios for the ACG and NM firms, although RN's comparisons are for 2 and 2.5 years after the merger. Contrary to

Bradford, they find significant differences.[17] Specifically, they find that for the ACG firms, the ratios of total operating expenses, compensation, occupancy expense, and advertising expense to total operating income fell more than at the NM firms. Although they also find weak evidence that the ratio of interest expense to total deposits and borrowings grew faster at the ACG firms, they conclude that profitability was clearly enhanced by the mergers.[18]

RN also look at changes in various risk measures for the two sets of firms and find little evidence of any significant differences in changes. They did find that the ACG SLAs had acquired fewer single-family mortgages and more multi-family and insured mortgages than the NM firms. Also, the fixed assets decreased at the ACG SLAs and increased at the NM ones. RN suggest this reflects the ACG firms dispersing redundant assets and the NM firms acquiring new branches to compete with the merging institutions. This speculation is certainly supported by Bradford's tests, which show that the merger rates in different states are significantly correlated with the branching restrictions, such that the easier the branching authority, the higher the merger rate.[19]

As if the dramatic differences in results between Bradford and RN are not confusing enough, it should be noted that Bradford's research design appears to contain at least one major flaw. In order to understand fully the impact of the merger, it would be necessary to know how the two merging firms would have performed separately. Since this information is obviously not available, then the next best alternative is to compare the changes in financial statements for the merging associations from a point prior to the merger to a date subsequent to the merger to comparable statements for the NM firms. Bradford, however, compares the difference in the financial statements between the ACG firm only (as opposed to the *pro forma* combination of the ACG and ACD firms) and the NM firm from a date prior to the merger to a date subsequent to the merger. The postmerger comparison involves the merged financial statements. Since he had already established that the ACG and ACD firms are financially different, one would expect that comparing the premerger statements of the ACG firms to the postmerger statements of the combined firms would show significant changes. The fact that he reports no significant differences in the changes between the ACG and NM firms is surprising and, in view of the RN results, also suspect.

Other Issues

Regulatory attitude has become somewhat more conducive to voluntary mergers in recent years. For example, as will be discussed in the next section in more detail, the FHLBB has eased its treatment of "goodwill" in analyzing the net worth requirements of the merged association. The Bank Board has also recently announced that it would be less restrictive in its analysis of the antitrust effects of proposed mergers. Specifically, it will now consider only actual violations of the antitrust law as opposed to the "general economic effect" on competition.[20] Even the Justice Department has encouraged a relaxation of some of the rules by suggesting that the Bank Board consider interstate voluntary as well as supervisory mergers.[21] The Bank Board has responded by indicating that it is considering approving interstate mergers by federal associations into states in which state-chartered associations are allowed to engage in interstate operations.[22]

The opportunity for voluntary interstate mergers does create a potential problem for the industry regulator. As long as such mergers are prohibited, then the federal associations may be willing to pay a premium to acquire a failing thrift if that is the only way to make an interstate acquisition. If interstate voluntary mergers are available, then the federal SLAs will be less likely to pay such a premium.

One of the few changes in recent years which may have discouraged some voluntary mergers has been the provision in the Community Reinvestment Act of 1978 which allows protestors to call for public hearings on mergers, and requires the Bank Board to consider the SLAs' performance under this act as part of the criteria for approval. For example, in order to get community approval for a recent merger, Glendale Savings and Loan in California had to agree to add two minority members to its 14-member board of directors and to commit itself to specified amounts of loans in certain inner-city areas.[23]

INVOLUNTARY MERGERS: THE ISSUES

Involuntary or supervisory mergers occur for two reasons. The first is that the FSLIC is attempting to minimize the cost of deposit insurance to the industry by minimizing its own operational costs. The second, related reason is that the FSLIC is attempting to minimize its presence in the resolution of an SLA's problems so as not to cast aspersion on the public's perception of the value of the FSLIC's insurance protection.[24]

The Value of the FSLIC's Reserves

Since the FSLIC can adjust its insurance premiums, one way of measuring the burden to the industry of deposit insurance is to evaluate the magnitude of the FSLIC's actual reserves relative to "desired" reserves. One way to make this comparison is to examine the "market value" of the SLA industry relative to the reserve fund. The market value of the industry could be defined as the market value of the assets less the market value of the liabilities. A second way to make this comparison is to compare the actual insurance payments by the FSLIC to its available resources.

The market value of the industry is not a measurable statistic, but a reasonable estimate can be made. Recall from Table 2.1 that total mortgages held by the SLAs at the end of 1981 were $518,350 million. The interest income from mortgage loans was $49,541 million, so the estimated coupon rate on these mortgages was 9.56 percent (mortgage interest income divided by total mortgage loans). In December 1981, the interest rate on new single-family homes was 15.23 percent, and on existing single-family homes it was 15.53 percent.[25] Loan repayments for the year totaled $34,432 million.[26] At this rate, the current mortgage portfolio would be completely paid off in a little more than 15 years (mortgage loans outstanding divided by loan repayments). Let us make the noble assumptions that the average mortgage held by the SLAs has a 9.56 percent coupon rate, an average remaining life of 7.5 years, and a market value based on an average yield-to-maturity of 15.38 percent.[27] Based on these assumptions, the mortgages have a market value of $427,428 million. To simplify the discussion, let us assume that for all the other assets, market value equals book value. This means that if the assets were all liquidated at these assumed values, the SLAs would lose $90,922 million from book value.

The losses on the assets, however, would be partially recaptured from gains derived from some of the liabilities. Deposits in fixed-rate certificates would also have a market value less than book value if the coupon rate is less than the current market rate. But this gain will not be large because, as pointed out in Chapter 7, nearly two-thirds of the deposits are already in certificates which pay market rates. In fact, an examination of the breakdown by types of deposits as presented earlier in Table 7.1 shows that less than 15 percent of the deposits are in what are probably fixed-rate, below-market certificates. The terms on these certificates are probably no more than eight years at most and perhaps closer to two years on average. So, even if these certificates have a market value of only 85 percent of their book value, and all the other deposits and other liabilities were liquidated at book value, SLAs would save $15,732 million. The difference between the $90,921 million lost from liquidating the assets and the $15,732 million gained from liquidating the deposits is a rough estimate of the amount that would have been needed to be covered by the net worth of the industry and the FSLIC insurance fund if the industry were liquidated at the end of 1981. This difference is $75,189 million, and the industry net worth, as had been shown in Table 2.1, is $28,392 million. However, the book value of the FSLIC fund is roughly $6.8 billion.[28] Clearly, the combined total of the FSLIC reserves and the industry net worth are not sufficient to cover an immediate liquidation of the SLA industry.[29]

It should also be noted that not all accounts at an FSLIC-insured association are insured. Only about 95 percent of the deposits are actually covered by the FSLIC insurance.[30,31] This means that approximately $26 million in deposits are not insured. Thus, even if the uninsured deposits are considered, the FSLIC reserves are still inadequate to cover the insured deposits in the event of liquidation.

A second way in which to view the appropriateness of the size of the FSLIC reserves is to compare the income and expenses of the FSLIC. These numbers for 1935 to 1979 are shown in Table 9.1. Two facts are clear from the table. The first is that since 1937 total expenses have exceeded "other income" (that is, income from other than insurance premiums) in only two years (1965 and 1966). The second is that the expenses have never exceeded the sum of insurance premiums and other income. Thus, measured in terms of *ex post* need, the FSLIC fund through 1979 appears to have been grossly larger than was nec-

Table 9.1
FSLIC Annual Income and Expense Items since Inception
($ Millions)

	Income from Insurance Premiums	Other Income (Primarily from Investments)	Total Expenses (Including Insurance Losses and Operating Costs)	Net Income
1979[a]	357	428	155	630
1978	331	379	135	575
1977	293	330	137	486
1976	250	299	122	427
1975	212	289	143	358
1974	190	241	125	306
1973	176	208	67	318
1972	154	173	97	230
1971	129	158	152	135
1970	111	154	114	151
1969	162	125	80	205
1968	103	102	86	115
1967	97	78	59	117
1966	92	63	75	80
1965	85	47	66	67
1964	76	40	37	79
1963	66	27	20	73
1962	57	18	9	66
1961	50	12	2	60
1960	44	10	1	53
1959	38	8	2	44
1958	33	7	2	38
1957	29	7	2	34
1956	25	6	2	29
1955	21	6	1	25

Table 9.1 (continued)

	Income from Insurance Premiums	Other Income (Primarily from Investments)	Total Expenses (Including Insurance Losses and Operating Costs)	Net Income
1954	17	5	2	21
1953	14	6	3	17
1952	12	5	3	14
1951	10	5	2	13
1950	8	5	3	10
1949	11.0	5.0	1.0	15.0
1948	9.0	5.0	1.0	13.0
1947	8.1	4.3	.5	11.9
1946[a]	6.7	4.0	.3	10.5
1946[a]	6.1	3.9	.1	9.9
1945	5.1	3.5	.4	8.2
1944	4.2	3.3	.3	8.2
1943	4.0	3.6	(1.7)[d]	9.3
1942	3.5	3.5	.2	6.8
1941	3.1	3.5	.3	6.3
1940	2.6	3.4	.1	5.9
1939	2.3	3.4	.3	5.4
1938	1.9	3.3	.2	5.0
1937	1.3	3.1	.1	4.4
1936	.8	3.0[b]	3.2	.7
1935	.2	3.0[c]	3.1	.1

SOURCE: Henry J. Cassidy, "An Approach for Determining the Capital Requirement for Savings and Loan Associations," Research Working Paper No. 97, Office of Policy and Economic Research, Federal Home Loan Bank Board, May 1980.

[a] 1979 is through September 30. 1946-1978 is through December 31. 1935-1946 is through June 30. Hence 1946 is shown both ways.
[b] $3.0 million was for a "special reserve for contingencies."
[c] $3.0 million was for a "reserve for three percent cumulative dividend."
[d] This $1.7 million is actually a net cash inflow. There is no indication in the above material as to why total expenses in 1943 is reported as a cash inflow.

essary. It is probable that this trend was broken in 1980. Although the income data for that year was unavailable at the time of this writing, the amount paid out for merger assistance was $1.3 billion, which is substantial compared to the $815 million paid out in the entire history of the FSLIC program for 1934 to 1979.[32]

The Cost of Involuntary Mergers

Whether or not the actual size of the FSLIC fund is adequate relative to the "desired" level, it is important that the public believes it is adequate. One strategy to minimize any doubt about the FSLIC's ability to provide insurance protection is to minimize whatever cash payments are necessary to resolve the problem of a failing institution and to minimize the public presence of the FSLIC when an SLA fails. This is frequently accomplished by forcing the failing institution into an involuntary merger. In other words, the involuntary merger becomes the cheapest cure for a failing SLA, keeps the FSLIC out of the limelight, and thus minimizes the development of public concern about other institutions failing.

In fact, some involuntary mergers may actually be virtually cost-free from the FSLIC's perspective. This occurs when the failing institution is deemed by other SLAs to have sufficiently attractive characteristics to justify the acquisition of an unattractive balance sheet. These characteristics would include such things as the location and the number of the offices of the failing institution. The most attractive locations are those areas of the country which have rapidly growing populations and thus rapidly growing savings deposits.

If a "free" merger partner cannot be found, then the FSLIC would look for the "cheapest" merger partner in terms of the price asked for the merger. In 1980, the FSLIC arranged 31 supervisory mergers but had to put up a dowry in only 11 of them.[33] The price can take several forms. It can be a direct cash payment, although this practice has been replaced with the purchase of "income capital certificates," as first approved in September 1981, although versions of these instruments had been used as far back as the early sixties.[34] The certificates are essentially conditional installment notes in which payment would always be less than the association's net income when the latter is positive, and zero when the SLA loses money.[35] These certificates give the FSLIC the power to veto any proposal by the issuing SLA to sell assets, reorganize, or borrow money over a certain amount.[36] The last, and perhaps most important, feature about the certificates is that the FHLBB has modified its net worth rules and will count the certificates as part of net worth.

In lieu of purchasing income capital certificates from the failing associations, the FSLIC also might purchase some of the loans or "weak assets" of the failing thrift, with the acquiring institution taking over the rest of the assets and liabilities.[37] Still another form of price paid in a merger has been a guarantee of the mortgage portfolio of the acquired thrifts against default, combined with the gift of enough assets to bring the net worth of the acquired institution up to zero.[38] When United Financial, a subsidiary of National Steel, merged with West Side Federal Savings and Loan Association of New York and Washington Savings and Loan Association of Miami,[39] the FSLIC protected United Financial against losses at its two subsidiaries by tying compensation to a cost-of-funds index at competing thrifts. The generosity of these terms was partially offset by the fact that the FSLIC required that National Steel first provide $75 million to the acquired subsidiaries.[40] In one recent case, the FSLIC merely agreed to protect the acquiring association against any liabilities which were not disclosed in the financial statements of the failing institutions.[41]

The price has even been as high as a guarantee to the acquiring institution that the FSLIC will cover the losses at the acquired associations for ten years.[42] This was the case when the FSLIC paid Great Western Financial Corp. of Los Angeles to acquire Lytton Financial Corp. in 1970. The final price over the ten-year period was $53 million.[43]

One of the more innovative arrangements used to promote a supervisory merger was that used for the acquisition of First Federal Savings and Loan Association of Broward County, Florida, by Glendale Federal Savings and Loan Association of California. As part of this agreement, an index was specified based on "the average coupon equivalent rates of 90-day, six-month and two-year Treasury bills and notes."[44] If the index moved up more than 100 basis points, the FSLIC would, over the next five years, make payments to Glendale. If the index dropped more than 100 basis points, then Glendale would reimburse the FSLIC, for up to five years after allowance for a one-time, $20 million deductible.[45]

One political aspect of the forced merger policy is that it clearly provides protection for all the creditors of the failing SLA, not just the insured depositors. This is far beyond the legal description of the FSLIC coverage. It is possible, however, that the FSLIC would argue that if the uninsured creditors were always forced to swallow their losses, then in the public's mind this might be viewed as the same as insured creditors taking losses, and the value of the FSLIC to forestall deposit runs would be greatly diminished.

Two trends are particularly noteworthy in the FSLIC's rescue efforts in the last few years. The first has been a move toward guarantees involving future compensation, which is motivated by a desire to preserve cash resources. For example, in the last seven months of 1981, the FSLIC facilitated 16 mergers with cash outlays of $63.7 million, even though the projected total additional outlays for those 16 mergers would be approximately $570 million.[46]

The FSLIC's second rescue effort has been to increase the number of bidders for failing institutions. This is accomplished by permitting interstate mergers and permitting commercial banks and industrial corporations to enter into consideration.[47] The move to allow interstate mergers was formally voted as a policy statement by the FHLBB in March 1981,[48] and the move to allow banks to take over thrifts did not occur until well into 1982.[49] This interstate merger policy was immediately challenged by the Independent Banker's Association of

Table 9.2
Balance Sheet for Company B

	Book Value	Fair Market Value
Mortgages	1,000,000	1,100,000
Other Assets	100,000	100,000
Total Assets	1,100,000	1,200,000
Deposits	1,050,000	1,050,000
Capital Stock	25,000	
Retained Earnings	25,000	
Total	1,100,000	

America, who argued that the Bank Board had exceeded its congressional mandate. The Bank Board's position was upheld in August 1982 by Federal Judge Gerhard Gesell.[50] It should be noted that interstate and intrastate branching has long been a controversial issue for commercial banks. Many of the small banks, who are the dominant members in the Independent Banker's Association, fear the competitive capability of the large urban banks. Also, many industry observers fear that this competitive edge of large banks will lead to a concentration of industry assets. Thus, the move to interstate acquisitions by SLAs and especially the move to interstate acquisitions by commercial banks represents the *start* of significant structural changes in the financial industry. For those who believe that the benefits of the resultant increased competition will outweigh any ill effects of oligopolistic concentration, this new merger policy is a long overdue development.

Goodwill

Not all involuntary mergers have occurred between a healthy and one or more failing associations. In some instances in recent years, several failing associations have been joined together for the primary purpose of creating the illusion of a healthy institution. This illusion is accomplished by the creation of an asset called goodwill that arises in the accounting entries used to record the merger. Since this is primarily an accounting issue, let us look at the accounting treatment of mergers.

Two accounting treatments are used to report mergers and acquisitions.[51] One is the purchase method, and the other is the pooling of interest method. In order to describe the purchase method, let us assume that Company A wishes to acquire Company B. A balance sheet for Company B is shown in Table 9.2, along with estimates of the "fair market value" of the assets and liabilities. For

Company B, the net fair market value of the company, as computed by the difference between the fair market values of the assets and liabilities, is $150,000. Suppose that Company A pays the shareholders of Company B $200,000 for the acquisition. Then the difference between the purchase price and the net fair market value will be treated as goodwill. The accounting entries in Company A's books would be as follows:

Entry	Debit	Credit
Mortgages	$1,100,000	
Other Assets	100,000	
Goodwill	50,000	
Deposits		1,050,000
Cash		200,000

In effect, the assets and liabilities of Company B are transferred from B's books to A's books and are stepped up to fair market value. The difference between the net fair market value and the acquisition price ($50,000) is entered on A's books as goodwill so that a reader of A's financial statements will be aware that A has acquired some potential earnings beyond that indicated by the net fair market value.[52]

The pooling of interest method is required whenever ownership groups have merely contributed assets (or pooled resources) to carry on operations in an organization which is substantially a continuation of the preceding entities.[53] In other words, the pooling of interest method must be used when the previous owners of both companies retain an ownership in the new company and do little more than exchange voting common stock in a ratio determined by the value of their contributions.

To continue the previous example, suppose that Companies A and B had engaged in a pooling of interest. Further suppose that Company A is the surviving company, and rather than pay $200,000 in cash, it issues stock with a market value of $200,000 and a par value of $10,000. Then Company A would make the following entries:

Entry	Debit	Credit
Mortgages	$1,000,000	
Other Assets	100,000	
Deposits		1,050,000
Retained Earnings		25,000
Capital Stock		10,000
Capital Surplus		15,000

Note that under this procedure, the market value of the issued stock is not relevant to the entries, only the book values of the assets and liabilities are germane.

There are several disadvantages to structuring a merger as a purchase rather than as a pooling of interest. In the case of a purchase, some cash is usually removed from the organization, which is not necessarily the case in a pooling of interest.[54] A second disadvantage is that the reserve for bad debts of the acquired entity must be treated as taxable income in the acquired association's final tax year. This inclusion will likely create an additional tax liability without any additional cash inflows to pay the liability. Still another disadvantage is that it may result in the owner of the acquired association having to pay capital gains taxes.

If the purchase method is used and goodwill is created, then it must be amortized, and the amortization period becomes a crucial issue. Theoretically, goodwill is supposed to represent future superior earnings that are not apparent in the new book value of the acquired assets. These earnings are supposedly associated with some feature of the acquired entity, which in the case of SLAs would be features such as office location or special management skills. Generally accepted accounting principles (GAAP), as defined in *APB Opinion No. 17,* states that goodwill should be amortized over the period during which the firm estimates it will benefit by these special features, but that this should not exceed 40 years. More recently, however, the Financial Accounting Standards Board has adopted a new position on the amortization period for financial institutions. It is that the period should be "tied more closely to the income-producing assets of the acquired institutions."[55] However, no description is provided as to how one determines the life of the income-producing assets.

Somewhat independently of GAAP, regulatory bodies can set their own accounting rules for purposes of evaluating such things as net worth positions. In the case of goodwill, the FHLBB at one time promulgated the guideline that the period to be benefited could not exceed ten years.[56] This guideline has been recently changed, however, and the FHLBB now allows a maximum amortization period of 40 years for interstate mergers and 25 years for intrastate mergers.[57] A less significant aspect to the amortization issue is the method of amortization. Previously, the Bank Board had allowed only straight-line amortization, but new regulations in 1981 require the method be the same as that used in amortizing the discount on the mortgages which are acquired. This means that the thrifts may now use straight-line, sum-of-the-years digits, or the level yield method.[58]

The treatment of goodwill under GAAP and regulatory accounting policies is not necessarily the same as its treatment under Internal Revenue Service (IRS) accounting policies. The IRS does not allow the amortization of goodwill as a tax-deductible expense. This means that the treatment of goodwill is immaterial in terms of its tax effects.

Despite the fact that goodwill and the discount on the mortgages will be amortized with the same method (for example, straight-line), most of the mortgages acquired in the merger will be paid off within a period of 10 to 15 years, and the goodwill will be amortized over a period of 40 years. This difference in amortization period creates an opportunity for reporting a substantially higher net income in the years immediately following the merger as the discount on the mortgages is amortized into current income at a faster rate than the goodwill is amortized.[59] In fact, as interest rates started to fall in late 1982, some of the SLAs sold their discounted mortgages and reported the gain as part of net income.[60] Such action simply aggravates the distortion already created by this accounting gimmickry.

In economic terms, of course, nothing has happened to the merging associations which makes them into financially stronger institutions. All that has happened is that anybody who is not familiar with the accounting issues may think the merged institutions are financially stronger, and the regulators can now act as if the merged associations are financially stronger.[61]

This encouragement by the regulators for failing thrifts to use the purchase method of accounting and its attendant creation of goodwill is in stark contrast with its desire to discourage the use of goodwill in voluntary mergers. Current FHLBB policy states that when voluntary mergers are evaluated for approval, the *pro forma* financial statements of the merged institution must meet the net worth requirements. If goodwill is created but is less than 20 percent of net worth, then no adjustments are made. If goodwill is created and is greater than 20 percent and less than 30 percent, then no adjustments are made if the acquiring association can document the value of the benefits which give rise to the goodwill (that is, can justify the purchase price). If the newly created goodwill exceeds the amount allowed by the Bank Board, which may be up to 30 percent, then the "excess" goodwill will be deducted from the net worth in regulatory evaluations of the net worth position.

CONVERSIONS

As mentioned at the start of the chapter, conversions within the SLA industry can take two forms. One is the conversion from one form of charter to another, and the other is the conversion of organizational form. Although neither type of conversion has occurred in large numbers, it is the latter which has grown in numbers in recent years and has certainly been the more controversial.

Charter conversions occur because of differences in regulatory stances. Specifically, the state regulatory body grants or denies some authority that is denied or granted by the FHLBB. These differences are usually minimized in that the FHLBB frequently specifies that the federally chartered associations are subject to state regulations when the latter are more restrictive. Nonetheless, the federal and state regulations are not always uniform. Thus, for example, federally chartered associations in Texas have converted to state charters to obtain broader consumer lending authority, federally chartered associations converted in Massachusetts in the late sixties to escape the interest rate ceilings, and state-chartered associations in California have converted recently to avoid the restrictions of the Wellenkemp decision.[62]

There have also been instances where state-chartered associations converted because the state regulators would not approve merger applications or would approve them only under terms unacceptable to the SLA, and the FHLBB would approve the merger without the unaccepted terms. For example, in 1981, Great Western Financial Corporation and Financial Federation Inc. were contemplating a merger which required the approval of the California Department of Savings and Loan Associations since the former was a state-chartered association. The conditions set down for the approval included that "Great Western lend up to $1.25 billion over the next four years for mortgages in low-income neighborhoods and purchase $100 million in loans from financial institutions owned by minorities."[63] Great Western found these terms unacceptable. The main economic benefits to the SLA industry of charter conversions appear to be that the conversion opportunity helps to minimize the regulatory burden and any predatory actions by one particular regulator.

The more interesting case is that of organizational form conversion. Specifically, there has been recurring interest by mutual organizations in converting to stock associations.[64] A list of the arguments favoring conversion was outlined over ten years ago by F. Marion Donahoe and is still pertinent today. The list, not necessarily in order of importance or accuracy, includes the following points:[65]

1. most directors are more comfortable with the stock form of organization, and it is better understood by the public;
2. the sale of stock increases reserves;
3. the ability to issue stock enables the SLA to sell debt more cheaply;
4. it is easier to facilitate mergers for stock institutions; and
5. the potential to grant stock options facilitates the acquisition and retention of management.

Some of these reasons require elaboration. Not only are stock associations more easily understood than mutuals, but they also provide a better mechanism for transferring profits to owners. Since the interest rate ceilings were imposed in 1966, the mutuals have by law been restrained in their ability to transfer their profits to their depositor-owners. No such restriction has ever existed on the payment of dividends on stock. Unfortunately, there is no indication that boards of directors were any more responsive to the owners of stocks than to the owners of mutuals.[66] So even though the stock organization is better understood, it is still effectively controlled by a self-perpetuating board of directors, just as the boards of mutuals are.

The ability to increase reserves through the sale of stock is crucial only in areas where rapid growth in deposits causes an SLA to move toward the minimum regulatory level of reserves. In areas with more modest growth, the ability to sell stock to acquire reserves conveys no special advantage because both stock and mutuals can meet the increased reserve requirements associated with the growth in deposits through the profits that are retained each year.[67,68]

That the ability to sell stock will reduce the interest rate on debt financing is not necessarily true. For example, the ability to issue stock enables an association to issue convertible debt. Although it is true that, *ceteris paribus,* convertible debt will always have a cheaper coupon than straight debt, the value of the conversion option makes the expected cost of the convertible debt more expensive than the cost indicated by the coupon rate. So while it is true that the ability to issue stock gives an SLA more financing options to choose from, it is not necessarily true that the resultant expected average cost of financing will be lower because of the ability to issue stock.

That stock organizations can more easily develop merger terms and that voluntary mergers are beneficial to the industry is fairly straightforward, as is the final argument that stock options facilitate the hiring and retention of quality management. This latter point is a result of tax law provisions which result in the Treasury providing a subsidy on stock options that is not provided on direct compensation.

In view of these various advantages to the stock form of organization, it would seem that there must be some disadvantages since on December 31, 1981 only 883 (20.3 percent) out of a total of 4,347 associations were stocks.[69] Some reasons that there are not more stocks include: many states simply do not allow stock SLAs; federal charters have never been granted to a *de novo* stock association; and only recently has the FHLBB reallowed stock associations to convert to federal charters.[70] During most of the post-World War II period, the Bank Board has imposed moratoriums on the conversion process. In addition, Congress passed its own moratorium (Public Law 93-100) in August 1973 which was to be effective through June 30, 1974.[71] In October 1974, Congress extended the moratorium until June 30, 1976 with Public Law 93-495. However, this second moratorium allowed for several "test cases" of conversions. Specifically, the number of test cases was allowed to equal 1 percent of all insured associations plus all applications to convert which were received prior to May 1973.[72] This number of potential test cases turned out to be 49. The expiration of this second congressional moratorium has not been followed by any additional congressional action.

The critics of the conversion process usually provide two arguments. The first is that since stock associations tend to be run as more aggressive and thus riskier operations, they have a greater tendency to destabilize the mortgage financing and thus the housing construction industries. The second is that conversions simply cannot be done equitably and may lead to windfall profits by the manager and severe disruption of net cash flows among financial institutions.

Conversions have been accomplished in two ways. One is a "free distribution" in which the shares of stock are given to the depositor-owners. It is analogous to a rights offering with a zero subscription price. A prominent conversion using this method was that of Citizens Federal Savings and Loan Association of San Francisco in 1971. In recent years, "free distributions" have been prohibited, and converting SLAs have been allowed only to sell their shares. There is a well-defined sequence as to who the prospective buyers must be, which starts with the depositors.[73]

Free distributions are not permitted because the FHLBB strongly believes that this option creates major disruptions in the net cash-flows among financial institutions. Based on a staff study, the Bank Board starts with the assumption that if free conversions were allowed, then current and prospective savers would simultaneously estimate the potential value of the windfall distribution of stock, the probability of a particular institution converting, and the time until the conversions might occur.[74] These estimates would then be translated into an incremental yield that the depositors might expect from placing their money on deposit in a mutual which might convert. The staff study assumes that a reasonable time until conversion would be three years, the probability of conversion would be approximately 50 percent, and the value of the distribution would be equal to the book value of the converting association. The study concludes based on these estimates that depositors would act as if the expected yields on deposits at those mutuals which might convert is augmented by 77 basis points.[75]

They then look at three econometric simulation models for 1974 to estimate how this augmented yield would have affected cash flows.[76] The one parameter which was changed with each simulation was the proportion of SLAs which had no probability of converting during that period. When as many as 79.8 percent of the SLAs were considered as possible converters, it was projected that the mutuals would pick up from $15.3 billion to $17.0 billion in deposits during 1974 due to conversion speculations. Included in these estimates are estimated losses of deposits by existing stock SLAs which range from $1.3 billion to $2.4 billion and losses of deposits by non-SLA firms which ranged from $12.9 billion to $15.9 billion. At the other end of the spectrum, when it was assumed that only 32.3 percent of the industry were potential converters, the gains in deposits by mutual thrifts ranged from $6.8 billion to $7.3 billion. The losses in deposits by the stock associations ranged from $1.7 billion to $3.3 billion, and the losses of deposits by non-SLA firms ranged from $3.5 billion to $5.5 billion.

This entire analysis depends on the estimate of the augmented expected yield that depositors could obtain by switching their deposits to those mutuals which might convert. However, the empirical estimate of 77 basis points is high for several reasons. First, the estimate of a three-year time horizon, based in part on the assumption that "a longer period would discourage potential depositors," is too low.[77] The analysis assumes that depositors will move their money to the potential converters. If this is true, then once conversions occur, these same depositors should then be expected to take their money to another potential converter. Therefore, to maximize the life of these deposits, the management would *optimally* hint at but perpetually delay conversion. In actual application, management action to delay the shifts of this speculative money would suggest a time horizon of longer than three years and thus a lower augmented yield.

A second problem with this model is that it assumes that depositors could identify potential converters from nonconverters. Although industry people are quite sensitive to the distinction between mutuals and stocks, it is far from clear that much of the public is aware of this difference. The inability of the public to appreciate the difference between mutuals and stocks, and thus to recognize the potential value of conversion, can be supported by some of the problems that Citizens Federal had in their free conversion. The FHLBB study describes these problems as follows:

> Even with the large potential windfall available to depositors, Citizens had difficulty obtaining the necessary proxies due to the lack of understanding on the part of depositors about converting. While it might have been expected that all accountholders would enthusiastically return their proxies in order to receive their windfall, this did not occur. At one point during the proxy solicitation, it became clear to management that a strong possibility existed that the required proxies would not be obtained. As a result, management again contacted depositors who had not responded to the initial appeal and urged them to send their proxies to the association. Finally, enough votes were cast to approve the plan of conversion.[78]

Perhaps the most valid assumption in the model used in the FHLBB conversion study is that depositors would assign an equal probability of conversion to all the potential converters. Beverly and Samuel Hadaway recently reported the results of their extensive and statistically sophisticated efforts to define a model which would predict which SLAs might convert. They simply could not construct a model which worked better than random chance.[79]

Although the Bank Board concluded that windfall conversions would be disruptive for the industry, they nonetheless supported conversions wherein the stock was sold following certain prescribed procedures. The intent of the procedures was to avoid the disruption of free conversions and to avoid any group such as management from acquiring an "unfairly" large percentage of the newly issued stock. To avoid the free distribution problem, the proceeds of the sale are placed in a liquidation account, and the depositor-owners of the mutual at the time of the conversion are the owners of this account. If the SLA is liquidated, these funds would be distributed to these previous owners. However, as these original depositor-owners eventually close out their passbook accounts, their percentage ownership in this liquidation account is transferred to the new stockholders. Obviously, ownership of the entire account will eventually pass to the stockholders. This eliminates the "free conversion" problem but replaces it with a windfall gain for the buyers of the stock because the buyers will eventually recapture complete control of the money they paid to buy the association.[80]

As mentioned earlier, the stock has to be offered for sale in a specified order to avoid the problem of unfair insider accumulation of the stock.[81] First, it must be offered to eligible account holders as of some specified date. The individual account holder may acquire no more than 5 percent of the stock. Then the stock can be offered to "supplemental account holders," also subject to the 5 percent limitation.[82] Any other association member can then be offered shares, up to a limit of 200 shares each. Finally, any remaining shares must be sold to the community or at large, with a limit of no more than 2 percent of the shares to any one purchaser. In addition to specifying this pecking order for the sale of shares, the Bank Board specifies that the management of the SLA as a group cannot purchase more than 25 percent of the shares, and no one manager can purchase more than 5 percent of the shares.[83] Managers are also restricted from selling any stock obtained in the initial subscription for three years. Finally, the converting SLA must report any changes in the accounts of any manager for a period of two years prior to the conversion if that manager's account exceeds $5,000.

Although all of these restrictions were not in place by 1977, it has been shown that on average only 3.8 percent of the depositor-owners purchased stock during conversions.[84] A survey performed recently by the Office of the Comptroller General contacted 647 former depositor-owners of several converted SLAs. Of the roughly two-thirds usable responses, one-half of the responders indicated they did not understand or were not interested in the conversion process. Of those who expressed an opinion, the ones who were pleased with the conversion exceeded those who were dissatisfied by a ratio of more than three to one. Those favoring conversion usually expressed satisfaction in the opportunity to acquire stock, while those opposing were usually dissatisfied at being forced to purchase stock in order to retain their ownership rights. This complaint would seem unjustified in view of the fact that ownership rights have no economic value in a mutual SLA.

It would seem, then, that despite all the public policy concern about protecting the depositor-owners, windfall gains nonetheless occur, and the depositor-owners do not particularly seem to care. It also appears that when they do care, their causes for concern are generally misplaced.

A final issue to consider is what effect conversions actually seem to have on the operating characteristics of the SLAs. Fortunately, there has recently been a flurry of studies on this topic by two researchers, and not surprisingly the conclusions from all of their studies are highly consistent.[85] The general methodology used in these studies starts with the selection of a group of SLAs which converted during a particular period. Matched samples are made with a set of mutuals which did not convert and a set of associations which were stocks all along. Multiple discriminant analysis tests are then performed using data prior to and subsequent to the conversion period for the entire sample. The conclusions derived are that the converting associations act more like mutuals than stocks prior to the conversion and more like stocks than mutuals after the conversion.

One fairly common feature about the converting associations is that after a few periods they do not have the higher net-worth-to-deposits ratios which one might expect from the sale of new equity. It appears that the converting associations tend to have higher growth rates in both mortgage lending and deposits. In many cases, the converting associations actually evolve to lower net-worth-to-deposits ratios than comparable nonconverting mutuals.

The differences between mutual and stock associations, in terms of operating efficiency, were discussed in Chapter 2. Suffice it to say that the evidence implies that stock associations do take greater risks, as their critics claim, but they also appear to be more profitable as one might expect from the higher levels of risk.[86]

SUMMARY AND CONCLUSIONS

As was mentioned at the start of the chapter, the SLA industry has been undergoing structural changes in recent years due to mergers and conversions. The number of mergers has risen dramatically from 37 in 1979 to 217 in 1981. A large part of this increase has certainly been due to the economic problems of the industry. Not all of the mergers were involuntary, but many of those classified as voluntary were probably only a few steps ahead of FSLIC involvement.

Although the motives for a voluntary merger are most likely the economic benefits of more income or less risk, empirical tests do not really tell us much. For example, we know that large firms typically acquire small firms. But we cannot say based on financial data why a particular large firm acquires a particular small firm. The data on whether economic benefits are realized on an *ex post* basis are somewhat conflicting, but it is likely that some benefits occur. It appears then that the voluntary mergers are making the industry more efficient by eliminating the smaller, less efficient firms.

The involuntary mergers are occurring to protect the integrity of the FSLIC reserves and to minimize the long-run, average cost to the industry of providing deposit insurance. Based on the market values of industry assets and liabilities, the FSLIC reserves are inadequate. Based on historical payouts, the FSLIC reserves appear excessive. Because of the trend toward contingent and delayed payouts, it is becoming less clear each year as to how much the FSLIC is paying out in settlements. It is clear that the interstate and interindustry mergers that the FSLIC is promoting may well lead to major competitive realignments during the next decade. It would seem inevitable that involuntary interstate mergers will eventually lead to voluntary interstate mergers.

The opportunity to convert charters has been economically beneficial to the industry in that it has enabled firms at times to escape to a less burdensome regulatory environment. Organizational form conversions usually occur with mutuals converting to stocks. The major economic benefit would seem to be the ability to acquire additional net worth. It appears that this additional equity from the sale of the stock is used to support above-average growth in deposits and total assets.

There are unquestionably some economic inequities which occur with organizational form conversions. But such conversions should be encouraged because of the overwhelming evidence that stock associations are on average more efficient than mutual associations.

NOTES

1. *'82 Savings and Loan Sourcebook*, United States League of Savings Associations, Chicago, Illinois, p. 41.

2. I use the word "ostensibly" because it is certainly possible that mergers may occur due to noneconomic motives such as managers wishing to build empires. We will, however, limit ourselves to economic considerations for mergers.

3. Eugene F. Brigham and R. Richardson Petit, "Effects of Structure on Performance of the Savings and Loan Industry," in Irwin Friend (ed.), *Study of the Savings and Loan Industry*, Washington, D.C., Government Printing Office, 1969, p. 1069.

4. Ibid., p. 1062.

5. The full study is provided in William Bradford, *Mergers in the Savings and Loan Industry*, Michigan Business Reports, Number 59, Division of Research, Graduate School of Business Administration, University of Michigan, 1977; but selected portions of the study are provided in William Bradford, "Savings and Loan Association Mergers: Analysis of Recent Experience," *Review of Business and Economic Research*, Fall 1977, pp. 1-18; and William Bradford, "The Performance of Merging Savings and Loan Associations," *Journal of Business*, January 1978, pp. 115-25.

6. David P. Rochester and Walter P. Neeley, "New Evidence of Synergy from Merging Savings and Loan Associations," a paper presented at the November 1981 Southern Finance Association annual meeting in New Orleans, Louisiana.

7. Bradford, *Mergers*, p. 52.

8. Ibid., p. 54.

9. Ibid.

10. Ibid., p. 64.

11. Bradford, "Savings and Loan," p. 13.

12. Bradford, "Performance," p. 118.

13. Ibid.

14. Ibid., p. 123.

15. Ibid.

16. Rochester and Neely, "New Evidence," p. 10.

17. It is certainly possible that the differences in results between Bradford's and RN's works are due to the different time periods used. But I do not think the changes in economic conditions between the 1969 to 1974 period and 1976 are all that are significant.

18. Rochester and Neely, "New Evidence," p. 15.

19. Bradford, *Mergers*, p. 32.

20. "Bank Board Eases Its Merger Rules for Healthy S&Ls," *Wall Street Journal,* October 30, 1981.

21. "Plan to Widen Bank Regulators' Powers for Emergencies as Approved by Reagan," *Wall Street Journal,* June 1, 1981.

22. "Bank Board Says It May Lower Rules on Federal S&Ls," *Wall Street Journal,* April 27, 1983, p. 3.

23. Pamela G. Hollie, "Savings and Loans Opposing Conditions Imposed on Mergers," *New York Times,* May 21, 1981, Sect. 2, p. 30.

24. See Henry J. Cassidy, "An Approach for Determining the Capital Requirement for Savings and Loan Associations," Research Working Paper No. 97, Office of Policy and Economic Research, Federal Home Loan Bank Board, May 1980, p. 2.

25. *'82 Savings and Loan Sourcebook,* p. 27.

26. Ibid, p. 31.

27. The average remaining life is assumed to be one-half of the remaining life based on current loan repayments, and the market yield-to-maturity is the arithmetic average of the interest rates on mortgages on new and existing single-family homes.

28. Although the book value is $6.8 billion, the actual value is more like $5.0 billion due to contingent liabilities associated with some supervisory mergers and losses on investments. See G. Christian Hill and Paul A. Gigot, "Federal Regulators Are Said to Sanction Merger among Ailing Savings and Loans," *Wall Street Journal,* February 18, 1982, p. 4.

29. The FSLIC, of course, has a statutory line of credit of $750 million with the Treasury. This line and any other borrowing capacity is not herein considered. The Bank Board has recently requested this line be expanded to $3 billion, but at this time it appears that the line will not be increased.

30. See Cassidy, "Determining the Capital Requirement," p. 8.

31. This is consistent with the figures which show that slightly over 95 percent of the deposits were insured at Economy Savings and Loan Association of Chicago, when it was liquidated in 1981. See Sue Shellenberger, "Demise of an S&L in Chicago is Linked to Belief That Interest Rates Would Fall," *Wall Street Journal,* June 5, 1981.

32. Brooks Jackson, "Mergers Are Set for 2 Failing S&Ls; Cost to U.S. Agency is Called Substantial," *Wall Street Journal,* June 2, 1981.

33. Brooks Jackson, "Regulators Seek to Ease Anxieties over Dismal State of S&L Industry," *Wall Street Journal,* March 20, 1981.

34. "Bank Board Plan to Fund Failing S&Ls Seems Unswayed by Reagan Opposition," *Wall Street Journal,* June 4, 1981.

35. "New Plan to Aid S&Ls is Adopted By Bank Board," *Wall Street Journal,* September 8, 1981.

36. "Two Illinois S&Ls Merged With Help of Federal Agency," *Wall Street Journal,* October 8, 1981.

37. G. Christian Hill, "FSLIC's Rescue Efforts Criticized as Unsound Use of Agency's Capital," *Wall Street Journal,* January 9, 1981.

38. G. Christian Hill and John Andrew, "U.S. Expected to Cut Costly Efforts to Force Mergers of Troubled S&Ls," *Wall Street Journal,* February 17, 1982, pp. 23, 42.

39. United Financial was formerly Citizens Savings and Loan Association of San Francisco, which was involved in an interesting organizational form conversion in 1972, which will be discussed later in this chapter. The resultant merger of those three firms is referred to as First Interstate.

40. John Andrew, "Acquired Had Little to Say in S&L Merger," *Wall Street Journal,* September 14, 1981, pp. 29, 34.

41. "Sooner S&L Unit Sets Rescue of 2 Texas S&Ls," *Wall Street Journal,* October 25, 1982.

42. Hill and Andrew, "U.S. Expected to Cut Costly Efforts."

43. Hill, "FSLIC's Rescue Efforts Criticized."

44. "Bailout Plan Protecting Glendale Federal in Florida S&L Merger May Be Prototype," *Wall Street Journal,* November 23, 1981, p. 6.

45. Ibid.

46. Timothy D. Schellhardt, "U.S. Assisted S&L Mergers Seen Topping 1981's Record 23, Bank Board Aide Says," *Wall Street Journal,* January 18, 1982.

47. See, for example, Andrew, "Acquired Had Little to Say in S&L Merger."

48. "Bank Board to Let S&L Buy Thrifts in Other States." *Wall Street Journal,* March 24, 1981, p. 2. Only four interstate mergers occurred in 1981, and 16 occurred in 1982. See "Mergers for 10 S&Ls Arranged by Bank Board," *Wall Street Journal,* December 21, 1982, p. 10.

49. "Fed Starts Study on Citicorp's Bid for Ailing S&L," *Wall Street Journal,* September 9, 1982, p. 7.

50. "Interstate Merger to Rescue Ailing S&Ls Can Be Done by Bank Board, Judge Rules," *Wall Street Journal,* August 5, 1982, p. 34.

51. The following description is based on David Hawkins, *Financial Reporting Practices of Corporations,* Dow Jones-Irwin, Inc., 1972, pp. 297-99.

52. A second, rather obvious reason for the goodwill entry is that it is necessary to keep the balance sheet balanced.

53. For an excellent description of determining when a pooling of interest has occurred, see Rudolph Lindbeck and John S. Jahera, Jr., "Thrift Institution Mergers: Income Tax Effects," *Federal Home Loan Bank Board Journal,* October 1982, pp. 8-11.

54. It is possible for a pooling of interest merger to result in a cash drain at an association. For example, suppose a stock SLA acquires a mutual SLA and gives each mutual investor-owner account an amount equivalent to the amount on deposit at the acquired institution as well as quantity stock based on the depositor-owners' share of the accumulated equity at the acquired SLA. If the depositor-owner is dissatisfied with having money on deposit at the merged association, he could withdraw his deposit, thus generating a cash drain.

55. "Accounting Board Rule Dims Allure of Buying Failing Banks, Thrifts," *Wall Street Journal,* March 1, 1983, p. 6.

56. FHLBB Memorandum #R-31a by William Sprague, March 8, 1974, unpublished.

57. Allan Sloan, "The Thrifts," *Forbes,* January 4, 1982, pp. 83-84.

58. Memorandum No. 8-654, Federal Home Loan Bank Board, October 23, 1980, p. 3.

59. Hill and Andrew, "U.S. Expected to Cut Costly Efforts."

60. "Bank Board's Chief Warns about S&Ls' Mortgage Portfolio," *Wall Street Journal,* October 28, 1982, p. 10.

61. Hill and Gigot, "Federal Regulators."

62. As the reader may recall from Chapter 4, the Wellenkemp decision declared that state-chartered associations in California could not enforce due-on-sale clauses in mortgage contracts.

63. Hollie, "Savings and Loans Opposing Conditions Imposed on Mergers."

64. Conversion from stock to mutual is a possibility but to this author's knowledge has not occurred in the SLA industry. Such conversions have, however, been a controversial feature of the insurance industry.

65. F. Marion Donahoe, "Conversion to a Stock Association," *FHLBB Journal*, August 1971, pp. 21-22.

66. This statement applies only to those corporations where there are no dominant stockholders, such that voting power is as dispered as it is in mutual organizations.

67. For an elaboration of this point, see J.R. Dixon III, "Going Stock: Escape from a Dilemma," *FHLBB Journal*, February 1979, pp. 22, 24.

68. It should also be pointed out that the number of new stock distributions *after* the conversions have occurred has been negligible. So although the conversion process brings in reserves, the sale of stock is not subsequently used to acquire reserves.

69. *'82 Savings and Loan Sourcebook*, p. 38.

70. The Garn-St. Germain Act which was passed in late 1982 allows all federal associations to convert to stock associations.

71. *Converting Savings and Loan Associations from Mutual to Stock Ownership— A National Policy Needed*, Report of the Comptroller General of the United States, General Accounting Office, October 1, 1979, p. 7.

72. "Conversions: Clamor Rises for Congress to Step In," *Savings and Loan News*, December 1979, p. 38.

73. This sequence will be described later.

74. The study on which the FHLBB arguments are based is reported in *The Impact of "Free Distribution" Conversion Windfalls on the Savings and Loan Industry*, a Study by the Staff of the Office of Economic Research, Federal Home Loan Bank Board, February 28, 1974. Summaries of selected portions of the study can be found in a Study by the Staff of the Office of Economic Research, "The Impact of 'Free Distribution' Conversion Windfalls on the Savings and Loan Industry (abstract)," *Journal of Finance*, May 1975, pp. 681-87; and Henry J. Cassidy, "Estimates of the Aggregate Impact of Expected Windfalls for a Portion of the S&L Industry," *Journal of Money, Credit and Banking*, November 1976, pp. 477-85.

75. Staff of the Office of Economic Research, *The Impact*, p. 140.

76. The models used were the Bosworth-Duesenberry model, the Data Resources, Inc. model, and what was then known as the Federal Reserve Board model. See Cassidy, "Estimates of the Aggregate Impact," p. 481.

77. Staff of the Office of Economic Research, *The Impact*, p. 136.

78. Ibid, p. 51.

79. Bevery L. Hadaway and Samuel C. Hadaway, "A Multiple Discriminant Model to Predict Savings and Loan Association Conversions," a paper presented at the October 1981 Financial Management Association annual meeting in Cincinnati, Ohio.

80. Walt Woerheide, "The Windfall Gains Associated with SLA Conversions: Reality or Myth?" *North Carolina Review of Business and Economics*, July 1980, pp. 15-16.

81. See Report by the Comptroller General, pp. 11-15.

82. These are depositors who have opened an account after the specified date used to determine eligible account holders.

83. It would appear that the managers could by-pass these restrictions on ownership by buying additional shares from the other shareholders immediately after conversions occur.

84. Report of the Comptroller General, p. 19.

85. See Beverly L. Hadaway, "An Evaluation of Performance Characteristic Differences between Converted and Mutual Savings and Loan Associations Using Discriminant Analysis," *Journal of Economics,* Fall 1980, pp. 126-30; Beverly Hadaway, "Conversions: Early Evidence of Their Impact on the Savings and Loan Industry," *The Housing Finance Review,* January 1982, pp. 23-42; Beverly Hadaway and Samuel C. Hadaway, "An Analysis of the Performance Characteristics of Converted Savings and Loan Associations," *Journal of Financial Research,* Fall 1981, pp. 195-206; Hadaway and Hadaway, "An Investigation of the Impact of Savings and Loan Association Conversions from Mutual to Stock Form of Ownership," Invited Research Working Paper No. 36, Federal Home Loan Bank Board, July 1980; Hadaway and Hadaway, "Converting to a Stock Company—Association Characteristics Before and After Conversion," *FHLBB Journal,* October 1980, pp. 20-22; and Beverly Hadaway, "Discretionary Managerial Behavior Effects of Savings and Loan Conversions: Competitive Implications for the Industry in a Deregulated Environment," a paper presented at the October 1982 Financial Management Association annual meeting in San Francisco, California.

86. Hadaway, "Conversions: Early Evidence," p. 41.

10

The Future

The greatest single determinant of the future of the thrift industry is certainly the level and the shape of the yield curve. As long as interest rates are at "high" levels, the thrift industry will be an ailing one. The longer the period of time over which the yield curve remains inverted, the more fatal the ailment is likely to be. Since the shape and location of the yield curve are beyond the control of the industry and its regulators, we shall proceed on the assumption that the interest rate environment in the future will at least be tolerable enough for an efficient thrift institution to survive.

As indicated at the start of this book, the various bail-out schemes for the industry which have been suggested in recent years would not be discussed. The reasons were twofold. First, such programs would at best only replenish some of the financial strength of the industry, without really changing the basic structure or risk exposure of SLAs. Even if the schemes were successful in shoring up the net worth of the industry, they would leave thrifts vulnerable to the same types of problems from which they are suffering today. This book has instead concentrated on those developments which have the promise of creating changes in the basic structure and risk exposure of the industry so that if it survives the current economic situation, future such situations should not have such disastrous effects. We have considered those topics affecting the long-term viability of the industry, ignored those topics affecting the immediate survival of the industry, and assumed that the industry will survive in some form.

The second reason for not discussing bail-out programs is that it appears in the current political environment that such schemes are not looked upon favorably. Certainly the Reagan administration is unenthusiastic about promoting a multitude of bail-out programs, and Congress seems intent on emphasizing deregulation where possible rather than governmental intervention. Even the President's Commission on Housing has heavily emphasized avoidance of government intervention and bail-out schemes.[1]

The conclusions from the various topics covered in the book are strongly suggestive that the changes occurring in the SLA industry will make it viable in the future. The most important changes are the deregulation of the mortgage instrument and the allowance of more efficient use of interest rate futures contracts. Both will enable SLA management to reduce substantially the duration mismatch which had previously been imposed. Other changes, such as the expansion of consumer lending authority, the authorization of NOW accounts, and the lifting of deposit rate ceilings, will provide some help for the duration mismatch, but their greatest contribution will likely be in the area of providing the ability to attract and retain customers for the SLAs' services.

If we accept the assumption that future interest rates will be such that efficient SLAs can survive, and the premise that the new powers afforded thrifts are sufficient to enable them to be efficient, then we are left only to ponder the structural changes that will likely occur in the industry. There are two specific structural issues. One is whether the industry will remain relatively homogeneous, and the second is whether the small associations are necessarily doomed to disappear.

FROM HOMOGENEOUS TO HETEROGENEOUS

In Chapter 2 we saw that the SLA industry was not a perfectly homogeneous industry in that SLAs were not identical in their operations, with financial statements that differed only by a scaling factor. Indeed, some SLAs acted somewhat like mortgage bankers, and others acted as "classical" thrifts which simply held their mortgages. There were also variations in the types of mortgages held (such as FHA and VA versus conventional, and single-family versus multi-family and commercial) and the types of financing utilized (such as more deposits and little borrowed money versus fewer deposits and more borrowed money). Despite these differences, the SLA industry could still be categorized as relatively homogeneous up through the late seventies in that they all had the vast majority of their assets invested in mortgages and financed these mortgages primarily with deposits.

The expanded asset and liability powers of recent years create the opportunity for the development of a more heterogeneous industry. Four different models of SLA operations may evolve. These include the "classical" thrift, a family finance center, an industrial-commercial lender, and a mortgage banker.[2] The "classical" thrift is probably the least likely to survive and will probably be found only in rural communities where there is not much competition. It would certainly suffer from the same interest rate risk exposure that SLAs have suffered from in the past. This "classical" SLA should continue as the dying part of the industry.

The family finance center model has long been touted by the FHLBB as the direction in which it sees the industry moving. This model is one in which the SLA attempts to provide as many of the financial services as any one family might want. The authorization of NOW accounts has been crucial in making the family finance center a reality. Once the SLA has grabbed a family's checking account business, then much of the other business should follow. This would include savings deposits, consumer loans, safe-deposit box rentals, stock brokerage transactions, debit and credit cards, and home insurance. This is not meant as an all-inclusive list but one which is representative of the broad services that could be offered. The family finance center would still make single-family home mortgages its primary asset, but consumer loans would become a significant asset holding.

It is not clear that all or even most SLAs will move toward this family finance center model since many of these services are in what are already highly competitive fields. Many banks, for example, are attempting to position themselves as family finance centers. Credit unions, many of which have grown large enough in recent years to offer a multitude of services, are also positioning themselves to be the dominant provider of financial services for families. Finally, even such operations as brokerage firms and retail stores are moving into offering many of the services that a family finance center would offer. This does not mean that an SLA would not find the family finance center profitable; it just means that there is a limit as to how many thrifts could compete in this area. By the end of this decade, perhaps less than half of the current members of the FHLBS would be identified as full-fledged family financial centers.

The third model is that of industrial-commercial lender. This type of thrift is the antithesis of the family finance center. As Dick Marcis describes it, "such an S&L will emphasize builder/developer business which may involve more short-term construction lending, acquisitions and real estate development loans."[3] This type of institution would likely not be a large part of the business, but it should be fairly distinctive. It would place less emphasis on deposits and more emphasis on borrowed money than would the family financial center.

The fourth model is that of mortgage banker. There should be ample opportunity for growth in the mortgage banking aspects of the SLA industry. The reasons include the continued development of a secondary market for all types of mortgages, coupled with an increased demand for pass-through securities such as the GNMA pass-through. The increased demand is shared both by individuals and institutions. Many older investors like the relative safety and monthly payments associated with the mortgage pass-through securities. Institutions such as pension funds have greater authority to hold mortgages in their portfolios and have shown a willingness to move into holding more mortgages. Like the industrial-commercial lender model, the mortgage banker operation would have less reliance on deposits and make greater use of borrowed money.

SURVIVAL OF THE BIGGEST?

Based on the few models of the various types of SLA operations that should evolve, a related issue that will evolve is whether small thrifts will be able to survive. The evidence to date indicates that if size is an issue in survival, then there is going to be difficulty in finding enough merger partners, but size is not necessarily a critical ingredient for survival.

The first point has been demonstrated recently by F. E. Balderston, who bases his study on four assumptions.[4] The first is that the "survivor" firms in any industry shake-up would be those which currently have over $300 million in total assets. The second is that all mergers would be made on an intra-district basis. The third is that 50 percent of all the firms within each district which have less than $300 million in total assets would become takeover candidates. The final assumption is that the number of acquisitions by each survivor firm is equal to the nationwide ratio of takeover candidates to survivor firms. Based on the 4,032 SLAs, as of June 30, 1980, Balderston identifies 378 as survivors and 1,827 as takeover candidates. The number of acquisitions by each survivor is rounded up to five, and the resultant number of unabsorbed firms is 428 located in eight districts.

When Balderston redefines a survivor firm as having $1 billion in total assets, the acquisition rate jumps to 20 and the number of unabsorbed firms rises to 687, also located in eight of the districts. The two conclusions from these data are that if size is a measure of survivorship, then a massive number of acquisitions will likely take place within the industry; and unless interdistrict and inter-industry mergers are given more serious consideration, there will be some districts in which there will not be the necessary absorption capacity.

Although Balderston indicates that several people have suggested that SLAs will need at least $1 billion in total assets to survive in the post-DIDMCA economy, he does not cite his sources for this observation.[5] Recent evidence by Rhoades and Savage would suggest that, at least in the pre-DIDMCA period, small SLAs were able to compete effectively against the larger associations.[6]

Rhoades and Savage used the financial statements of FSLIC-insured SLAs for the years 1974 to 1979. They arbitrarily allocated all SLAs located in SMSAs to eight size categories based on total assets. The smallest asset size class was $0 to $4.9 million in assets, and the largest was over $1 billion in total assets. Within each SMSA, they defined the smallest SLAs size as those SLAs in the smallest class which had at least one SLA provided the class was under $100 million in total assets. Similarly, the largest SLAs were those in the largest size category which had at least one SLA, provided the category was over $100 million in total assets. There were 204 SMSAs which provided comparisons for large and small SLAs and 99 SMSAs which provided comparisons for the second largest and second smallest SLAs. The largest and smallest and the second largest and second smallest SLAs were compared in the four categories of profitability, aggressiveness in making loans, risk, and deposit growth.

Rhoades and Savage found the larger SLAs more profitable when measured in terms of net income to total assets, but they found no significant differences when measured in terms of net income to net worth. The larger SLAs paid substantially more interest on deposit and nondeposit liabilities than the smaller associations, but the smaller ones had higher noninterest expenses. The smaller SLAs also had higher average mortgage yields than the larger ones. Although Rhoades and Savage find that the larger SLAs have a larger portion of their assets in loans and a larger portion specifically in real estate loans, they find no significant difference in deposit growth over the 1974 to 1979 period. They also find that the larger SLAs consistently have higher risk exposure. The larger associations have lower net-worth-to-total-assets ratios, higher nondeposit-liabilities-to-total-assets ratios, higher high-cost-deposits-to-total-deposits ratios, and lower liquid-assets-to-total-assets ratios.

The lower risk exposure of the smaller SLAs is certainly consistent with the lower ratios of net-income-to-total-assets. In fact, on a risk-adjusted basis, it may well be that the smaller SLAs have performed comparably to the large associations. Simply put, "there is *no* evidence that smaller institutions are not viable competitors in the big markets where they face large competitors."[7]

THE VALUE OF DEPOSIT INSURANCE

As was pointed out in Chapter 9, the thrift industry has technically been bankrupt for the last few years, in the sense that the market value of liabilities has exceeded the market value of the assets. Indeed, some writers have gone so far as to suggest that this market value insolvency has been the cause of the "silent run" on thrifts that has been occurring.[8] This "silent run" is the fact that withdrawals have been exceeding deposits for the majority of the months in recent years, yet there has been no specific event which has brought attention to this phenomenon. Recent evidence would suggest that it is not concern about the safety of the deposits at the thrifts that has produced this run but simply a desire to attain higher yields.[9] In a nationwide survey of the chief financial decision makers in 3,014 randomly selected households, 49 percent of the respondents indicated they had neither heard nor read about thrift difficulties, and only 5 percent of the survey sample indicated they believed thrifts were less safe than other financial institutions.[10]

Another interesting observation about the thrift industry is that many involuntary mergers still occur without the need for an endowment to the acquiring association. Obviously, the acquiring associations must believe that the bankrupt institutions are worth more than what is indicated by the market values of their assets and liabilities.

The lack of depositor concern about safety and thrift willingness to acquire bankrupt SLAs suggest the presence of values not recorded on financial statements. Edward Kane has argued that this valuable, intangible asset is the FSLIC deposit insurance.[11] Arguing that the cost of FSLIC insurance consists of implicit and explicit components, Kane suggests that the combined premiums have represented a substantial subsidy to the industry. The explicit premium is at the rate of one-twelfth of one percent per year of insured deposits. The implicit premium is the taxes the SLAs paid but could have avoided had they been willing to realize the losses on the market value of their mortgages over the years.[12] The losses were not realized because they would have reduced net worth below the amount required by FSLIC's net worth requirements.

Kane goes on to argue that not only has deposit insurance been a valuable, intangible asset to thrifts but that it has actually encouraged additional interest rate risk exposure. The reason is that the deposit premiums are insensitive to the interest rate risk exposure of a thrift. Thus, a thrift actually increases the value of its deposit insurance by increasing its interest rate risk exposure.[13]

These perverse consequences of deposit insurance have not gone unnoticed by the regulators. As pointed out in Chapter 1, an asset-composition-based net worth index was introduced in the late seventies. Insured SLAs were required to hold the larger net worth based on the traditional liability measures or based on the asset composition measures. The problem here is that using adjustable net worth requirements as an implicit risk premium is somewhat inefficient. It creates an opportunity cost of foregone leverage, and such a cost would be difficult to measure.

A more efficient method for controlling for risk is to make the explicit cost of the premiums directly dependent on the risk exposure of each thrift. Indeed, one such proposal is now being considered by the FHLBB.[14]

The most obvious technique to prevent the abuse of deposit insurance and to encourage the reduction of interest rate risk exposure would be to tie the level of deposit premiums to the magnitude of the duration mismatch.[15] This suggestion is made with the understanding that such a task would not be easy. As we have seen in the previous chapters, simply measuring the duration of any one asset or liability is a difficult task requiring several empirical assumptions. The calculation of the exact duration mismatch for a particular association will probably never be more than a calculated guess. Nonetheless, it is the most important direction in which industry regulation should now move.

CONCLUDING COMMENTS

One of the problems in past thinking about the SLA industry was the frequent assumption, either explicit or implicit, that a healthy thrift industry was a prerequisite for a healthy housing industry. In other words, the amount of mortgage money provided by thrifts was seen as an argument in the demand function for housing. But as Allan Meltzer has pointed out, that is simply not the case.[16] Rather, the demand for mortgage money is a derived function based on demand for housing. Efforts to increase the supply of mortgage money or decrease the cost of mortgage money will only tend to shift the demand for housing forward or backward in time. It has little effect on the aggregate demand for housing over time.[17] This means that all of the regulatory protection given the thrifts over the years in the name of the housing industry may have accomplished little for the housing industry.

This does not mean that nothing has been accomplished by such protection. The beneficiary has actually been the house-buying consumer. The incremental mortgage money which has been made available as a result of the regulatory favors given the thrift industry has provided the home buyer greater choice over the amount of equity money he invests in his own home and the amount of money he has available to make other purchases. As Meltzer points out, thrifts do not finance homes; they finance balance sheets.[18] The real by-product of the trend toward larger and longer mortgages (and thus lower downpayments and usually smaller monthly payments) has been a larger amount of debt on consumer balance sheets and more money available for other investments and other consumer purchases. Indirectly, SLAs have been in the consumer finance business for years.

The point here is that deregulation which makes the thrifts into a competitive rather than a sheltered industry will not necessarily hurt the housing industry. The home-buying consumer may well find that he has fewer choices in how much debt he issues. But his long-run demand for housing will not be drastically altered.

The reader has probably gathered by now that this author is reasonably optimistic about the future of the thrift industry. The duration mismatch from which the industry has long suffered can now be better managed through the use of adjustable mortgages, financial futures, interest rate options, consumer loans, market-rate deposits, and NOW accounts. Thrift associations will continue to exist, although as modified versions of what the industry has been.

NOTES

1. Dave F. Seiders, "The President's Commission on Housing Perspectives on Mortgage Finance," *Housing Finance Review,* October 1982, p. 325.

2. See, for example, Richard G. Marcis, "Implications of Financial Innovation and Reform for the Savings and Loan Industry," in "The Savings and Loan Industry in the 1980's," Research Working Paper No. 100, Office of Policy and Economic Research, Federal Home Loan Bank Board, December 1980; and Jack C. Harris, "Future Directions in American Home Finance," a paper presented at the 1982 meeting of the Southwestern Federation of Administrative Disciplines in Dallas, Texas.

3. Marcis, "Implications of Financial Reform," p. 6.

4. F.E. Balderston, "The Structural Option for the Savings and Loan Industry," *Housing Finance Review,* April 1982, pp. 193-207.

5. Balderston, "The Structural Option," p. 196.

6. Stephen A. Rhoades and Donald T. Savage, "Survival of the Small S&Ls," *The Bankers' Magazine,* September/October 1981, pp. 79-85.

7. Rhoades and Savage, "Survival of the Small S&Ls," p. 85.

8. Charlotte Chamberlain and Robert R. Shullman, "How Consumers See Thrifts: Safety, Rates, and Service," *Federal Home Loan Bank Board Journal,* September 1982, p. 2.

9. Ibid., p. 8.

10. Ibid., p. 3.

11. See Edward J. Kane, "S&Ls and Interest-Rate Reregulation: The FSLIC as an In-Place Bailout Program," *Housing Finance Review,* July 1982, pp. 219-43; and Edward J. Kane, "Regulation, Savings and Loan Diversification and the Flow of Housing Finance," *Savings and Loan Asset Management under Deregulation: Proceedings of the Sixth Annual Conference,* Federal Home Loan Bank of San Francisco, 1980, pp. 81-110.

12. Kane, "S&Ls and Interest-Rate Reregulation," p. 232.

13. Ibid., p. 241.

14. See, for example, Christopher Conte, "Bank Board May Raise Deposit Premiums to Cover Expected Costs of Aiding S&Ls," *Wall Street Journal,* March 31, 1983, p. 12.

15. See, for example, Gerald O. Bierwag, George G. Kaufman, and Alden Toevs, "Management Strategies for Savings and Loan Associations to Reduce Interest Rate Risk," *New Sources of Capital for the Savings and Loan Industry: Proceedings of the Fifth Annual Conference,* Federal Home Loan Bank of San Francisco, 1979, p. 196.

16. Allen Meltzer, "The Thrift Industry in the Reagan Era," *Managing Interest Rate Risk in the Thrift Industry: Proceedings of the Seventh Annual Conference,* Federal Home Loan Bank of San Francisco, 1981, pp. 5-13.

17. Ibid., p. 11.

18. Ibid., p. 10.

Bibliography

Albaum, Gerald, and George Kaufman. "Variable Rate Residential Mortgage: Implications for Borrowers." *Alternative Mortgage Instrument Research Study,* Vol. 1. Washington, D.C.: Federal Home Loan Bank Board, January 1978.

Alwan, Hadi, and Paul Hanchatt. "Reverse Mortgages, Estate Planning and the Financing of Real Estate." A paper presented at the 1981 Midwest Business Administration Association meeting in Chicago, Illinois.

American Mortgage Insurance Company. "Survey of Savings and Loan Associations' Adjustable Mortgages." Raleigh, N.C.: September 1981.

Altman, Edward I. "The Development of a Performance-Predictor System for Savings and Loan Associations." Invited Research Working Paper No. 10, Office of Economic Research, Federal Home Loan Bank Board, 1975.

_____. "Predicting Performance in the Savings and Loan Association Industry." *Journal of Monetary Economics,* 3 (October 1977), 443-66.

Andrew, John. "Acquired Had Little to Say in S&L Merger." *Wall Street Journal,* September 14, 1981, pp. 29, 34.

_____. "Assumable-Mortgages Ruling Seen further Hurting Market." *Wall Street Journal,* June 30, 1982, p. 25.

_____. "S&Ls Wary about Flexing New Muscles in the Riskier Commercial-Loan Arena." *Wall Street Journal,* October 5, 1982, p. 18.

Anreder, Steven S. "Built on Stilts: Overspeculation, Thin Margins Shake the Market for Ginnie Maes." *Barron's,* November 12, 1979.

Asay, Michael R. "Effects of NOW Accounts on Earnings and Competition in Commercial Banking: A Review of Theory and Evidence." Working Paper No. 26, Financial Studies Section, Board of Governors of the Federal Reserve System, April 1979.

_____ and Thomas Eric Kilcollin. "The Competitive Effects of NOW Accounts on Financial Institutions in New England." Working Paper No. 35, Financial Studies Section, Board of Governors of the Federal Reserve System, April 1980.

Atkinson, Jay. "The Structure of Cost in the Savings and Loan Industry during 1974." Research Working Paper No. 67, Office of Economic Research, Federal Home Loan Bank Board, March 1977.

_____. "Firm Size in the Savings and Loan Industry." Invited Research Working Paper No. 29, Office of Economic Research, Federal Home Loan Bank Board, December 1979.

Balderston, F.E. "The Structural Option for the Savings and Loan Industry." *Housing Finance Review,* Vol. 1, No. 2 (April 1982), 193-207.

Basch, Donald L. "Circumvention Innovations: The Case of NOW Accounts in Massachusetts, 1972-77." *Journal of Bank Research,* 13 (Autumn 1982), 160-67.

Benston, George. "Cost of Operations and Economies of Scale in Savings and Loan Associations," in Irwin Friend (ed.), Vol. 2, *Study of the Savings and Loan Industry,* Washington, D.C., GPO,1969.

Bercovici, Liza. "Shared Equity Mortgages Break New Legal Ground." *Real Estate Review,* 11 (Winter 1982), 58-61.

Biederman, Kenneth R., and John A. Tuccillo. *Taxation and Regulation of the Savings and Loan Industry.* Lexington, Mass.: D.C. Heath, 1976.

Bierwag, G.O., and George G. Kaufman. "Coping with the Risk of Interest Rate Fluctuations: A Note." *Journal of Business,* 50 (July 1977), 364-70.

———, ——— and A.L. Toevs. "Management Strategies for Savings and Loan Associations to Reduce Interest Rate Risk." *New Sources of Capital for the Savings and Loan Industry: Proceedings of the Fifth Annual Conference,* Federal Home Loan Bank of San Francisco, 1980.

Bleiberg, Robert. "Forgotten Man No Longer: The Saver of Modest Means May Finally Get His Due." *Barron's,* May 28, 1979, pp. 7-8, 10.

Board of Governors of the Federal Reserve System. *Ways to Moderate Fluctuations in Housing Construction.* Washington, D.C.: Government Printing Office, 1972.

Boltz, P.W. "Commercial Banking under Coordinated Ceiling Rates Payable by Banks and Thrift Institutions." Working Paper, Board of Governors of the Federal Reserve System, April 1978.

Booth, James R. "NOW Accounts: Competition in Western States." A paper presented at the 1981 Financial Management Association meeting in Cincinnati, Ohio.

Boudreaux, Kenneth J. "Managerialism and Risk Return Performance." *Southern Economic Journal,* 39 (January 1973), 366-72.

Boulding, Kenneth E. and Thomas Frederick Wilson, eds. *Redistribution through the Financial System.* New York: Praeger, 1978.

Boyce, Byrl N., and Keith B. Johnson. "Adjustable Rate Mortgages: The Experience in New England Thrifts prior to May 1981." A paper presented at the 1981 Eastern Finance Association meeting in Newport, Rhode Island.

Bradford, William. *Mergers in the Savings and Loan Industry.* Michigan Business Reports, No. 59, Division of Research, Graduate School of Business Administration, University of Michigan, 1977.

————. "Savings and Loan Association Mergers: Analysis of Recent Experience." *Review of Business and Economic Research,* 13 (Fall 1977), 1-18.

————. "The Performance of Merging Savings and Loan Associations." *Journal of Business,* 51 (January 1978), 115-25.

Brigham, Eugene F., and R. Richardson Petit. "Effects of Structure on Performance in the Savings and Loan Industry," in Irwin Friend (ed.), *Study of the Savings and Loan Industry,* Vol. 3, Washington, D.C., GPO, 1969, 971-1210.

Buckley, John M., Jr. "The Federal Home Loan Bank Board." *Federal Home Loan Bank Board Journal,* 15 (April 1982), 4-12.

Carberry, James, and G. Christian Hill. "Some Mortgage Firms Swap Lower Rates for Share in the Gain When Home is Sold." *Wall Street Journal,* August 22, 1980.

Carron, Andrew S. *The Plight of Thrift Institutions.* Washington, D.C.: Brookings Institution, 1982.

Cassidy, Henry J. "Estimates of the Aggregate Impact of Expected Windfalls for a Portion of the S&L Industry." *Journal of Money, Credit and Banking,* 8 (November 1976), 477-85.

_____. "The Changing Home Mortgage Instrument in the United States." *Federal Home Loan Bank Board Journal,* 11 (December 1978), 11-17.

_____. "S&L Branching and Operating Costs." Research Working Paper No. 75, Office of Economic Research, Federal Home Loan Bank Board, 1978.

_____. "Comparison and Analysis of the Consumer Safeguards of Variable Rate and Renegotiable Rate Mortgage Instruments." Research Working Paper No. 95, Office of Policy and Economic Research, Federal Home Loan Bank Board, 1980.

_____. "An Approach for Determining the Capital Requirement for Savings and Loan Associations." Research Working Paper No. 97, Office of Policy and Economic Research, Federal Home Loan Bank Board, 1980.

_____. "The Role of the Savings and Loan Associations in the 1980s," in "The Savings and Loan Industry in the 1980s." Research Working Paper No. 100, Office of Policy and Economic Research, Federal Home Loan Bank Board, December 1980.

_____. "Price Level Adjusted Mortgages versus Other Mortgage Instruments." *Federal Home Loan Bank Board Journal,* 14 (January 1981).

Chamberlain, Charlotte, and Robert R. Shullman. "How Consumers See Thrifts: Safety, Rates, and Service." *Federal Home Loan Bank Board Journal,* 15 (September 1982), 2-8.

Chase, Kristine. "Interest Rate Deregulation, Branching, and Competition in the Savings and Loan Industry." *Federal Home Loan Bank Board Journal,* 14 (November 1981).

Clotfelter, Charles, and Charles Liberman. "On the Redistribution Impact of Federal Interest Rate Ceilings." *Journal of Finance,* 33 (March 1978), 199-213.

Cohn, Richard, and Stanley Fischer. "An Analysis of Alternative Nonstandard Mortgages." *Mortgage Study Reports,* Report No. 5, December 1974.

Cole, David W. "Measuring Savings and Loan Profitability." *Federal Home Loan Bank Board Journal,* 4 (October 1971), 1-7.

Colton, Kent W. "Financial Reform: A Review of the Past and Prospects for the Future." Invited Research Working Paper No. 37, Office of Policy and Economic Research, Federal Home Loan Bank Board, September 1980.

_____, Donald Lessard, and Arthur Solomon. "Borrower Attitudes toward Alternative Mortgage Instruments." Invited Research Working Paper No. 31, Office of Policy and Economic Research, Federal Home Loan Bank Board, January 1980.

Comptroller General of the United States. *Converting Savings and Loan Associations from Mutual to Stock Ownership—A National Policy Needed.* Washington, D.C.: General Accounting Office, 1979.

Conte, Christopher. "Bank Board May Raise Deposit Premiums to Cover Expected Costs of Aiding S&Ls." *Wall Street Journal,* March 31, 1983, p. 12.

Cox, John C., Jonathon E. Ingersoll, Jr., and Stephen A. Ross. "Duration and the Measurement of Basis Risk." *Journal of Business,* 52 (January 1979), 51-61.

Cox, William N. "NOW Pricing: Perspectives and Objectives." *Economic Review of the Federal Reserve Bank of Atlanta,* (February 1981), 22-25.

Crockett, John, and A. Thomas King. "The Contributions of New Asset Powers to the S&L

Earnings: A Comparison of Federal- and State-Chartered Associations in Texas." Research Working Paper No. 110, Office of Policy and Economic Research, Federal Home Loan Bank Board, July 1982.

Dann, Larry, and Christopher James. "An Analysis of the Impact of Deposit Rate Ceilings on the Market Values of Thrift Institutions." *Journal of Finance,* 37 (December 1982), 1259-75.

Diller, Stanley. "Near-Term Optimization or Duration as Measure of Bond Price Volatility." *The Money Manager,* February 5, 1979.

Dince, Robert R., and James A. Verbrugge. "The Right Way to Save the S&Ls." *Fortune,* August 10, 1981.

Dixon, J. R., III. "Going Stock: Escape from a Dilemma." *Federal Home Loan Bank Board Journal,* 12 (February 1979), 22, 24.

Donahoe, F. Marion. "Conversion to a Stock Association." *Federal Home Loan Bank Board Journal,* 4 (August 1971), 21-22.

Donlan, Thomas G. "Fall from Grace." *Barron's,* December 7, 1981, p. 30.

Draper, Daniel C. "Alternative Mortgage Instruments." *Real Estate Review,* 11 (Fall 1981), 32-38.

Edmister, Robert O. *Financial Institutions: Markets and Management.* New York: McGraw-Hill, 1980.

Eisenbeis, Robert A., and Myron L. Kwast. "The Implications of Expanded Portfolio Powers on S&L Institution Performance." A paper presented at the 1982 Financial Management Association meeting in San Francisco, California.

Federal Home Loan Bank Board. *A Financial Institution for the Future: Savings, Housing Finance, Consumer Services: An Examination of the Restructuring of the Savings and Loan Industry.* Washington, D.C.: Government Printing Office, 1975.

Feldstein, Martin. "Why Short-Term Interest Rates are High." *Wall Street Journal,* June 8, 1982, p. 26.

Findlay, M. Chapman, III, and Dennis Capozza. "The Variable-Rate Mortgage and Risk in the Mortgage Market: An Option Theory Perspective." *Journal of Money, Credit and Banking,* 9 (May 1977).

Fisher, Larry, and Roman Weil. "Coping with the Risk of Interest Rate Fluctuations: Returns to Bondholders from Naive and Optimal Strategies." *Journal of Business,* 44 (October 1971),408-31.

Follain, James, and Raymond Struyk. "Homeownership Effects of Alternative Mortgage Instruments." *American Real Estate and Urban Economics Association Journal,* 5 (Spring 1977), 1-43.

Frankle, Charles T., and Andrew J. Senchack, Jr. "Economic Considerations in the Use of Interest Rate Futures." *The Journal of Futures Markets,* 2 (Spring 1982), 107-16.

Fraser, Donald R. "DIDMCA and the Savings and Loan Industry: Evidence from a Survey." *Federal Home Loan Bank Board Journal,* 15 (January 1982), 2-8.

Freiberg, Lewis. "The Problem with SAM: An Economic and Policy Analysis." *Housing Finance Review,* Vol. 1, No. 1 (January 1982), 73-91.

Friend, Irwin, ed. *Study of the Savings and Loan Industry.* 4 vols. Washington, D.C.: Federal Home Loan Bank Board, 1969.

Frodin, Joanne H., and Richard Startz. "The NOW Account Experiment and the Demand for Money." Working Paper No. 11-79, Rodney F. White Center for Financial Research, University of Pennsylvania, 1979.

_____ and _____. "The NOW Account Experiment and the Demand for Money." *Journal of Banking and Finance,* 6 (June 1982), 179-93.

Gilbert, R. Alton. "Will the Removal of Regulation Q Raise Mortgage Interest Rates?" *Federal Reserve Bank of St. Louis Review,* 63 (December 1981), 3-12.

Glassman, Cynthia A., and Stephen A. Rhoades. "Owner vs. Manager Control Effects on Bank Performance." *The Review of Economics and Statistics,* 62 (May 1980), 263-70.

Grebler, Leo. *The Future of Thrift Institutions in the United States.* Danville, Ill.: Joint Savings and Loan and Mutual Savings Banks Exchange Groups, 1969.

Griffith, Reynolds, and Zack E. Mason. "The Adjustable Rate Mortgage: Which Index is Best?" A paper presented at the 1982 Southwestern Federation of Administrative Disciplines meeting in Dallas, Texas.

Grove, M.A. "On 'Duration' and the Optimal Maturity Structure of the Balance Sheet." *The Bell Journal of Economics and Management Science,* 5 (Autumn 1974), 696-709.

Grover, Allan M. "Choosing the Right VRM Index." *Federal Home Loan Bank Board Journal,* 13 (August 1980), 4-7.

Guenther, Robert. "Two Mortgage Ideas Fizzle . . . Granny Flats . . . Rental Advice." *Wall Street Journal,* March 31, 1982.

Hadaway, Beverly L. "An Evaluation of Performance Characteristic Differences Between Converted and Mutual Savings and Loan Associations Using Discriminant Analysis." *Journal of Economics,* Fall 1980, 126-30.

_____. "Conversions: Early Evidence of Their Impact on the Savings and Loan Industry." *The Housing Finance Review,* Vol. 1, No. 1 (January 1982), 23-42.

_____. "Alternative Mortgage Activity in the Ninth Federal Home Loan Bank District." *Federal Home Loan Bank Board Journal,* 15 (August 1982), 6-11.

_____. "Discretionary Managerial Behavior Effects of Savings and Loan Conversions: Competitive Implications for the Industry in a Deregulated Environment." A paper presented at the 1982 Financial Management Association meeting in San Francisco, California.

_____ and Samuel C. Hadaway. "An Investigation of the Impact of Savings and Loan Association Conversions from Mutual to Stock Form of Ownership." Invited Research Working Paper No. 36, Office of Policy and Economic Research, Federal Home Loan Bank Board, July 1980.

_____ and _____. "Converting to a Stock Company—Association Characteristics Before and After Conversion." *Federal Home Loan Bank Board Journal,* 13 (October 1980), 20-22.

_____ and _____. "A Multiple Discriminant Model to Predict Savings and Loan Association Conversions." A paper presented at the 1981 Financial Management Association meeting in Cincinnati, Ohio.

_____ and _____. "An Analysis of the Performance Characteristics of Converted Saving and Loan Associations." *Journal of Financial Research,* 4 (Fall 1981), 195-206.

Halloran, John A. "Mortgage Risk in a Portfolio Theory Context." *Journal of the Midwest Finance Association,* 7 (1978), 107-20.

Harris, Jack C. "The Cloudy Future for S&Ls." *Collegiate Forum,* Fall 1981.

_____. "Future Directions in American Home Finance." A paper presented at the

1982 Southwestern Federation of Administrative Disciplines meeting in Dallas, Texas.

Hartzog, B.G., Jr. "The Impact of NOW Accounts on Savings and Loan Behavior and Performance." *Quarterly Review of Economics and Business,* 19 (Autumn 1979), 97-108.

―――――. "Nationwide NOW Accounts: Questions and Answers." *Federal Home Loan Bank Board Journal,* 13 (January 1980), 2-5.

―――――, Robert Losey, and Walt Woerheide. "The Effect of the 'Wild Card' Experiment on Savings Flows at SLAs." A paper presented at the 1979 Southern Finance Association meeting in Atlanta, Georgia.

Hess, Alan C. "Duration Analysis for Savings and Loan Associations." *Federal Home Loan Bank Board Journal,* 15 (October 1982), 12-14.

Higgins, Byron. "Interest Payments on Demand Deposits: Historical Evolution and the Current Controversy." *Monthly Review,* Federal Reserve Bank of Kansas City, 62 (July-August 1977), 3-15.

Hill, G. Christian. "Lenders Pushing Second Mortgages to Ease Pinch of Long-Term Loans." *Wall Street Journal,* November 4, 1980.

―――――. "FSLIC's Rescue Efforts Criticized as Unsound Use of Agency's Capital." *Wall Street Journal,* January 9, 1981.

―――――. "Growing-Equity Home Loans are Gaining Popularity because of Quick Repayments." *Wall Street Journal,* October 6, 1982.

――――― and John Andrew. "U.S. Expected to Cut Costly Efforts to Force Mergers of Troubled S&Ls." *Wall Street Journal,* February 17, 1982, pp. 23, 42.

――――― and ―――――. "Power to Call in Mortgages upon Sale of Homes is Seen Being Given All Thrifts." *Wall Street Journal,* June 29, 1982.

――――― and Paul A. Gigot. "Federal Regulators Are Said to Sanction Merger among Ailing Savings and Loans." *Wall Street Journal,* February 18, 1982, p. 4.

Hirshen, Alvin, and Susan Evans. "Revitalizing America's Older Communities: More than 400 S&L's Using $1.13 Billion in CIF Funds." *Federal Home Loan Bank Board Journal,* 12 (February 1979), 2-10.

Holdren, Don. "NOW Accounts: A Comment on Competitive Pricing." A paper presented at the 1981 Financial Management Association meeting in Cincinnati, Ohio.

Holland, Daniel. "Tax and Regulatory Problems Posed by Alternative Nonstandard Mortgages." *New Mortgage Designs for an Inflationary Environment: Proceedings of a Conference Held at Cambridge, Massachusetts, January 1975,* edited by Franco Modigliani and Donald Lessard.

Hollie, Pamela G. "Savings and Loans Opposing Conditions Imposed on Mergers." *New York Times,* May 21, 1981, Sect. 2, p. 30.

Hunt Commission. *Report of the President's Commission on Financial Structure and Regulation.* Washington, D.C.: Government Printing Office, 1971.

Iezman, Stanley L. "The Shared Appreciation Mortgage and the Shared Equity Program." *Real Estate Review,* 10 (Fall 1981), 40-52.

Institutions, Policies and Economic Performance. Carnegie-Rochester Conference Series on Public Policy, Vol. 4, 1976.

Jackson, Brooks. "Regulators Seek to Ease Anxieties over Dismal State of S&L Industry." *Wall Street Journal,* March 20, 1981.

―――――. "Mergers Are Set for 2 Failing S&Ls; Cost to U.S. Agency is Called Substantial." *Wall Street Journal,* June 2, 1981.

Jaffee, Dwight M. "Eliminating Deposit Rate Ceilings." *Federal Home Loan Bank Board Journal,* 6 (August 1973), 4-12.

_____. "What to Do about Savings and Loan Associations?" *Journal of Money, Credit and Banking,* 6 (November 1974), 537-49.

_____. "The Federal Home Loan Bank System Since 1965." *Institutions, Policies and Economic Performance,* Carnegie-Rochester Conference Series on Public Policy, Vol. 4, 1976.

_____. "Interest Rate Hedging Strategies for Savings and Loan Associations." *Managing Interest Rate Risk in the Thrift Industry: Proceedings of the Seventh Annual Conference,* Federal Home Loan Bank of San Francisco, 1981, 83-106.

_____ and Kenneth T. Rosen. "A Monthly Forecasting Model of Deposits, Mortgages, Advances, and Housing." A paper presented at the 1978 Mid-Year American Real Estate and Urban Economics Association meeting in Washington, D.C.

_____ and _____. "Mortgage Credit Availability and Residential Construction." *Brookings Papers on Economic Activity,* No. 2 (1979), 333-76.

_____ and _____. "The Changing Liability Structure of Savings and Loan Associations." *Journal of the American Real Estate and Urban Economics Association,* 8 (Spring 1980), 33-49.

_____ and _____. "Deposit Costs and Mortgage Rates: Reply." *Housing Finance Review,* Vol. 1, No. 1 (January 1982), 49-53.

Kalish, Lionel, and Joseph A. McKenzie. "The Influence of Portfolio Drag on a Savings and Loan Association's Current Mortgage Lending Policy." Research Working Paper No. 69, Office of Economic Research, Federal Home Loan Bank Board, January 1978.

Kane, Edward J. "Short-Changing the Small Saver: Federal Government Discrimination against Small Savers during the Vietnam War." *Journal of Money, Credit and Banking,* 2 (November 1970), 513-22.

_____. "Getting Along without Regulation Q: Testing the Standard View of Deposit Rate Competition during the 'Wild-Card Experience.'" *Journal of Finance,* 33 (June 1978), 921-32.

_____. "Reregulation, Savings and Loan Diversification and the Flow of Housing Finance." *Savings and Loan Asset Management Under Deregulation: Proceedings of the Sixth Annual Conference,* Federal Home Loan Bank of San Francisco, 1980.

_____. "S&Ls and Interest-Rate Reregulation: The FSLIC as an In-Place-Bailout Program." *Housing Finance Review,* Vol. 1, No. 3 (July 1982), 219-43.

Kaplan, Donald M., and David L. Smith. "The Role of Short-Term Debt in Savings and Loan Liability Management." *New Sources of Capital for the Savings and Loan Industry: Proceedings of the Fifth Annual Conference,* Federal Home Loan Bank of San Francisco, 1979.

Kaufman, George. "The Questionable Benefit of Variable Rate Mortgages." *Quarterly Review of Economics and Business,* Vol. 13, No. 3 (Autumn 1973), 43-52.

_____. "Duration, Planning Period, and Tests of the Capital Asset Pricing Model." *The Journal of Financial Research,* 1 (Spring 1980), 1-10.

_____ and Eleanor Erdevig. "Improving Housing Finance in an Inflationary Environment: Alternative Residential Mortgage Instruments." *Economic Perspectives,* Federal Reserve Bank of Chicago, 5 (July/August 1981), 1-23.

_____, Larry Mote, and Harvey Rosenblum. "Implications of Deregulation for Product Lines and Geographical Markets of Financial Institutions." A paper presented at the Eighteenth Conference on Bank Structure and Competition, Federal Reserve Bank of Chicago, April 1982.

Kichline, James L. "Prospects for Institutional Reforms of the Major Depository Intermediaries," in Board of Governors of the Federal Reserve System, *Ways to Moderate Fluctuations in Housing Construction,* Washington, D.C., 1972, 282-300.

Kidwell, David S., and Richard Peterson. *Financial Institutions, Markets, and Money.* Hinsdale, Ill.: Dryden Press, 1981.

Kilcollin, Thomas Eric, and Gerald A. Hanweck. "Regulation Q and Commercial Bank Profitability." Research Papers in Banking and Financial Economics, Federal Reserve System, March 1981.

Kimball, Ralph C. "The Maturing of the NOW Account in New England." *New England Economic Review,* July/August 1978, 27-42.

_____. "Variations in the New England NOW Account Experiment." *New England Economic Review,* November/December 1980, 23-39.

King, A. Thomas. "The Deposit Rate and the Mortgage Rate: Does Regulation Q Promote Homeownership?" Research Working Paper No. 85, Office of Economic Research, Federal Home Loan Bank Board, September 1979.

_____. "Discrimination in Mortgage Lending: A Study of Three Cities." Research Working Paper No. 91, Office of Policy and Economic Research, Federal Home Loan Bank Board, February 1980.

Kling, Arnold. "Son of SAM: A Proposal for a Deferred-Payment Mortgage." *Housing Finance Review,* Vol. 1, No. 1 (January 1982), 93-102.

Kolb, Robert, John Corgel, and Raymond Chiang. "Effective Hedging of Mortgage Interest Rate Risk." *Housing Finance Review,* Vol. 1, No. 2 (April 1982), 135-46.

_____ and Gerald D. Gay. "Immunizing Bond Portfolios with Interest Rate Futures." *Financial Management,* Vol. 11, No. 2 (Summer 1982), 81-89.

Kreutz, Oscar R. *The Way It Happened.* St. Petersburg, Fla: St. Petersburg Printing Company, 1972.

Lapp, John S. "The Determination of Savings and Loan Association Deposit Rates in the Absence of Rate Ceilings: A Cross-Section Approach." *Journal of Finance,* 33 (March 1978), 215-30.

Lindbeck, Rudolph, and John S. Jahera, Jr. "Thrift Institution Mergers: Income Tax Effects." *Federal Home Loan Bank Board Journal,* 15 (October 1982), 8-11.

Long, Jody. "Florida S&Ls, Expecting Deregulation to Step Up Competition, Grid for Battle." *Wall Street Journal,* April 28,1983, p. 54.

Losey, Robert L., and Susan Kelsey. "Interest Rate, Default, and Basis Risk in Hedging Fixed Rate Conventional Mortgages." *Federal Home Loan Bank Board Journal,* 14 (November 1981), 10-12.

Lundsten, Lorman, and Lewis Mandell. "Consumer Selection of Banking Space—Effects of Distance, Services, and Interest Rate Differentials." *Proceedings of a Conference on Bank Structure and Competition,* Federal Reserve Bank of Chicago, April 28-29, 1977, 260-86.

Macaulay, Frederick R. *Some Theoretical Problems Suggested by the Movements of Interest Rates, Bond Yields, and Stock Prices in the United States since 1856.* New York: Columbia University Press, 1938.

Managing Interest Rate Risk in the Thrift Industry: Proceedings of the Seventh Annual Conference. San Francisco, Calif.: Federal Home Loan Bank of San Francisco, 1981.

Mandell, Lewis, and Neil B. Murphy. "NOW Accounts: The First Decade." A paper presented at the 1981 Financial Management Association meeting in Cincinnati, Ohio.

Maness, Terry S., and A. J. Senchack. "Hedging the Cost of Money Market Certificates by Savings and Loan Associations." A paper presented at the 1982 Southwestern Federation of Administrative Disciplines meeting in Dallas, Texas.

Marcis, Richard G. "Implications of Financial Innovation and Reform for the Savings and Loan Industry," in "The Savings and Loan Industry in the 1980's." Research Working Paper No. 100, Office of Policy and Economic Research, Federal Home Loan Bank Board, December 1980.

_____ and Dale Riordan. "The Savings and Loan Industry in the 1980's." *Federal Home Loan Bank Board Journal,* 13 (May 1980), 2-15.

_____ and Jerry Hartzog. "NOW Accounts: Significant Advantages for New England." *Federal Home Loan Bank Board Journal,* 11 (June 1978), 2-6, 38.

Maris, Brian. "Consumer Lending by S&Ls: The Prospects." *Federal Home Loan Bank Board Journal,* 13 (May 1980), 20-26.

_____. "Savings and Loans and Consumer Credit: An Assessment." Research Working Paper No. 94, Office of Policy and Economic Research, Federal Home Loan Bank Board, April 1980.

Marvell, Thomas B. *Federal Home Loan Bank Board.* New York: Praeger, 1969.

McEnally, Richard W. "Duration as a Practical Tool for Bond Management." *Journal of Portfolio Management,* 3 (Summer 1977), 53-57.

_____. "A Comprehensive Look at Shared-Appreciation Mortgages." *Federal Home Loan Bank Board Journal,* 13 (November 1980), 11-15.

McKenzie, Joseph A. "Simulation Analysis of Rollover Mortgage Portfolios." Research Working Paper No. 98, Office of Policy and Economic Research, Federal Home Loan Bank Board, June 1980.

_____. "A Comprehensive Look at Shared-Appreciation Mortgages." *Federal Home Loan Bank Board Journal,* 13 (November 1980), 11-15.

_____. "A Borrower's Guide to Alternate Mortgage Instruments." *Federal Home Loan Bank Board Journal,* 15 (January 1982), 16-22.

McLean, Ken. "Legislative Background of the Depository Institution Deregulation and Monetary Control Act of 1980." *Savings and Loan Asset Management Under Deregulation: Proceedings of the Sixth Annual Conference,* Federal Home Loan Bank of San Francisco, 1980.

McNulty, James E. "Real Estate Financing." *Real Estate Review,* 11 (Winter 1982), 12-14.

_____ and William E. Chalker. "The Forward Commitment Market for Mortgage-Backed Securities." *Federal Home Loan Bank Board Journal,* 13 (June 1980), 2-15.

Meador, Mark. "The Effects on Mortgage Repayments of Restrictions on the Enforcement of Due-on-Sale Clauses: Aggregate and Micro California Results." Research Working Paper No. 107, Office of Policy and Economic Research, Federal Home Loan Bank Board, August 1982.

Meagher, James P. "Due-on-Sale: A Day in Court." *Barron's,* April 19, 1982.

_____. "Fast-Payoff Mortgages Win a Fan." *Barron's,* July 19, 1982.

_____. "An Office Space Glut . . . More on GEMs." *Barron's,* August 2, 1982.

Meltzer, Allen. "The Thrift Industry in the Reagan Era." *Managing Interest Rate Risk*

in the Thrift Industry: Proceedings of the Seventh Annual Conference, Federal
　　Home Loan Bank of San Francisco, 1981, 5-13.
Meyer, Thomas, and Harold Nathan. "Mortgage Rates and Regulation Q." Working Paper
　　Series No. 171, Department of Economics, University of California-Davis, July
　　1981.
Modigliani, Franco, and Donald Lessard, eds. *New Mortgage Designs for an Inflationary
　　Environment: Proceedings of a Conference Held at Cambridge, Massachusetts.*
　　Federal Reserve Bank of Boston Conference Series, Vol. 14, 1975.
Monsen, Joseph R., John S. Y. Chiu, and David E. Colley. "The Effect of Separation of
　　Ownership and Control on the Performance of the Large Firm." *Quarterly Journal
　　of Economics,* 82 (August 1968), 435-51.
Morgan, George Emir, and Susan M. Becker. "Environmental Factors in Pricing NOW
　　Accounts in 1981." *Journal of Bank Research,* 13 (Autumn 1982), 168-78.
Morris, Frank. "The Test of Price Control in Banking." *New England Economic Review,*
　　Federal Reserve Bank of Boston, May/June, 1979.
Mortlock, E. M. "New Housing Law Benefits Savings and Loan Associations." *Commercial
　　and Financial Chronical,* September 1964.
Murphy, Neil B. "Testing the Effect of Thrift Institution Escape from Federal Deposit
　　Interest Ceilings: The Case of Co-operative Banks in Massachusetts." A paper
　　presented at the 1975 Midwest Finance Association meeting in Chicago, Illinois.
Myler, Kathleen. "Foreclosure Change Seen Aiding Illinois Mortgage Resales." *Chicago
　　Tribune,* October 11, 1981.
*New Sources of Capital for the Savings and Loan Industry: Proceedings of the Fifth
　　Annual Conference.* San Francisco: Federal Home Loan Bank of San Francisco,
　　1979.
Nicols, Alfred. *Management and Control in the Mutual Savings and Loan Association.*
　　Lexington, Mass.: D. C. Heath and Company, 1972.
Ozanne, Larry. "The Financial Stakes in Due-on-Sale: The Case of California's State-
　　Chartered Savings and Loans." Research Working Paper No. 109, Office of Policy
　　and Economic Research, Federal Home Loan Bank Board, July 1982.
Paulus, John D. "Effects of 'NOW' Accounts on Costs and Earnings of Commercial
　　Banks in 1974-5." Staff Economic Study No. 88, Board of Governors of the
　　Federal Reserve System, 1976.
Peterson, Richard L., and Debra A. Drecnik. "Second Mortgage Survey, 1979." Working
　　Paper No. 33, Credit Research Center, Purdue University, 1980.
_____. "Consumer Lending by S&Ls." *Savings and Loan Asset Management
　　under Deregulation: Proceedings of the Sixth Annual Conference,* Federal Home
　　Loan Bank of San Francisco, 1980.
Peterson, William M. "The Effects of Interest Rate Ceilings on the Number of Banking
　　Offices in the United States." Research Paper No. 8103, Federal Reserve Bank
　　of New York, 1981.
Phillips, Susan M., and Paula A. Tosini. "A Comparison of Margin Requirements for
　　Options and Futures." *Financial Analysts Journal,* November/December 1982,
　　54-58.
Pyle, David H. "Interest Rate Ceilings and Net Worth Losses by Savers," in Kenneth E.
　　Boulding and Thomas Frederick Wilson, eds., *Redistribution through the Fi-
　　nancial System,* Praeger Publications, 1978, 87-101.
_____. "The Losses on Savings Deposits from Interest Rate Regulation." *The*

Bell Journal of Economics and Management Science, 10 (Autumn 1979), 614-22.

_____. "Deposit Costs and Mortgage Rates." *Housing Finance Review,* Vol. 1, No. 1 (January 1982), 43-48.

Raper, H. David. "Converting the Elderly Homeowner's Equity into Income." *Real Estate Review,* 12 (Summer 1982), 123-27.

Rhoades, Stephen A., and Donald T. Savage. "Survival of the Small S&Ls." *The Bankers' Magazine,* 164 (September/October 1981), 79-85.

Riordan, Dale P., and Jerry Hartzog. "The Impact of the Deregulation Act on Policy Choices of the Federal Home Loan Bank Board." *Savings and Loan Asset Management Under Deregulation: Proceedings of the Sixth Annual Conference,* Federal Home Bank of San Francisco, 1980, 33-58.

Rochester, David P., and Walter P. Neeley. "New Evidence of Synergy from Merging Savings and Loan Associations." A paper presented at the 1981 Southern Finance Association meeting in New Orleans, Louisiana.

Rose, Peter S., and Kenneth D. Riener. "Competing for Consumer Dollars with NOW Accounts." *Business Horizons,* 23 (October 1980), 74-78.

Rosen, Kenneth T. "Deposit Deregulation and Risk Management in an Era of Transition." *Managing Interest Rate Risk in the Thrift Industry: Proceedings of the Seventh Annual Conference,* Federal Home Loan Bank of San Francisco, 1981, 15-34.

Rosenblum, Harvey. "Interest Rate Volatility, Regulation Q, and the Problems of Thrift Institutions." *Proceedings of a Conference on Bank Structure and Competition,* May 1 and 2, 1980, Federal Reserve Bank of Chicago, 16-42.

_____. "Liability Strategies for Minimizing Interest Rate Risk." *Managing Interest Rate Risk in the Thrift Industry: Proceedings of the Seventh Annual Conference,* Federal Home Loan Bank of San Francisco, 1982.

Savings and Loan Asset Management under Deregulation: Proceedings of the Sixth Annual Conference. San Francisco, California: Federal Home Loan Bank of San Francisco, 1980.

"The Savings and Loan Industry in the 1980's." Research Working Paper No. 100, Office of Policy and Economic Research, Federal Home Loan Bank Board, 1980.

Schellhardt, Timothy D. "U.S. Assisted S&L Merger Seen Topping 1981's Record 23, Bank Board Aide Says." *Wall Street Journal,* January 18, 1982.

_____. "S&Ls Had Record $4.6 Billion Loss in '81; $6 Billion Deficit Seen Possible This Year." *Wall Street Journal,* April 6, 1982.

_____. "Thrifts Cleared to Enter Securities Field by Bank Board; Legal Challenges Likely." *Wall Street Journal,* May 7, 1982.

Scholes, Myron S. "The Economics of Hedging and Spreading in Futures Markets." *The Journal of Futures Markets,* 1 (Summer 1981), 265-86.

Seiders, Dave F. "The Presidents' Commission on Housing Perspectives on Mortgage Finance." *Housing Finance Review,* Vol. 1, No. 4 (October 1982), 323-48.

_____. "Changing Patterns of Housing Finance." *Federal Reserve Bulletin,* Board of Governors of the Federal Reserve System, June 1981.

Sharma, Jandhyala L. "Creative Financing Techniques Will Not Save the S&Ls." *Real Estate Review,* 11 (Fall 1981), 111-14.

Shellenberger, Sue. "Demise of an S&L in Chicago is Linked to Belief That Interest Rates Would Fall." *Wall Street Journal,* June 5, 1981.

Sichelman, Lew. "'No-interest' Loans of Interest to FTC." *Chicago Tribune,* February 21, 1982.

Sloan, Allan. "The Thrifts." *Forbes,* January 4, 1982, 83-84.

Smith, David L., Donald M. Kaplan, and William F. Ford. "Profitability: Why Some Associations Perform Far above Average." *Federal Home Loan Bank Board Journal,* 10 (November 1977), 7-13.

Smith, James. "Measuring Economic Strain under Alternative Mortgage Instruments." Invited Working Paper No. 27, Office of Policy and Economic Research, Federal Home Loan Bank Board, September 1979.

Smith, Paul. "Response of Consumer Loans to General Credit Conditions." *American Economic Review,* 48 (September 1958), 649-55.

Smith, Shelby J. "Texas S&Ls: Implications for Consumer Lending." Invited Research Working Paper No. 13, Office of Economic Research, Federal Home Loan Bank Board, 1976.

Simonson, Donald G., and Peter C. Marks. "Breakeven Balances on NOW Accounts: Perils in Pricing." *Journal of Bank Research,* 11 (Autumn 1980), 187-91.

——————— and ———————. "Pricing NOW Accounts and the Cost of Bank Funds, Part One: Break Even Analysis of NOW Accounts." *The Magazine of Bank Administration,* November 1980, 28-31.

——————— and ———————. "Pricing NOW Accounts and the Cost of Bank Funds, Part Two: NOWs and the Cost of Funds." *The Magazine of Bank Administration,* December 1980, 21-24.

Spellman, Lewis J. "Deposit Ceilings and the Efficiency of Financial Intermediation." *Journal of Finance,* 35 (March 1980), 129-36.

———————. "Commercial Banks and the Profits of Savings and Loan Markets." *Journal of Bank Research,* 12 (Spring 1981).

Staff of the Office of Economic Research. *The Impact of "Free Distribution" Conversion Windfalls on the Savings and Loan Industry.* Washington, D.C.: Federal Home Loan Bank Board, 1974.

Stigum, Marcia L. "Some Further Implications of Profit Maximization by a Savings and Loan Association." *Journal of Finance,* 31 (December 1976), 1405-26.

Taggert, Robert A., Jr. "Effects of Deposit Rate Ceilings: The Evidence from Massachusetts Savings Banks." *Journal of Money, Credit and Banking,* 10 (May 1978), 139-57.

——————— and Geoffry Woglom. "Savings Bank Reactions to Rate Ceilings and Rising Market Rates." *New England Economic Review,* Federal Reserve Bank of Boston, September/October 1978, 17-31.

Theobald, A.D. *Forty-Five Years on the Up Escalator.* Private printing, 1975.

Thygerson, Kenneth J. "The Case for Savings and Loan Participation in the Consumer Credit Market." Working Paper No. 4, U.S. League of Savings Associations, Chicago, Ill., 1973.

———————. "The Effect of Government Housing and Mortgage Credit Programs on Savings and Loan Associations." Occasional Paper No. 6, U.S. League of Savings Associations, Chicago, Ill., 1973.

———————. "Futures, Options, and the Savings and Loan Business." *Savings and Loan Asset Management Under Deregulation: Proceedings of the Sixth Annual Conference,* Federal Home Loan Bank of San Francisco, 1980, 119-47.

Understanding the Delivery Process. Chicago: The Board of Trade of the City of Chicago, 1980.

Unger, Michael L. "The Community Reinvestment Act and the Community Lending Activities of Savings and Loan Associations." A paper presented at the 1979 Midwest Finance Association meeting in Chicago, Illinois.

U.S. Congress, House. Committee on Banking, Currency, and Housing. *Financial Institutions and the Nation's Economy (FINE) "Discussion Principles."* Hearing, 94th Congress, 1st and 2nd Sessions, 1975. Washington: Government Printing Office.

_____. *Adjustable Rate Mortgages: Hearings Before the Subcommittee on Financial Institutions Supervision, Regulation and Insurance of the Committee on Banking, Finance and Urban Affairs,* Ninety-Seventh Congress, First Session, Serial No. 97-34.

U.S. Congress, Senate. *Equity for the Small Saver,* Hearings on S. Con. Res. 5 before the Subcommittee on Financial Institutions, Senate Committee on Banking, Housing, and Urban Affairs, 96th Congress, 1st Session, 1979. Washington: Government Printing Office.

U.S. League of Savings Associations. *'82 Savings and Loan Sourcebook.* Chicago, Ill.: 1982.

Verbrugge, James A., and Steven J. Goldstein. "Risk, Return, and Managerial Objectives: Some Evidence from the Savings and Loan Industry." *Journal of Financial Research,* Vol. 4, No. 11 (Spring 1981), 45-58.

_____ and _____. "Profitability and Operating Efficiency Differences among Savings and Loan Associations." A paper presented at the 1982 Financial Management Association meeting in San Francisco, California.

_____ and John S. Jahera, Jr. "Expense-Preference Behavior in the Savings and Loan Industry." *Journal of Money, Credit and Banking,* 13 (November 1981), 465-76.

_____, Richard A. Schick, and Kenneth J. Thygerson. "An Analysis of Savings and Loan Profit Performance." *Journal of Finance,* 31 (December 1976), 1427-42.

Vrabac, Daniel J. "Savings and Loan Associations: An Analysis of the Recent Decline in Profitability." *Economic Review,* Federal Reserve Bank of Kansas City, 67 (July-August 1982), 3-19.

Walker, David A. "Effects of Financial Deregulation on Bank and Thrift Institution Competition." A paper presented at the 1981 Southern Finance Association meeting in New Orleans, Louisiana.

Webb, Bruce G. "Borrower Risk under Alternative Mortgage Instruments." *Journal of Finance,* Vol. 37, No. 1 (March 1982), 169-83.

Weinrobe, Maurice. "An Analysis of the Effectiveness of FHLBB Liquidity Policy, 1971-75." *Journal of Finance,* 32 (December 1977), 1617-37.

Wermiel, Stephen. "Mortgage Shift Can Be Blocked, Top Court Rules." *Wall Street Journal,* June 29, 1982.

Werner, Ruth. "The Federal Home Loan Bank System." *Federal Home Loan Bank Board Journal,* 15 (April 1982), 16-19.

West, Robert Craig. "The Depository Institutions Deregulation Act of 1980: A Historical Perspective." *Economic Review,* Federal Reserve Bank of Kansas City, 67 (February 1982), 3-13.

Weston, J. Fred, and Eugene F. Brigham. *Essentials of Managerial Finance.* 6th ed. Hinsdale, Ill.: Dryden Press, 1982.

White, Lawrence J. "Price Regulation and Quality Rivalry in a Profit-Maximizing Model: The Cost of Bank Branching." *Journal of Money, Credit and Banking,* 8 (February 1976), 97-106.

Wilson, John, William O'Connel, Jr., and Ronald Olson. *A Model for Savings and Loans.* Richmond, Va.: Robert F. Dame, 1982.

Winningham, Scott, and Donald G. Hagen. "Regulation Q: A Historical Perspective." *Economic Review,* Federal Reserve Bank of Kansas City, 65 (April 1980), 10-16.

Woerheide, Walt J. "S&L Operating Expenses—A Historical Record." *Federal Home Loan Bank Board Journal,* 12 (October 1979), 16-21.

_____. "Economies of Scale in the SLA Industry: The Historical Record." *Nevada Review of Business and Economics,* 4 (Summer 1980), 2-8.

_____. "The Evolution of SLA Susceptibility to Interest Rate Risk during the Seventies." *Journal of the Midwest Finance Association,* 9 (1980), 117-33.

_____. "The Windfall Gains Associated with SLA Conversions: Reality or Myth?." *North Carolina Review of Business and Economics,* 6 (July 1980), 15-16.

_____. "What Does It Take to Stay Even with Inflation?" *Journal of Institute of Certified Financial Planners,* Vol. 2, No. 4 (Summer 1981), 242-48.

Wofford, Larry E., and Richard C. Burgess. "Structuring Adjustable Rate Mortgages: Single Asset and Portfolio Considerations." A paper presented at the 1982 Financial Management Association meeting in San Francisco, California.

Wolkowitz, Benjamin, Michael Asay, and Ellen D. Harvey. "The Economics and Regulation of Alternative Home Mortgage Instruments." Research Papers in Banking and Financial Economics, Board of Governors of the Federal Reserve System (March 1979), Washington, D.C.

Wright, Thomas V. "Analysis of an Institutional Alternative to Residential Land Contract Sales." *Federal Home Loan Bank Board Journal,* 15 (September 1982), 9-12.

Yawitz, Jess. "The Relative Importance of Duration and Yield Volatility on Bond Price Volatility." *Journal of Money, Credit and Banking,* 9 (February 1977), 97-102.

_____ and William Marshall. "The Shortcomings of Duration as a Risk Measure for Bonds." *The Journal of Financial Research,* 4 (Summer 1981), 91-101.

Zabrenski, Stephen T., and Virginia K. Olin. "Characteristics of Adjustable Mortgage Loans by Large Associations." *Federal Home Loan Bank Board Journal,* 15 (August 1982), 21-24.

Index

About the Author

WALTER J. WOERHEIDE is Assistant Professor and Acting Head of the Department of Finance at the University of Illinois at Chicago. A former financial economist for the Federal Home Loan Bank Board, he is a frequent contributor to its *Journal* and other financial journals.